Foreword

Thank you very much for choosing this book!

Are you interested in the design and simulation of three-dimensional objects using Autodesk's "Inventor"? Do you have no CAD knowledge or already have some experience with other CAD programs, but would like to switch to "Inventor" or continue your education?

Then you are exactly right with this book! I am an engineer and would like to bring you from scratch, in a simple and easy to understand way the professional program "Inventor" in the practical application!

Here is the link to download and free trial version:

https://www.autodesk.com/products/inventor/overview

This comprehensive and detailed course is aimed specifically at beginners and shows from the beginning how CAD designs, animations and FEM simulations succeed. In addition to theoretical explanations on the use of the software and the approach, you will learn in this course primarily through practical and exciting design projects!

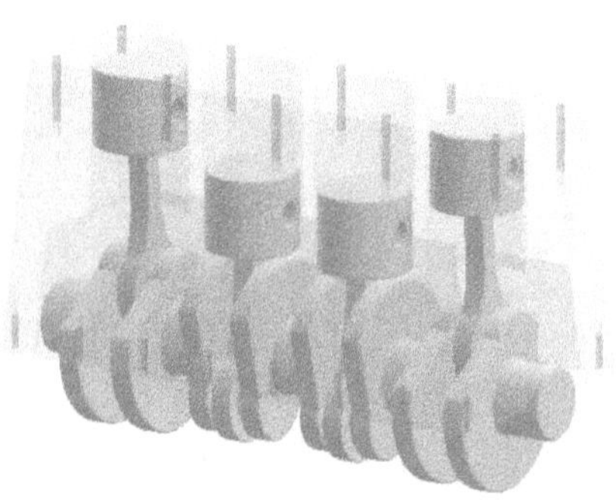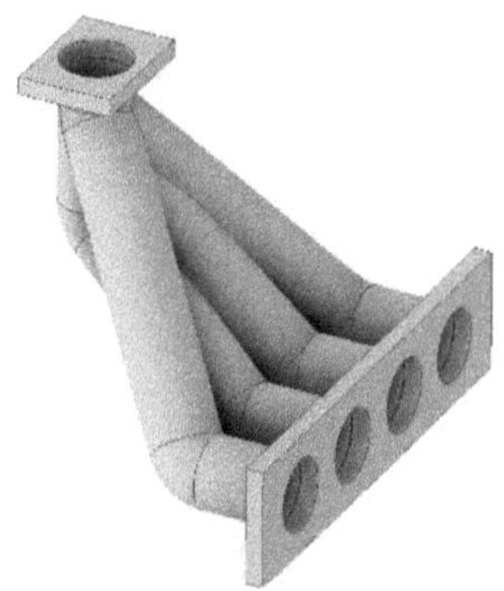

In this course you will learn everything you need to know as a beginner about "Inventor" and CAD design or FEM simulation! Start today with this book into the fascinating world of "Inventor"! Let's go!

Table of contents

1 Introduction: course scope and software

1.1 What to expect and what you will learn in this course

Welcome to the "Inventor" course for beginners!
Thank you for choosing this course!

In this course you will find an introduction to the basics of the great CAD program "Inventor" from Autodesk and learn in particular the CAD design in detail and understand. As an engineer, I will show you, step by step, my knowledge from my studies and professional practice, so that you can achieve optimal learning success with theoretical basics on the one hand, but above all with practical examples on the other hand. After a theoretical introduction, this course includes many practical design projects to learn the design and the program from scratch.

And with "Inventor" from Autodesk, as with other CAD programs, you can not only design. Rather, this program combines and links several engineering disciplines, such as CAD ("Computer Aided Design") and FEM ("Finite Element Method"), in one platform. So with "Inventor" you can not only create components or assemblies, but also perform simulations and animations as well as create renderings. The main focus of this course is on design with "Inventor", i.e. the CAD part of the program. But the other functions will not be neglected, don't worry!

As already mentioned, the abbreviation CAD stands for "Computer Aided Design". What is CAD software anyway? CAD software is used to virtually create or edit three-dimensional objects. Starting with simple individual parts, through complex parts, to entire assemblies that can be virtually assembled.

In this course, specially designed for beginners, you will learn how the "Inventor" environment is structured and how to make the most of its features to create three-dimensional objects. Each project of the course can be followed step by step and one by one, in order to get an easy introduction to the material and to become more familiar with the multiple functions of the program with each lesson.

In a nutshell, this means that you can learn the following in detail in this course:

- Find your way around the "Inventor" program quickly and confidently
- Master all the important functions of "Inventor" quickly and confidently
- To learn the basics of CAD design and the different ways of working / methods.
- Get to know 2D sketching and 3D object creation
- Create individual parts and assemblies
- Render and animate individual parts and assemblies

- simulate individual parts and assemblies, i.e. apply loads and display stresses and strains (FEM simulations)
- Learn the environment of technical drawings and create technical drawings

It is best to stay in the order that the course provides, as the lessons build on each other. If you do not understand individual functions or commands right away or miss the explanation for a function, just stick with it, the course is structured in such a way that all important and basic functions are explained sufficiently and in an intuitive way. Therefore, explanations in the chapters may overlap or certain functions may not be covered in detail until a later chapter.

1.2 The CAD program "Inventor"

The professional CAD program "Inventor" from Autodesk offers a clear and simple user interface, but it also has its price! A license currently costs about 350 € per month, annually about 2,900 €. If you buy a license for a longer period, you can save a little. Pupils and students have the possibility to get a license for the duration of their studies. All others can test the program at least for 30 days free of charge in its full extent. It is no longer possible to buy the software directly, there is only the possibility to subscribe to the software for a certain period of time. With a subscription, "Inventor" can then be installed on up to three computers. However, it can only be used on one computer at a time and only with the purchaser's login data.

The structure of the design features is relatively identical for all common CAD programs used by engineers or technicians in their daily work. There is a basic selection of professional CAD programs. In addition to "Inventor", the best known are: SolidWorks, Catia, SolidEdge, Pro/Engineer, also known as Creo, and probably the best known of them all: AutoCAD. There are basically no major differences in the prices, so these programs are usually only worthwhile for professional users and self-employed people.

And now we're ready to get started! Before we get to the basics of CAD design, we will make general program settings and familiarize ourselves with the program interface and functions.

2 Preparation: First steps with "Inventor "

2.1 Making general settings

When we start the program for the first time, we are initially presented with three windows and three menu bars. In the menu bar "Get started" we find standard options, such as creating a new file or opening an already created file. In addition, we can work through tutorials, see what is new in an update version of "Inventor" and request or look up help.

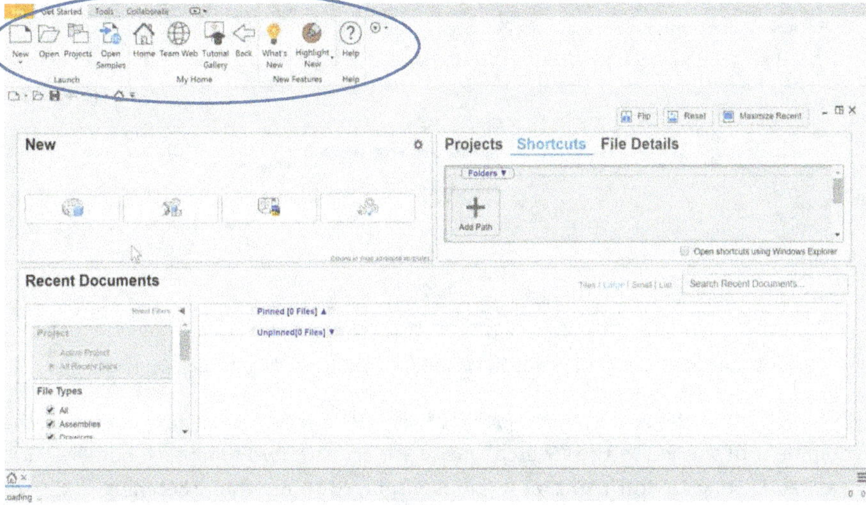

Figure 1: When starting the software for the first time, this display appears; tab "Get started" selected

In the "Tools" menu bar, we can use the "Application Options" button to make initial settings for the program or reactivate existing settings. With the help of these settings, the program can be individualized to some extent, e.g. the background color can be set in the "Colors" section - I prefer the white "Presentation" layout - or graphic settings, depending on the hardware, can be made in the "Hardware" menu tab.

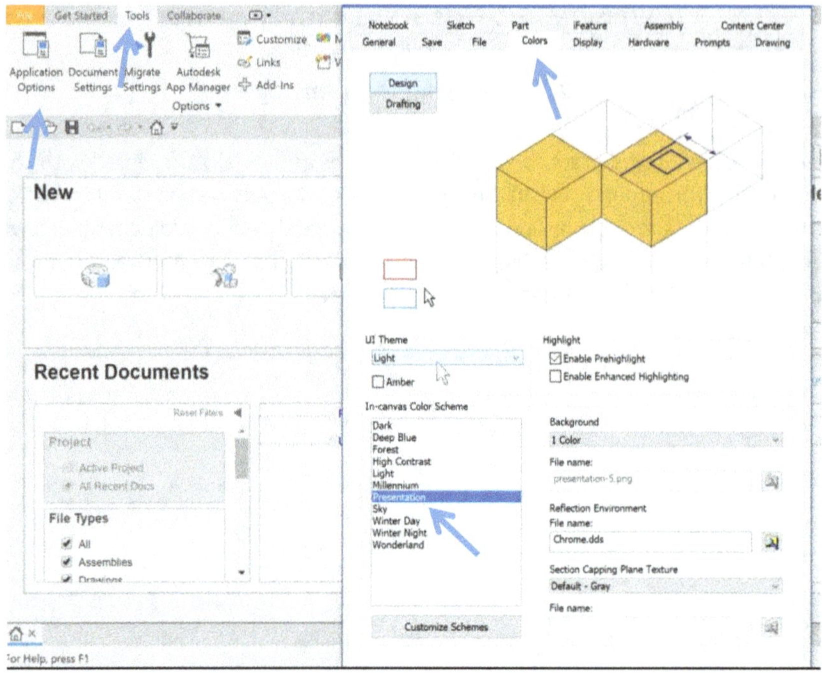

Figure 2: Making the first settings in the "Tools" tab with "Application Options

Here we have to choose between quality of display or performance, depending on the equipment of the PC. In the "Sketch" menu we activate two functions, namely "Grid lines" and "Snap to grid", so that a grid is displayed to us when sketching in the 2D environment and we can select the grid points more easily with the cursor. However, this setting is really just a matter of taste.

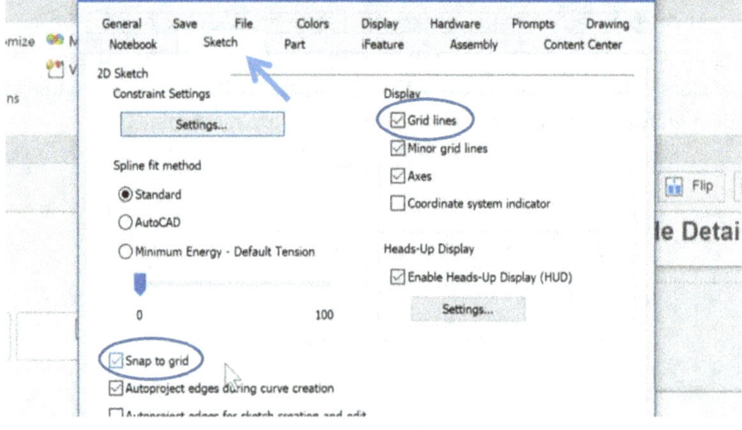

Figure 3: In the "Sketch" tab, activate the "Grid lines" & "Snap to grid" options

At last we want to make a setting for the units at "File". With a click on "Configure Default Template" we can change this to "mm" and set the "Drawing Standard" to "ISO".

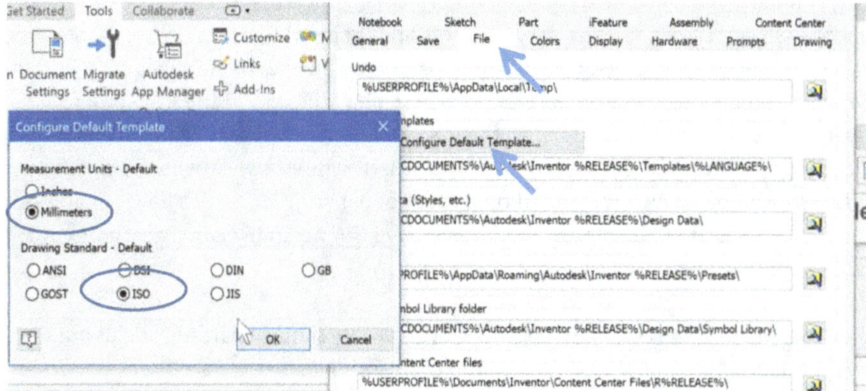

Figure 4: Set "Configure Default Template" to "mm" and "ISO"; "File" menu tab

For organizational reasons, the program language remains in English. This is also advantageous for you, in order to find your way around better in the international work routine on the one hand and in the mostly English-speaking Internet forums or community on the other hand. All other settings are not needed for the time being, they are much too special for the start and can be left at the default values.

We are now still in the start window of the program, in which there are still the three sections "New", "Projects" and "Recent Documents". These are relatively self-explanatory, in "Recent Documents" you will see the most recently used files, after the creation of the first files. In the "New" section we can choose between the creation of a single part "Part", an assembly "Assembly", a technical drawing "Drawing", as well as a "Presentation".

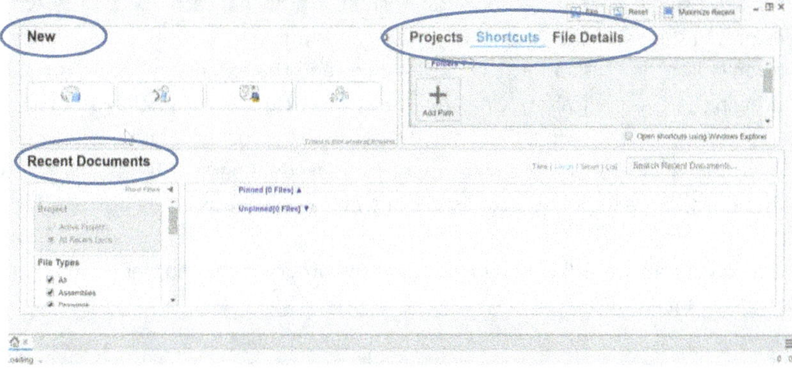

Figure 5: The three areas of the start window

If you have never worked with a CAD program before, you may wonder what the difference is between a single part: "Part" and an assembly: "Assembly" and why a distinction is made here. Think of it very simply. Just like in the real world, in the virtual environment of a CAD program, every more complex part is assembled from several individual parts. A car, for example, has thousands of individual parts, from the steering wheel to the smallest bolts. Each of these parts is an independent individual part that, when assembled as a whole, results in an assembly, the car. In the CAD program, an assembly is therefore made up of all the individual parts - just as in real assembly. With "drawing", a technical drawing, an individual part with views, dimensions and all the necessary information is described on a sheet of paper in 2D in such a way that it can be manufactured in a company by an employee. An assembly can also be described with a technical drawing.

Since we want to start constructing our first - still very simple - part as soon as possible, we therefore now first select the creation of a new single part: "Part".

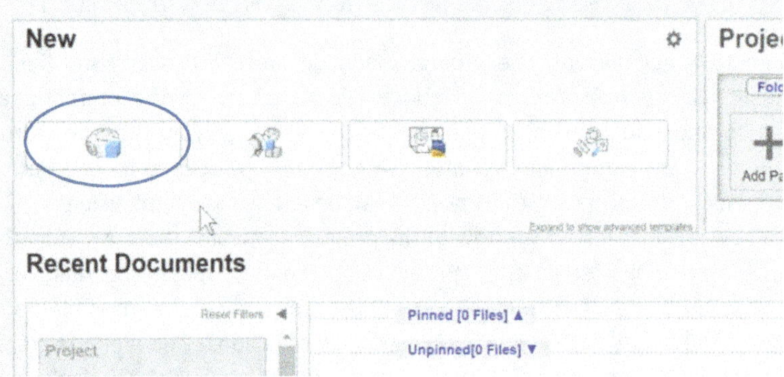

Figure 6: Creating a new single part: "Part

By the way, single part, assembly and technical drawing each have different file extensions. In this case, the extension ". ipt" stands for "part", i.e. individual parts, the extension ". iam" for "assembly", i.e. assemblies and the extension ". dwg" or ". idw" for "drawing", i.e. technical drawings. A look at this extension will help you to identify what you are dealing with in a file. Then we get to the actual program environment of "Inventor", in this case to the environment for individual parts ("Parts"). By the way, we can return to the initial window by clicking on the small box in the bottom bar.

In the next chapter we will take a first look at the program environment and functions of Autodesk "Inventor".

2.2 Overview of program environment and functions

Let's first take a look at the program environment and the menu bars located in the upper and side areas.

The menu bars in the upper area are different for each of the four environments: "Part", "Assembly", "Drawing" and "Presentation". While there are always some tabs that appear in several or all environments, such as "3D Model" or "Sketch", there are generally different tabs and functions depending on the environment. We will learn what the differences are during the course.

So now we are in the environment: "Part".

At the top left, "File" allows you to open, save or export files and other basic commands.

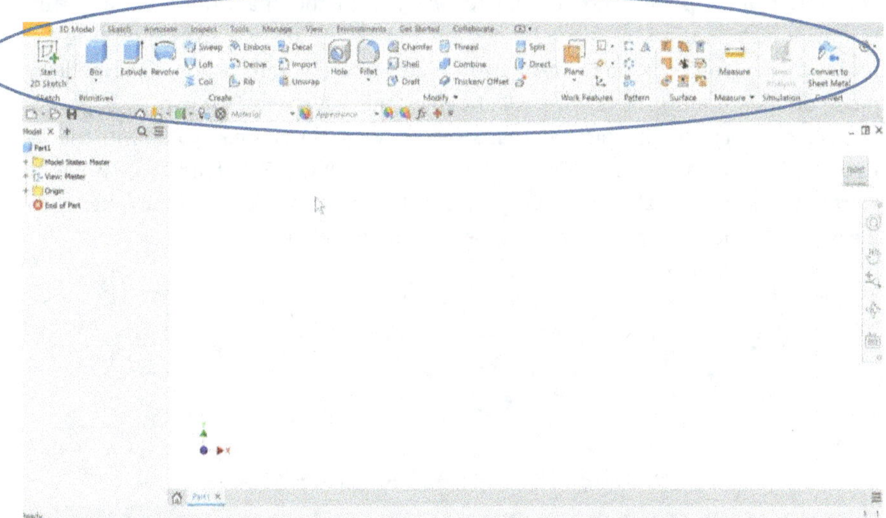

Figure 7: "Part" environment with selection tabs, bars, features and drawing environment

The selection tabs on the side of "File" can be used to switch between the individual submenus for the features in the respective environment. In this first section, "Part", we will first deal with the design features for a single part. There are ten different tabs here: "3D Model", "Sketch", "Annotate", "Inspect", "Tools", "Manage", "View", "Environments", "Get Started" and "Collaborate".

Figure 8: The ten different tabs in the "Part" environment

In the "3D Model" menu tab, you will find all the functions that are necessary for creating or editing a three-dimensional object. In the "Create" section you will find all the functions for creating a 3D part. In the "Modify" section you will find all the functions for editing a 3D part. What these functions can do and how to use them, we will learn in detail and step by step during the course.

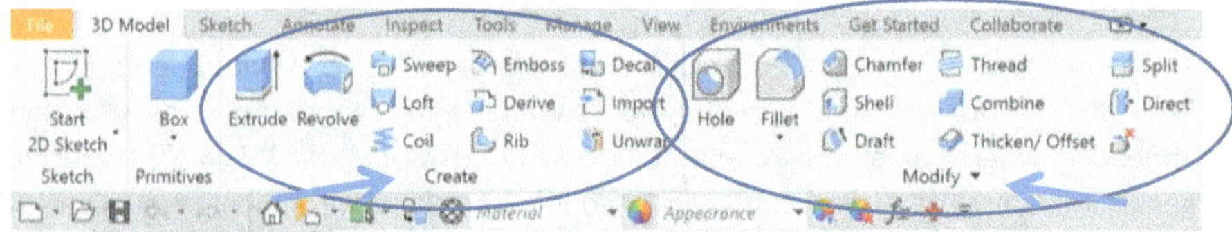

Figure 9: The "Create" and "Modify" sections in the "3D Model" tab

In this chapter, we first want to get an overview. The "Shape Generator" can be used to create an optimized component structure based on a load situation (keyword: topology optimization). In the "Work Features" we find all the tools for construction, i.e. axes, planes, points and coordinate systems. In the "Pattern" area, a pattern command can be used to save a lot of time and effort during construction. The two areas "Create Freeform and Surface" are intended for the freeform or surface modeling mode of operation. However, we will not cover this advanced CAD way of working in this beginner's course. It is also only necessary for very complex parts. And with the last two points "Simulation" and "Convert" on the one hand a FEM load analysis can be started or a sheet metal part can be designed. These two sections, on the other hand, we will very much cover in this course, because they are important and exciting.

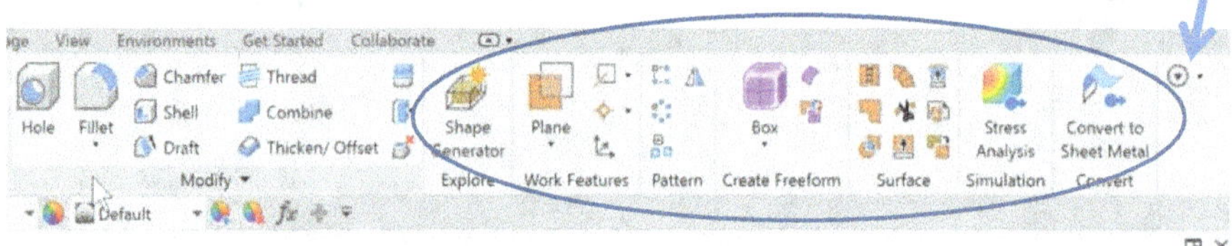

Figure 10: Additional features from the "3D Model" tab

By the way, with the small arrow on the far right, this bar can be customized in each of the menu tabs, i.e. needed or not needed sections can be shown or hidden. For us, for example, "Primitive" is still interesting, with which simple bodies such as a cube can be created directly, and the function "Measure", with which you can measure something in the 3D environment. In exchange we hide "Explore" and "Create Freeform".

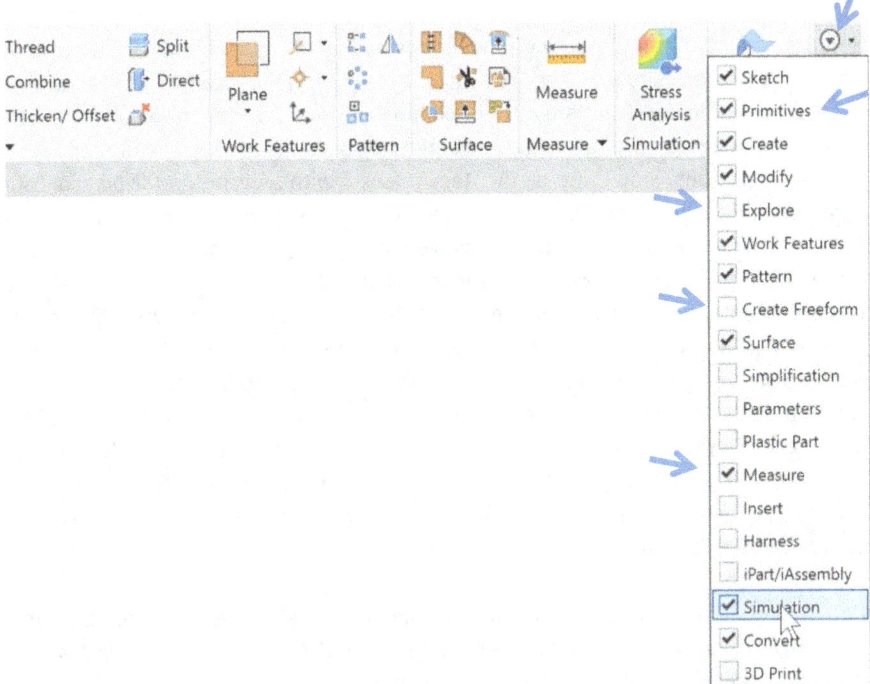

Figure 11: Making settings for the displayed features

You are also welcome to take a look at the other possible sections. In the next section "Sketch", which is intended for 2D sketches, we first find "Create", "Modify" and "Pattern" again. Here lines, circles or other 2D geometries can be created or modified.

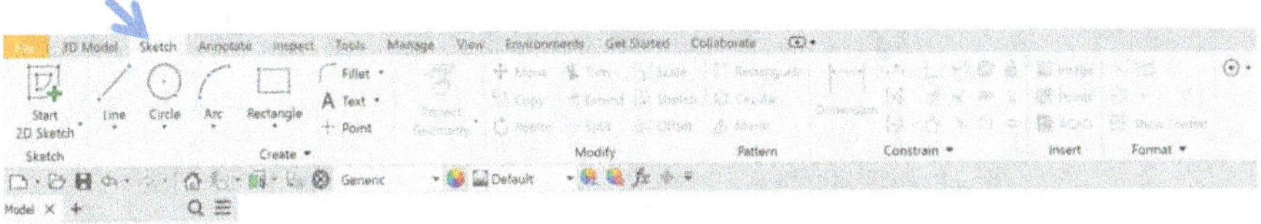

Figure 12: The features in the "Sketch" menu tab

If you do not have any previous knowledge, you must mentally divide the CAD program and the design of an individual part into a two-dimensional and a three-dimensional area. You start with a 2D sketch and then create a 3D body from it. But more about that later!

In the "Annotate" menu tab, tolerances, dimensions, surface specifications and other remarks can be applied directly to the 3D component as an annotation. However, this is normally not absolutely necessary and is usually noted on an engineering drawing. However, applying these annotations directly to the 3D part can have advantages when the 3D model is transferred to manufacturing in addition to a drawing. A tolerance analysis can also be started in this area. In the menu tabs "Inspect" and "Tools" you will find again the general measuring function, as well as the possibility to start various analyses, the possibility to change the material or the appearance of a part, as well as a few more commands that are rather unimportant for us for the time being. We will skip the "Manage" menu tab, since its content is also unimportant for this beginner's course. Important, however, is the tab "View", with which the display of our components can be controlled. Here, in addition to the general component display ("Visual Style"), the focus or shadow, as well as a background can be displayed. But more about this later. The last important area is the tab "Environment". In this tab you can switch to the other environments of "Inventor". In addition to the CAD design, "Inventor" can also be used to perform an FEM load simulation with "Stress Analysis" or to create an animation and a rendering with "Inventor Studio". Tolerance analysis can also be performed, and there is also a specific environment for creating castings and more. For us, the already mentioned possibility of sheet metal design with "Convert to Sheet Metal" is still important. The last two menu tabs "Get started" and "Collaborate" are very self-explanatory and contain rather general commands, feel free to click through here if needed.

Don't be afraid of the multitude of elements and features! In the course of the course we will get to know the individual elements step by step and in detail using practical examples. Therefore only this short clear explanation.

If we now look at the drawing layer area, we find the part browser of the construction file in the left area.

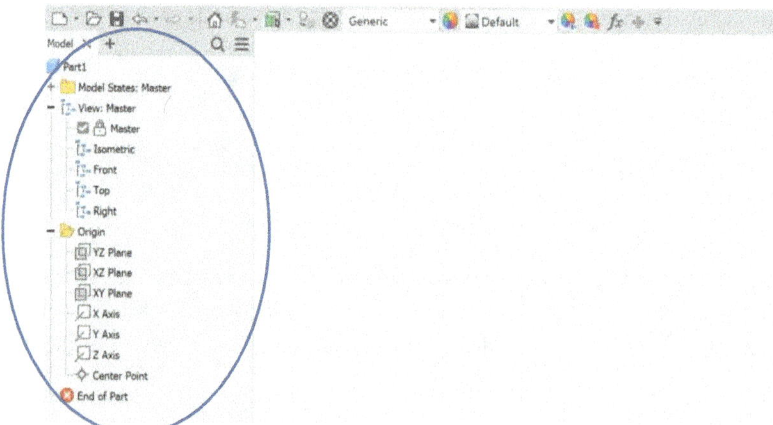

Figure 13: The left pane shows the part browser of the design file

If it is not displayed or if you have closed it by mistake, click on the small plus symbol and select "Model Browser".

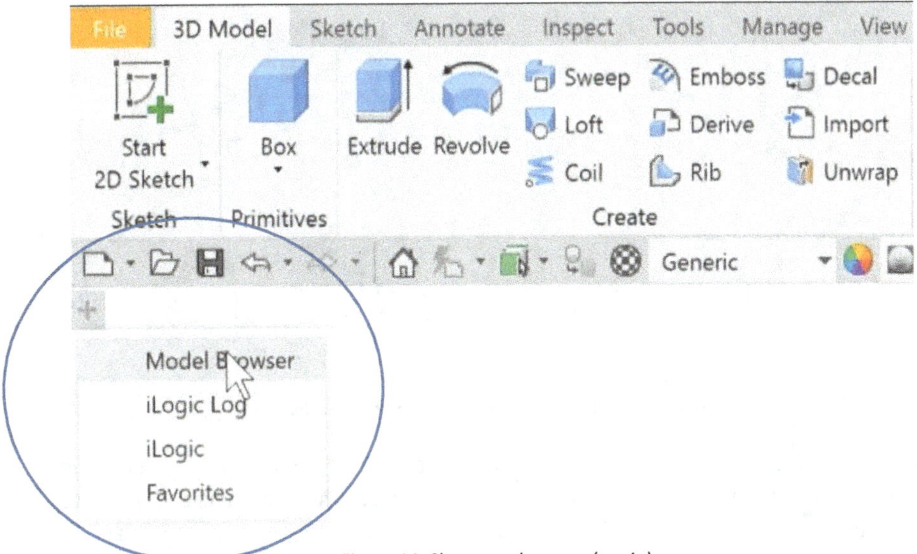

Figure 14: Show part browser (again)

This part browser contains all views, as well as the origin, the planes and the axes of a file. However, the main function of this part browser is to list the created sketches, construction elements, etc., in chronological order. , chronologically, in order to activate / deactivate or edit them with a right click on them. We will see later how this works. It is also very good if you get into the habit of naming the individual components and possibly sketches and layers right from the start, in order to find your way around a complex construction more easily later. Simply double-click on the element and enter a new name.

In the narrow bar above this part browser, you will once again find general functions such as "Open", "Save", "Undo", "Redo" and settings for selecting elements or features, as well as settings for the material and the appearance. It may be that this bar is also displayed at the top, with a click on the small arrow on the far right, you can change the display position if necessary.

Figure 15: General command bar above the part browser or at the very top

In the upper right area is the orbit cube. Here you can select views of the current construction and rotate the drawing environment including the object.

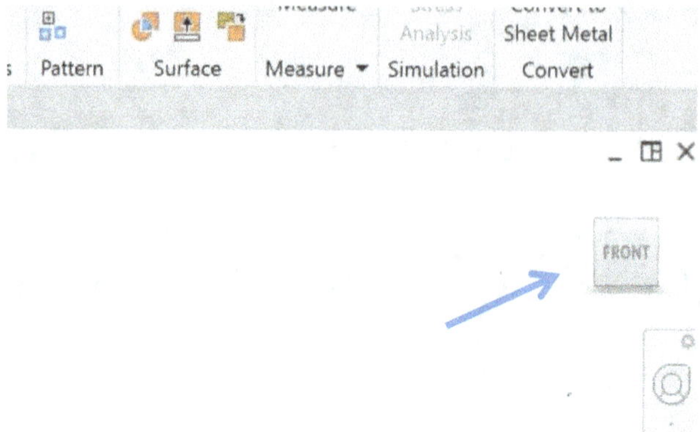

Figure 16: The orbit cube for rotations and object alignment

Rotation of the drawing environment is also possible with the SHIFT key pressed while moving the mouse. Shifting is possible with the mouse wheel pressed and a mouse movement. The zoom function is performed as usual by turning the mouse wheel.

By right-clicking on the drawing environment, we can access the quick selection menu, which can be used to quickly execute a variety of commands.

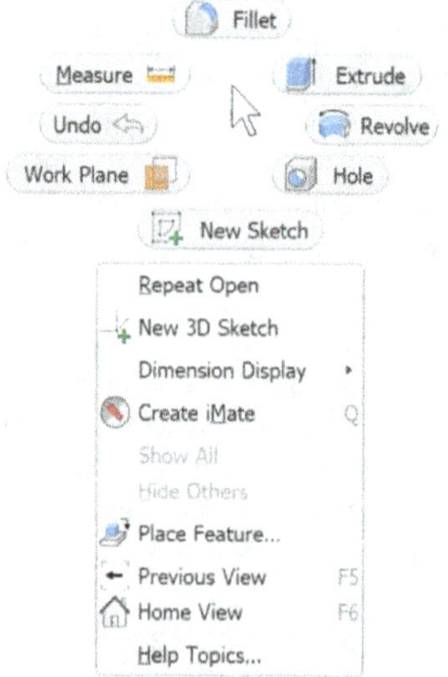

Figure 17: Quick selection menu of "Inventor"; opens with a right click on the drawing layer

In the lower part of the drawing environment we can switch between several open files.

The bar on the right side below the orbit cube also gives us the option to move or rotate the environment as well as the "Look at" command, which makes it very easy to look vertically at a selected area of a component. In addition, a navigation wheel can be activated in this bar, which is then permanently displayed and serves as a kind of quick selection menu. Here you can also choose between different designs.

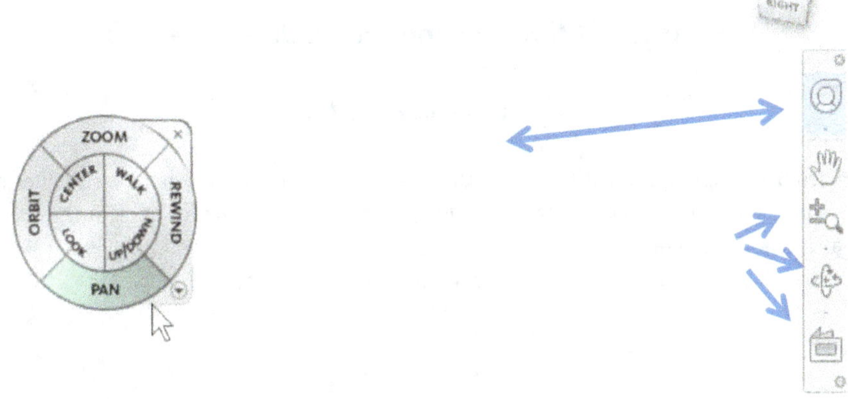

Figure 18: Quick selection bar (right) and activated navigation wheel (left)

Very well, after this chapter we can find our way around the program environment relatively easily and can start with the next chapter. As already mentioned, common CAD programs work in a very identical way. We would now like to look at this way of working in detail in the following.

Section I: CAD Construction / Design

3 Basics of CAD: Function and mode of operation

3.1 2D sketching environment

Each 3D component must first be started as a 2D sketch. This is where we define the "floor plan" of the object, so to speak. Imagine that you are taking a look at the top of a simple three-dimensional object. For example, what do you see in a cylinder when you look at it from above, at a perfect right angle to the axis?

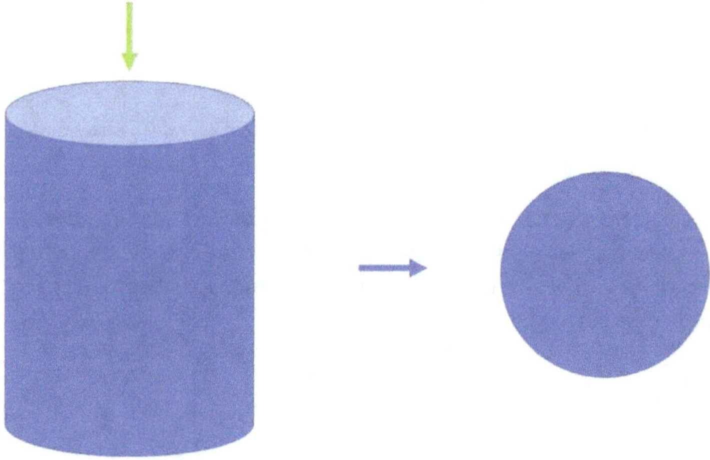

Figure 19: A three-dimensional cylinder has a 2D circle as its basic shape

Correct, a two-dimensional circle, nothing else. And it is exactly from this 2D shape that the cylinder, analogous to all other elements, is also created in the CAD program. It is exactly this circle geometry that we have to draw for this object, for example, in the first step. The three-dimensional shape is then obtained by further command steps. For the 2D sketch, e.g. also the top surface of an object or a side surface, or also a partial surface comes into question. Here you need some spatial imagination.

For each 3D part, as we said, we must first make a two-dimensional sketch. We will look at how to create a 2D sketch in detail in this chapter. At the beginning of a sketch, in the "3D Model" area, alternatively also in "Sketch", select the "Start 2D Sketch" command.

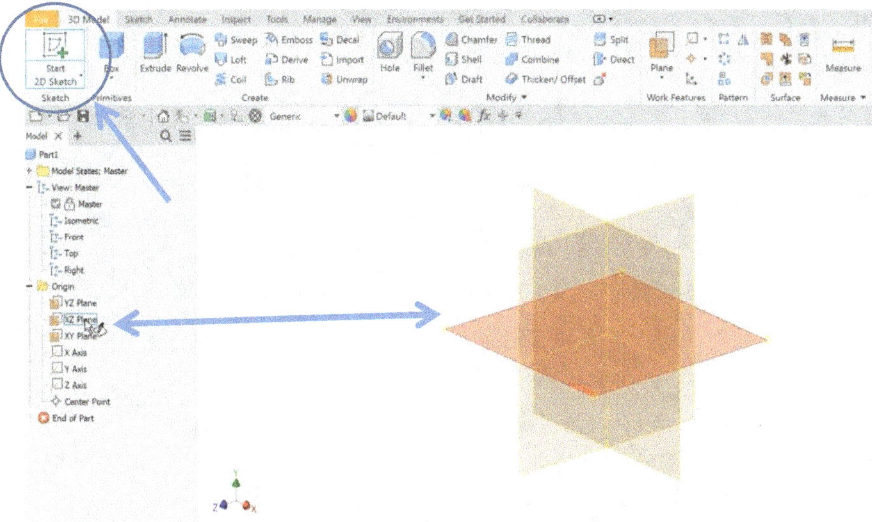

Figure 20: Starting a 2D sketch and selecting a layer

Then we are shown the planes of the coordinate system and we have to decide for a plane of the three-dimensional space on which we want to draw our 2D sketch. In our example, we want to look from above at the circular surface or top surface, so we should choose the x-z plane, that is, the plane that the x and z axes form. Which plane you choose is only important for the alignment of the views. The program then opens the selected sketching plane for us. As you will notice, the "Sketch" menu bar also opens automatically in the upper area, where you can find all the 2D commands.

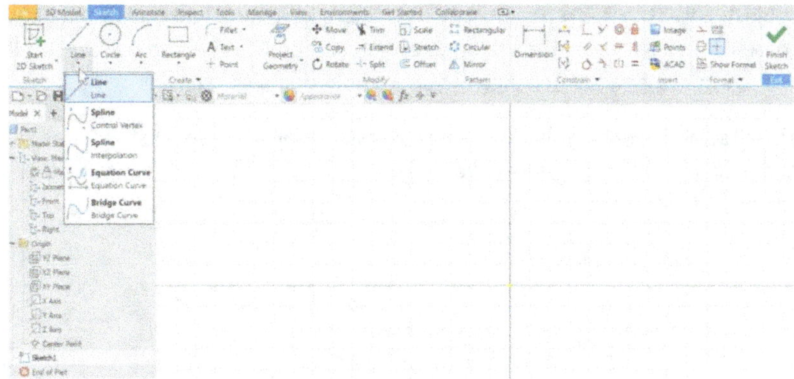

Figure 21: 2D sketching environment with the "Sketch" bar and the drawing grid

A variety of basic drawing elements are now available for creating the geometry of a 2D sketch. By selecting a "line", for example, a geometry can be formed from line-shaped elements. Let's try this out. To do this, simply click on any point, e.g. on the center of the coordinate system, and start a drawing by clicking and dragging with your mouse.

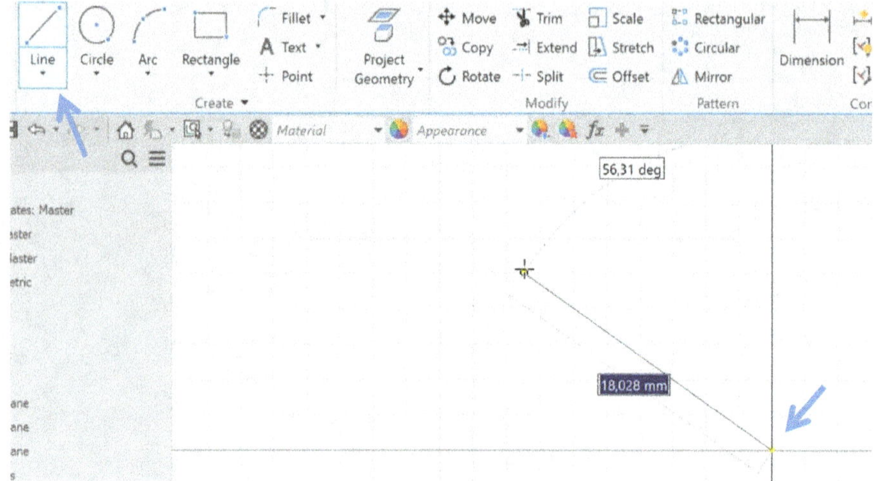

Figure 22: Creating a first line

With another click you create the line. If you then want to continue drawing directly after this line, simply continue drawing, if not use the "ESC" key and start again at a different position.

The drawing should correspond, for example, to the cross-section of the desired 3D object or, in the case of simple objects, to the upper surface or cross-sectional area of the object. Enter the desired dimensions using the keyboard. You can switch between dimension and angle using the tab key. You can also draw freely and use the displayed values as a guide, or add or change the dimensions and angles later.

The small symbols that are displayed for a rectangle, for example, are the "constraints" or "dependencies" of the respective lines. We will take a closer look at these in a moment.

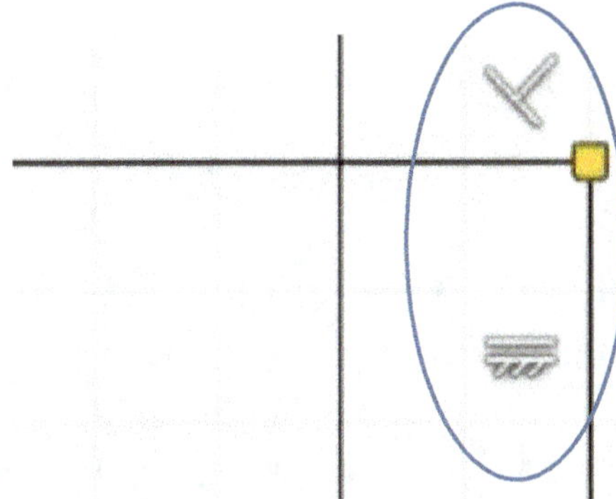

Figure 23: The "constraints" or conditions / dependencies of the sketch elements

Besides a line, you can also create a circle, an ellipse, a freeform curve, an arc, an oblong hole or a rectangle. Let's just try that out one after the other as well.

You will also find in the "Create" menu: a point, various arcs and several other elements.

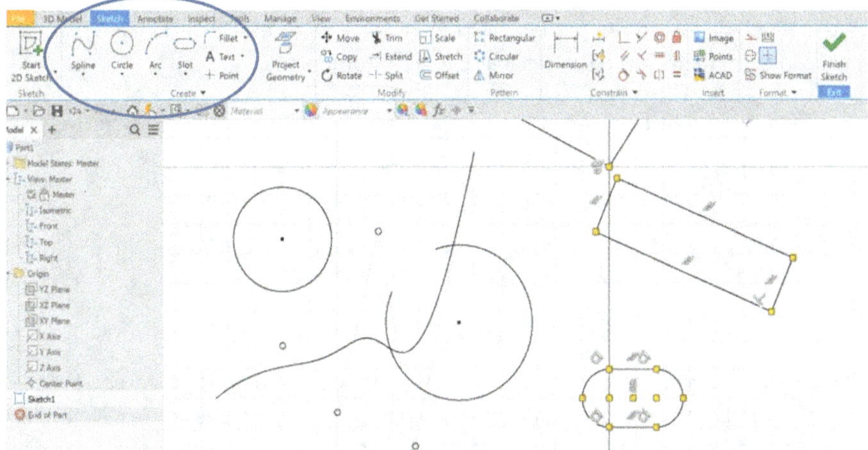

Figure 24: Sketching exercises with different commands, such as circle, rectangle, oblong hole, etc.

It is best to simply try out all elements at least once. To do this, simply pause briefly and start independently in the sketching environment of the CAD program. It is best to use this approach throughout the course. This is the most effective way to learn.

Another tip about the prefabricated geometry elements, such as rectangle or circle: When drawing, you will notice that the rectangle, for example, starts from a corner. However, if you want the rectangle to span from the center, you can also use the drop-down menu at "Rectangle" to select a "Center Rectangle" or also "2-Point Rectangle".

With the circle you can - if desired - also create a tangential circle instead of a center circle, for example.

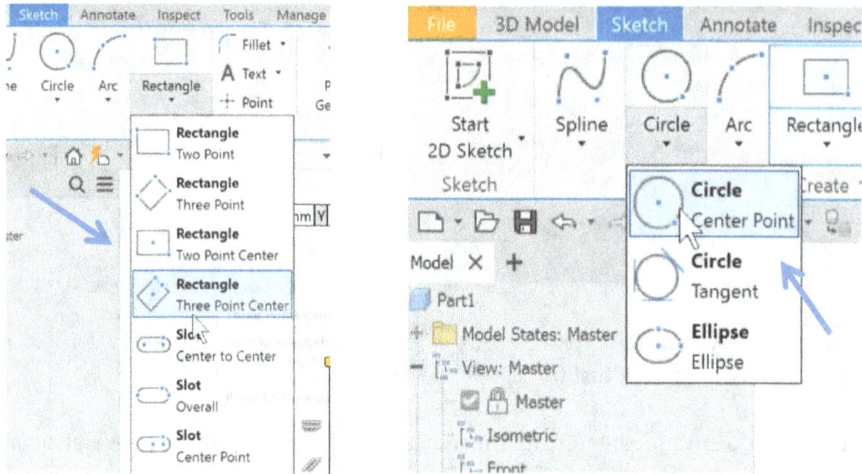

Figure 25: Don't forget the 2D elements drop-down menu

In the Modify area we can perform various operations to modify a sketch. First, let's take a look at the Move, Copy, Scale and Stretch commands.

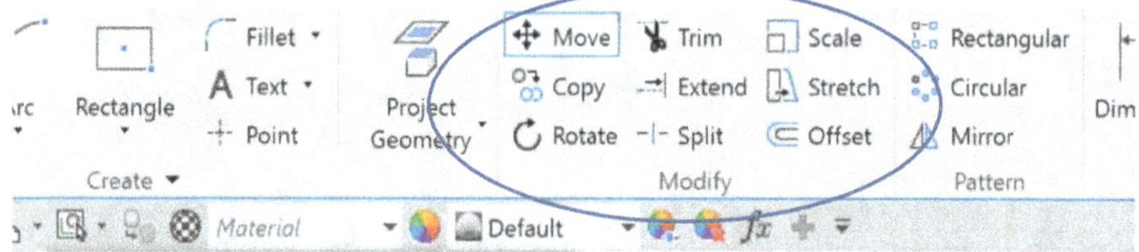

Figure 26: The Modify menu section in the Sketch panel

These work in a very similar way, but of course each does something different. Let's try the commands on the example of a rectangle. The way it works is as follows. First select the command, e.g. "Move", then select the cursor "Select" in the window. In the next step, select the rectangle or the individual lines or another geometry element with the mouse. Then select the "Base Point" cursor in the command window and define a reference point on the drawing plane. Now when we move our mouse, we can see how to move the part based on the reference point.

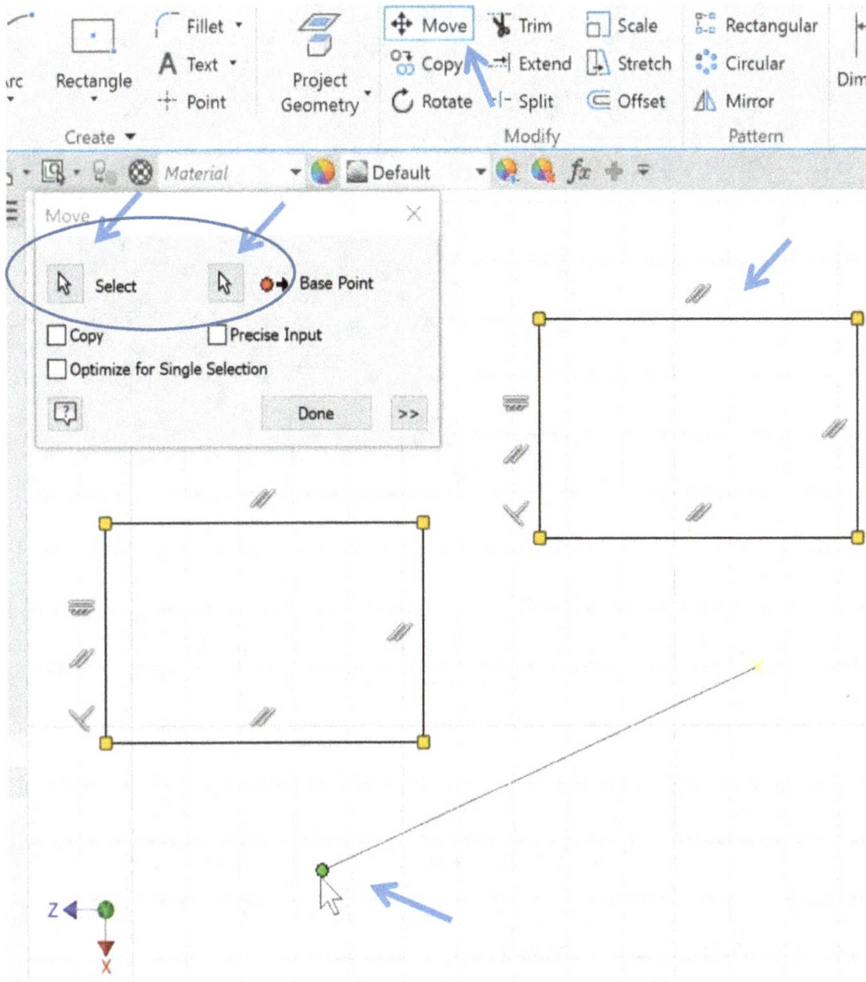

Figure 27: The "Move" command in the application; the rectangle on the upper right must already exist, so simply draw it; the lower left is then created with the command

You can then place the rectangle in the desired position with one click. For "Copy", "Scale" and "Stretch" this works - as said - in an identical way. For "Rotate" we don't need a "Base Point", but have to enter an angle for the rotation. "Trim" and "Extend" can be used to shorten or lengthen a line segment. Split" can be used to split a line into two lines at the closest point. And with "Offset" you can create an identical geometry element with a distance to the original one.

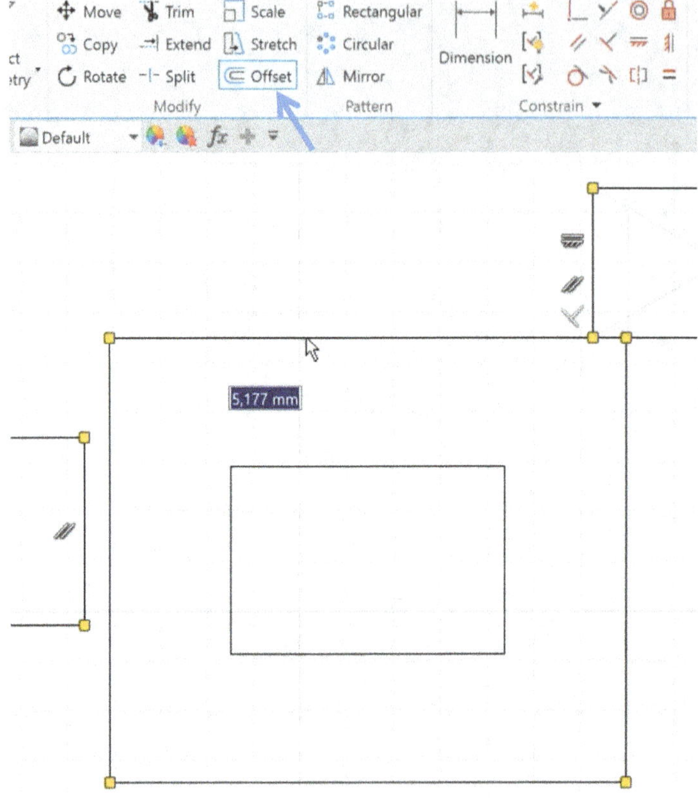

Figure 28: Create another rectangle with spacing using the "Offset" function

Here you can perform relatively basic drawing operations. We will get to know the menu area "Pattern" later in the course.

Before we conclude this chapter, as promised, let's get to know the world of "constraints" / "dependencies". You can use these in the 2D sketching environment and use them to create constraints between individual geometric elements. This is sometimes, but not always, necessary or helpful. By the way, in this area you will also find the "Dimension" function for creating dimensions.

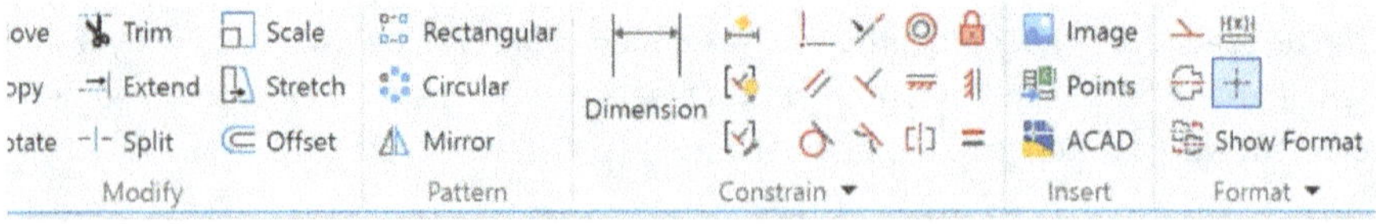

Figure 29: The Constrain area in the Sketch panel

We will now take a closer look at the most important "constraints". Let's start with the horizontal and vertical constraints. Let's assume that we try to draw a rectangle freehand and we get a polygon whose lines unfortunately do not represent a rectangle.

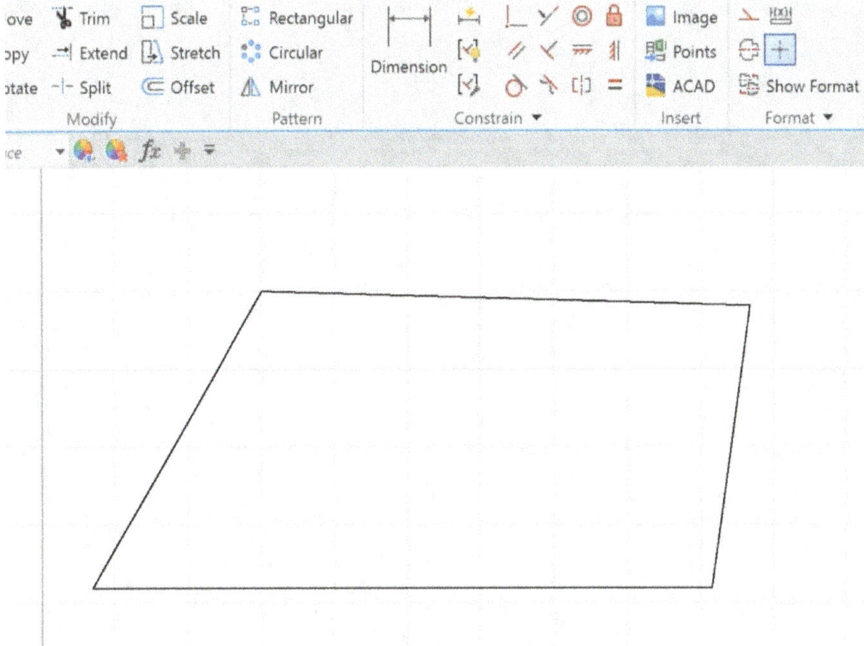

Figure 30: For the exercise, draw the following polygon from individual lines;
simply select dimensions / angles freely

By selecting the "horizontal" condition, we can create two perfectly horizontal lines by clicking the top and bottom lines. In an identical way, we apply the "vertical" condition to the lateral lines and end up with a rectangle. As you can see, these conditions are displayed to us as small icons next to the respective line and are also already suggested when creating a sketch.

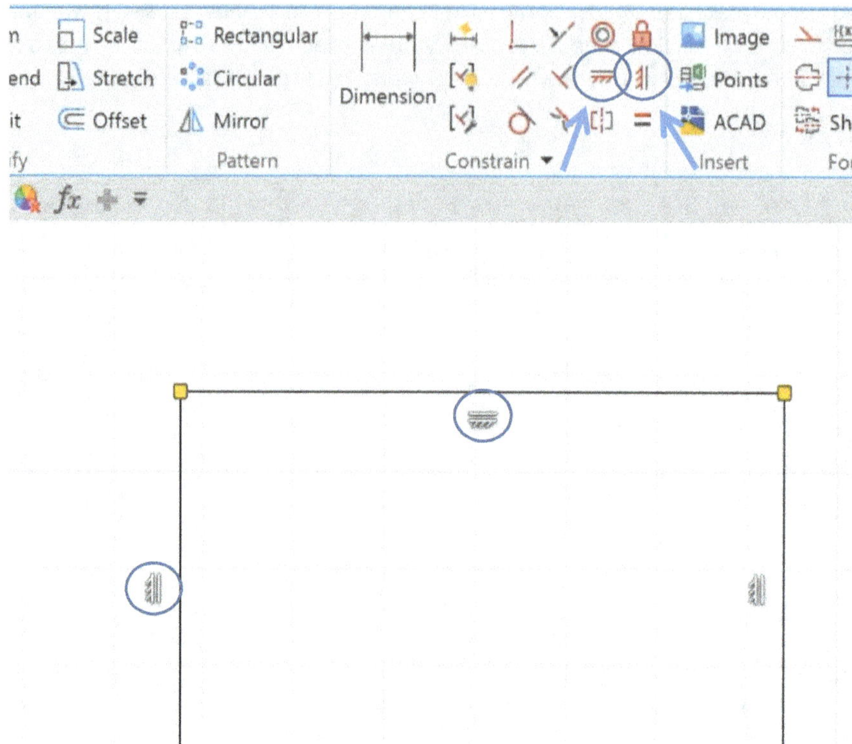

Figure 31: Apply constrain "horizontal" and "vertical"; always click on the opposite lines after the command has been selected.

In the bar at the bottom you can also hide the display of these conditions. In addition, you can use "Snap to Grid" to set whether the cursor should snap to the grid points when drawing, i.e. whether it should remain attached to the grid points for easier sketching, or not.

Figure 32: Show / hide dependencies ("Constrain") & activate / deactivate "Snap to Grid

Back to the "Constraints". With the relation "concentric" / "concentric" two circle structures can be set concentric to each other. For example, let's draw a large circle and a slightly smaller one. We want to get two concentric circles, i.e. two circles where the centers are congruent. We achieve this by selecting the appropriate dependency and the two circles.

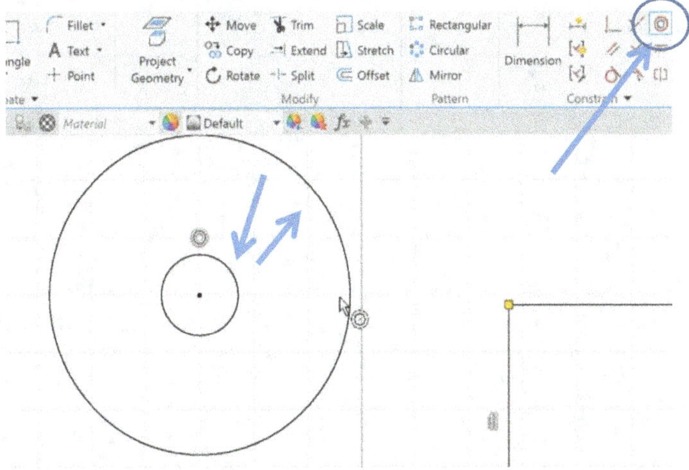

Figure 33: The "concentric" dependency; select command and select circles one after the other

The two "constraints": "Perpendicular" and "Parallel" are relatively self-explanatory. Nevertheless, let's look at a small example with two lines each. For the function "Perpendicular" / "plumb" we draw the following two lines. By selecting the condition and selecting the lines, we get as a result two lines that are perpendicular to each other.

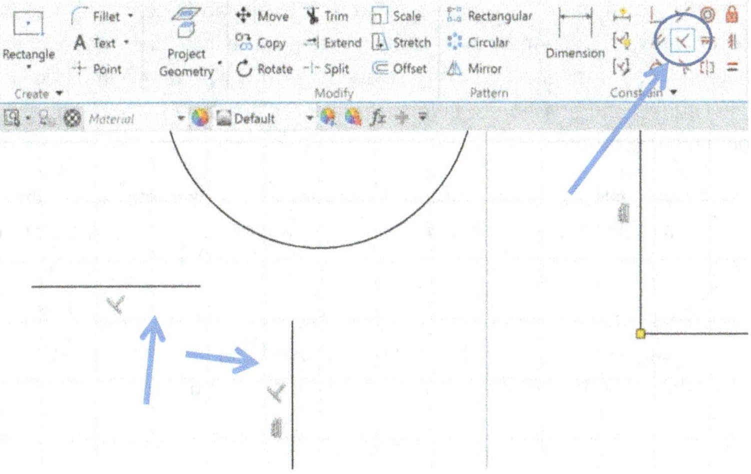

Figure 34: The "Perpendicular" dependency

For "Parallel" we draw two more lines and by selecting the condition we get two perfectly parallel lines.

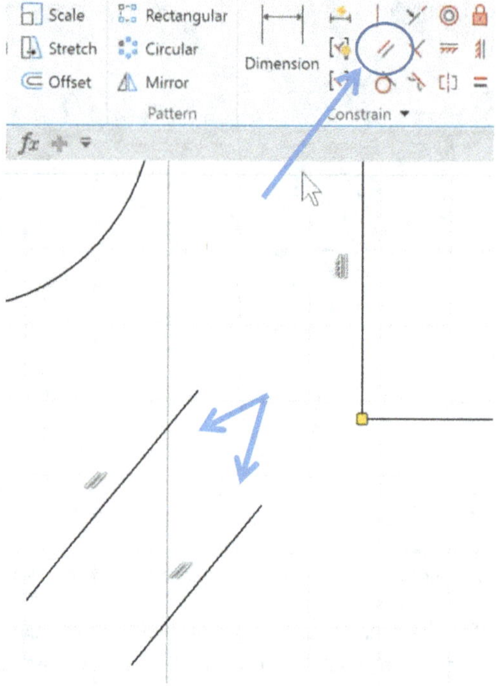

Figure 35: The "Parallel" dependency

We use the "constraints": "Coincident", i.e. congruent and "Colinear", i.e. colinear, whenever we want to connect two points or bring a line into linear dependence with another line of another element. To illustrate, let's draw a rectangle and two lines. We want to connect the first line to a vertex of the rectangle and make the second line colinear with the other line.

By the way, you can also apply multiple "constraints". For example, we could also still apply the constraint horizontally to a line that already has another constraint - except vertically.

Let's take a look at the "Tangent" condition. As the name and the small picture already indicate, we can use this to set a line tangential to a circle, for example. Let's try it out. First draw the circle, then a line and then apply the condition.

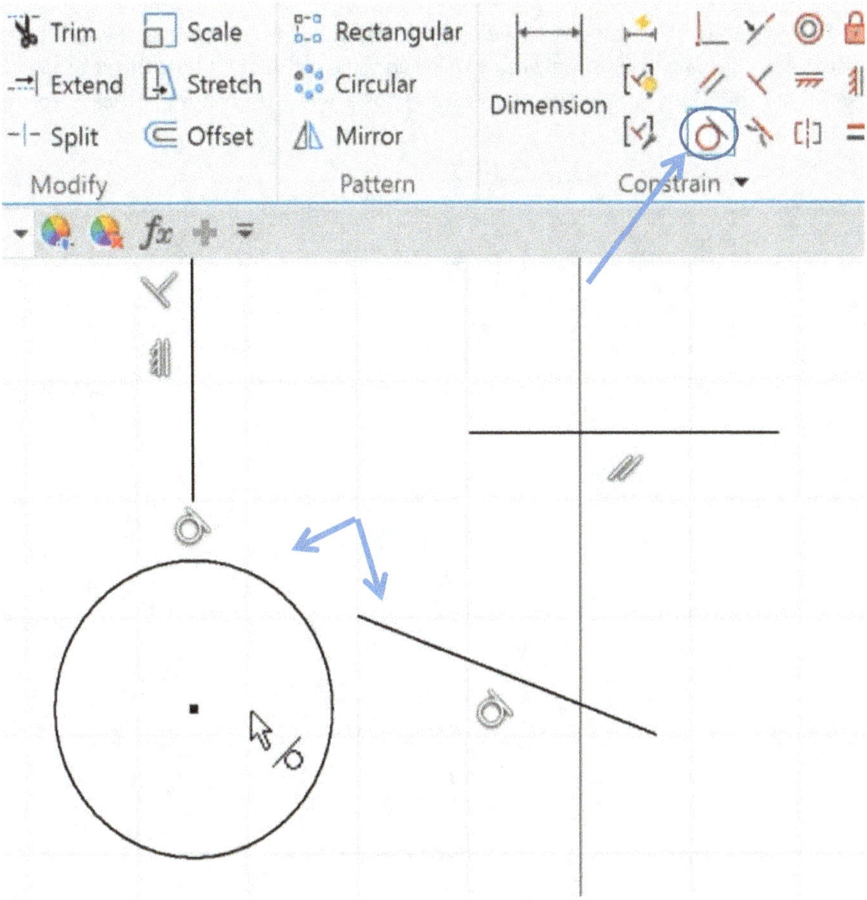

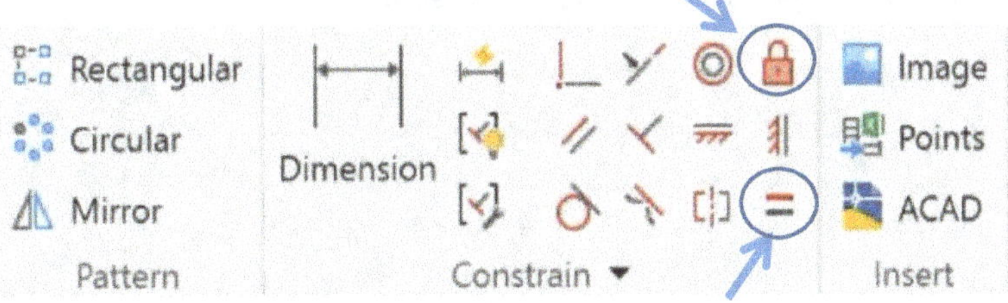

Figure 36: The "Tangent" dependency

Just try the two "constraints": "Fix" / "Fixing" and "Equal" / "Equal" once yourself. You can't go wrong and the name is relatively self-explanatory. The "Fix" constraint simply fixes an element in place in the drawing layer and "Equal" ensures that the same dimensioning exists between elements.

Figure 37: The "Fix" and "Equal" dependencies

With "Symmetric" you can set two elements, e.g. two lines, symmetrically to a third line, i.e. a symmetry axis. Simply draw three lines, select the first line, the second line and finally the third line and the two outer lines are aligned axisymmetrically to the middle one.

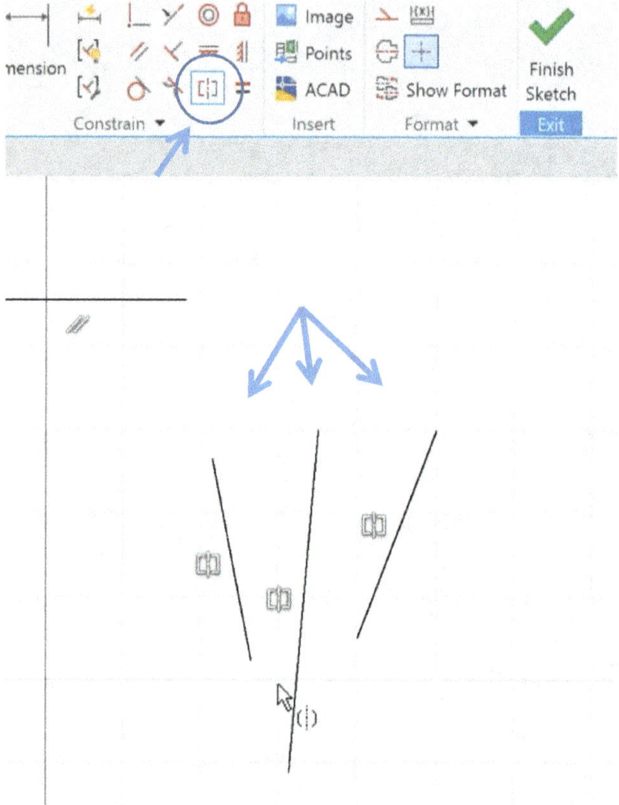

Figure 38: The "Symmetric" dependency using the example of three lines

With the command "Image" we could insert an image into the drawing environment, for example, if we simply want to trace a geometry.

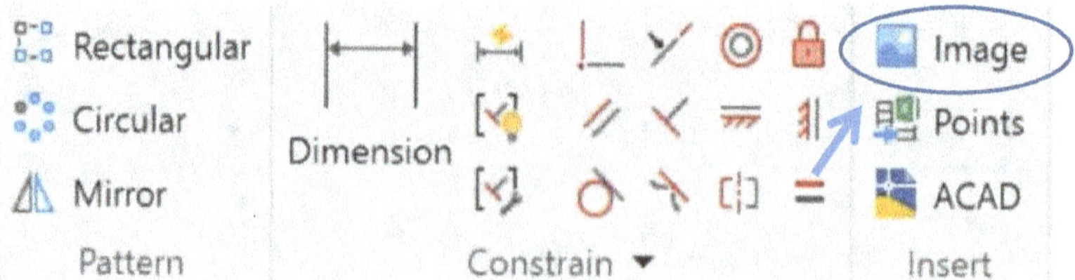

Figure 39: The "Image" command from the "Insert" section

To conclude these first 2D sketching exercises, please draw another circle in a new file, which you can then provide with fictitious dimensions using the "Dimension" function, i.e. "Dimensioning". For example, select a diameter of 50 mm. Simply draw the circle and select the "Dimension" tool. There are two ways with dimensions, both of which lead to the goal. You can draw a circle with the dimensions already correct by entering the values using your keyboard while drawing. Use the tab key to switch between the individual fields for entering the dimensions. Alternatively, you can draw any circle and then change the dimensions. You do this with the function "Dimension" / "Dimensioning" and a double click on the dimensioning. Then enter the desired value and confirm with the Enter key.

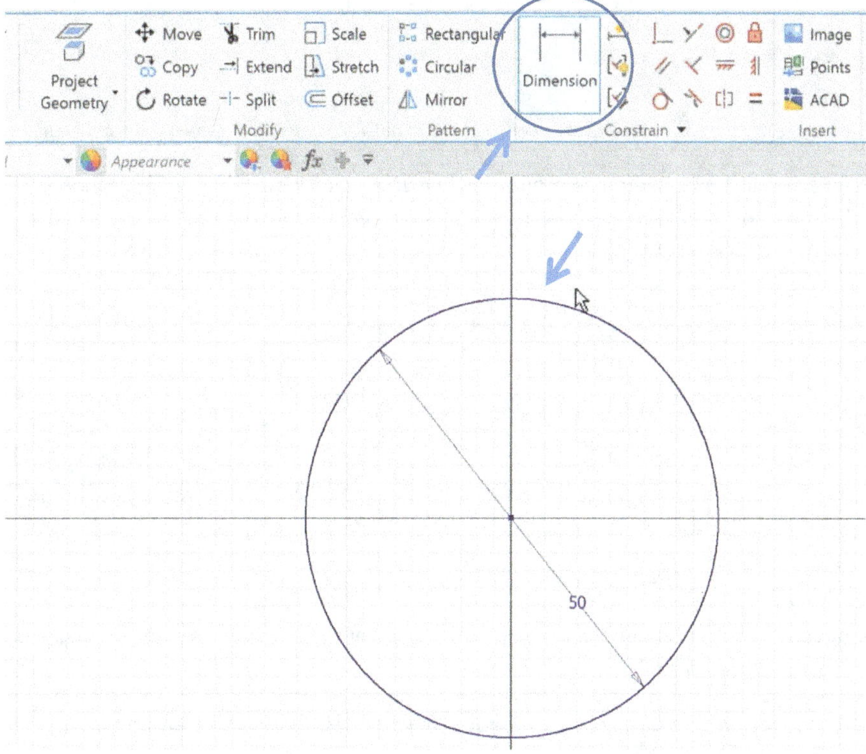

Figure 40: Drawing a circle with a diameter of 50 mm and dimensioning it with "Dimension

You can also use this command to dimension the distance between two lines. To do this, simply click first on the first line and then on the second line whose distance you want to dimension.

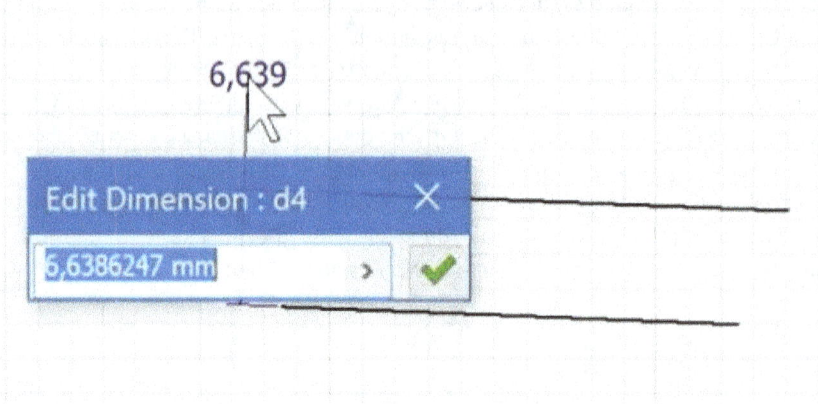

Figure 41: Dimension the distance between two parallel lines using the "Dimension" command

You can exit the 2D sketching mode with the green check mark in the upper menu bar. The program then switches back to the 3D environment and shows us our sketch as a profile on the selected plane.

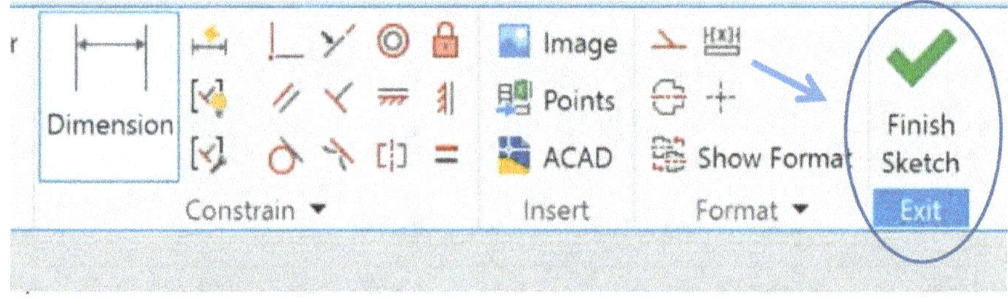

Figure 42: Exit 2D sketching mode and thus switch back to 3D mode

To create a three-dimensional object, it is important that the 2D sketch is completely closed and has no gaps.

By the way, with a double click on your mouse wheel you can fit an object into the current view. This is very helpful if you ever find yourself very far away in virtual space and can no longer see an object.

In the next chapter we will create a three-dimensional object from the 2D sketch we made. Very good, you are making good progress! Soon we will already get to the first real construction project!

3.2 3D object environment

In this chapter, we would now like to create a 3D object from the previously sketched 2D surface. To do this, we will use the functions from the "Create" section in the "3D Model" area. To create a cylinder, we use probably the most needed function from this menu. We use the command "Extrude" / "Extrusion". This function represents a so-called extrusion command. In other CAD programs you will therefore often find the term "Extrude" or "Extrude Linear" or similar.

Now simply select the function and the profile is normally already extruded automatically.

If not, simply click on the profile. Drag the displayed orange arrow with your mouse in the possible range of motion and change the dimensions of the 3D object in this way. Alternatively, you can also enter the desired dimension right away and confirm with Enter.

In the window that opens when you select the "Extrude" command and is called "Properties", you can select or deselect the profile and also specify the direction of the extrusion, i.e. to which side it should be extruded, or whether it should be extruded symmetrically in two directions from the sketch plane, for example. Under "Advanced Properties" you will find the option to make the object conical.

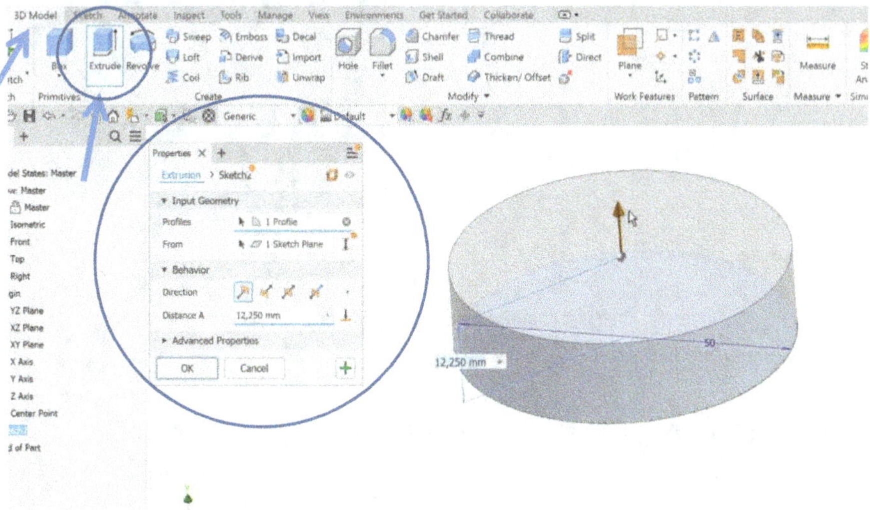

Figure 43: The "Extrude" command in the application; enter 50 mm as the dimension

Before we deal with the other commands from the "Create" menu, we will use the constructed cylinder to first get to know the most important commands from the

"Modify" section. We use this section whenever we want to modify an already constructed object.

For example, we can use the "Fillet" / "Round off" function to round one or more edges. Simply select the function and select one or more edges. An arrow appears again, which we use as with the "Extrude" command. In the "Properties" window we can then change further options.

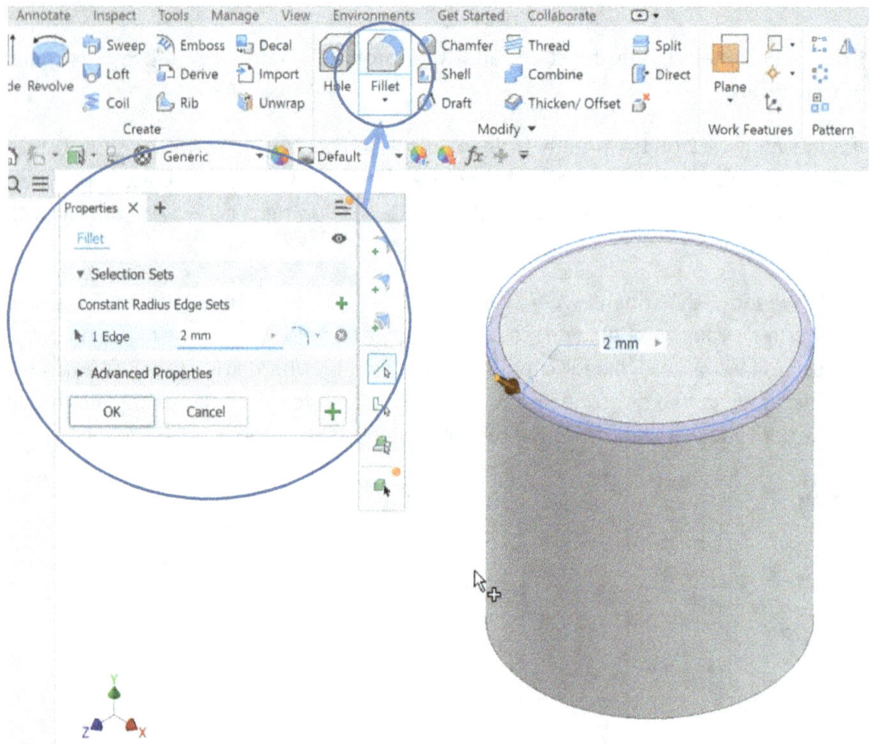

Figure 44: The Fillet command from the Modify section for edge fillets

In an analogous way, we can create a chamfer with "Chamfer" / "Chamfer".

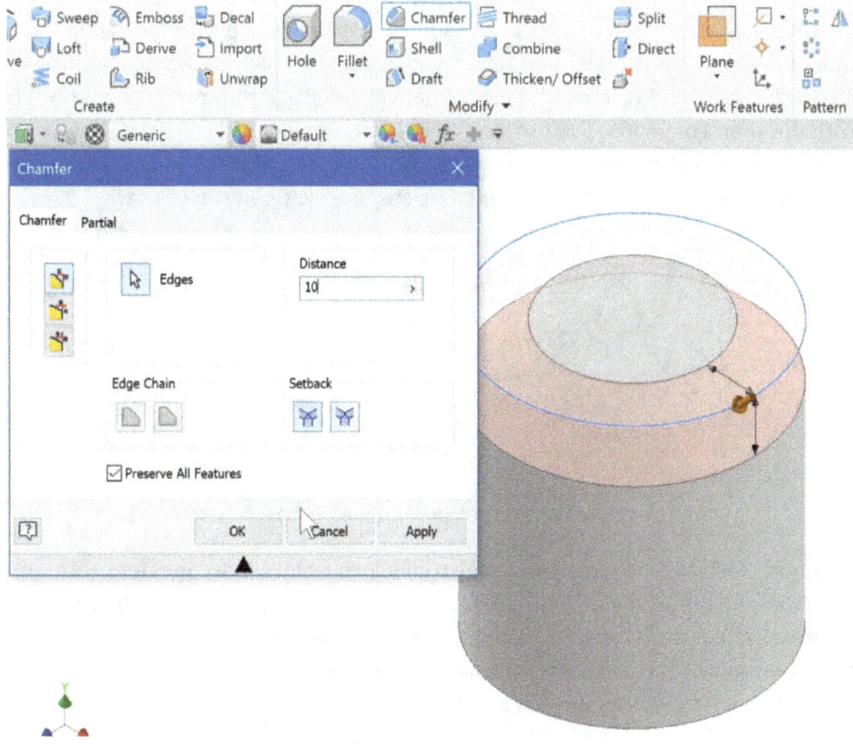

Figure 45: Creating a chamfer with "Chamfer"

Another important command is "Shell". With the help of this command you can easily hollow out an object, i.e. create a thin-walled 3D object. Select the command and the face of the cylinder and enter a wall thickness or use the arrow. Pretty simple, isn't it?

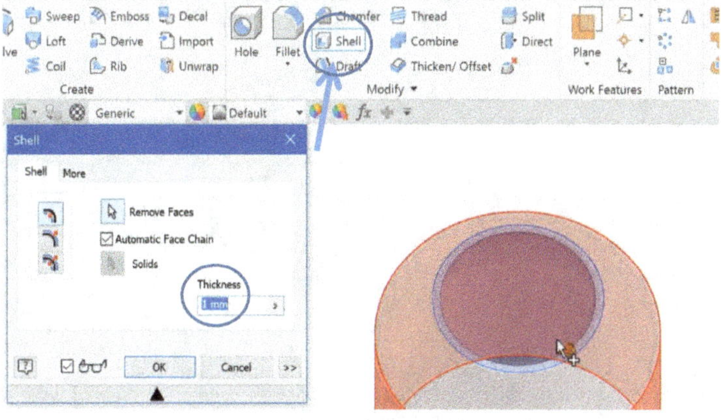

Figure 46: Hollowing out an object with "Shell"

The other commands are applied just as simply. With Hole a hole can be created, with Thread a thread. With Combine you can unite solids, with Split you can split them again. We will look at these commands in more detail later, using the construction projects. With the Draft command, you can quickly create a slope or incline. Simply select two faces of a 3D object and enter a slope angle. With "Thicken / Offset" you can strengthen a face with additional material and with "Delete Face" you can delete a face.

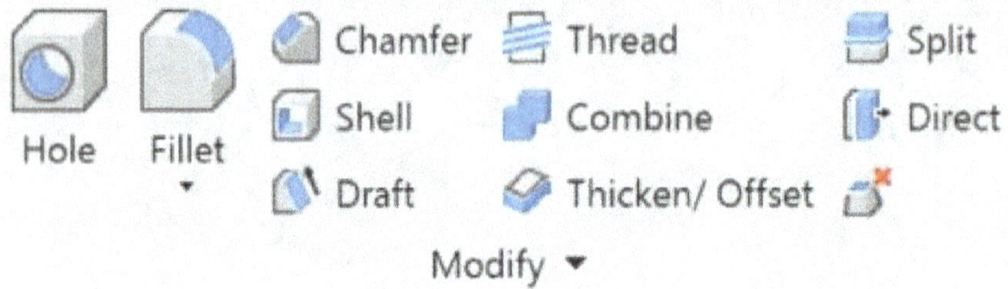

Figure 47: The remaining commands from the "Modify" section

Now that we know the most important commands from this section, let's turn once again to the "Create" menu. Besides "Extrude" we find here the important commands "Revolve" / "Rotate", "Sweep", "Loft" / "Elevation" and more. The explanations and sample images of the software are very clear and helpful here and already give us a first hint of what these commands can do.

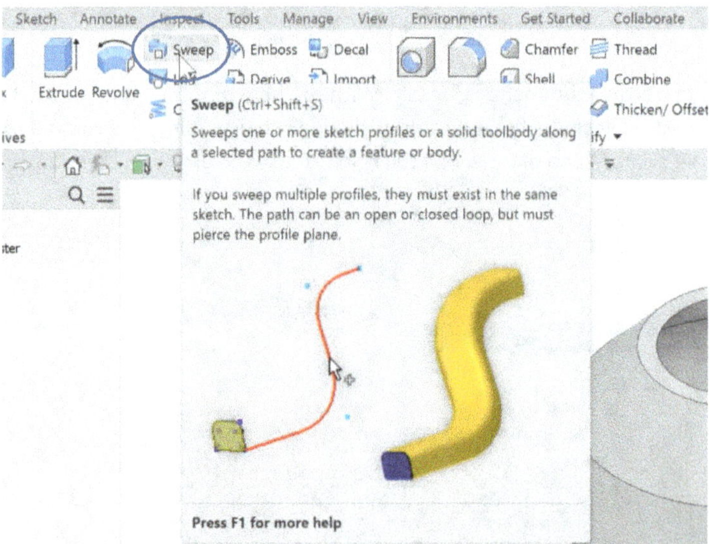

Figure 48: If you stay a little longer with the cursor on a feature, an explanation of the respective command often appears

We will look at how to use them in more detail in the next chapter, as this is related to how CAD design works.

By the way, in "Inventor" for some elements it is also possible to shorten the process from 2D sketch to 3D object by combining both steps, which can definitely save some time. For example, in the "Primitives" section of "3D Model" we can immediately construct a cuboid, a cylinder, a sphere and other elements with the respective command.

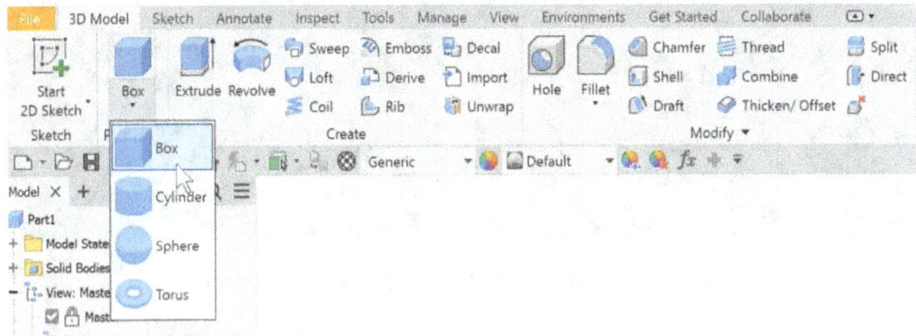

Figure 49: Create prefabricated 3D elements without detour

Simply select the command, sketch the footprint onto a plane of the 3D space and extrude the element.

And now, on to the next chapter!

3.3 Working methods of construction

As already briefly mentioned in the previous chapter, there are different approaches to the design of 3D objects. One possible approach to the design is, for example, to design as the actual machining - e.g. a milling or turning of a starting material, the so-called semi-finished product - would proceed.

Figure 50: "Turning" (left) and "Milling" (right) of a material

In the CAD program, you first create the raw material, in this case the cuboid material, and then work on it successively in further steps - using cutouts, holes, fillets and other design features virtually - so that you get the final element. That's why this method of construction is called subtractive. You reduce the initial material through individual processing steps until you get the desired object. But there are also other approaches, such as the additive method. Here, the CAD model or even the real object, as is the case with 3D printing, is built up element by element. We will take a look at how this works in concrete terms in a moment.

We will first deal with the classic subtractive approach. In the next steps, we want to make a hole and a cutout in rectangular form in a simple cube. I have already prepared the cube. The dimension is, for example, 50 mm in all directions.

Figure 51: Our starting material; a cube with the dimensions 50x50x50 mm

To create the hole, we can use the "Hole" function from the "Modify" section. Simply select the command and the surface on which you would place the drill in reality. Then select two edges and enter dimensions to determine the position of the hole on the surface.

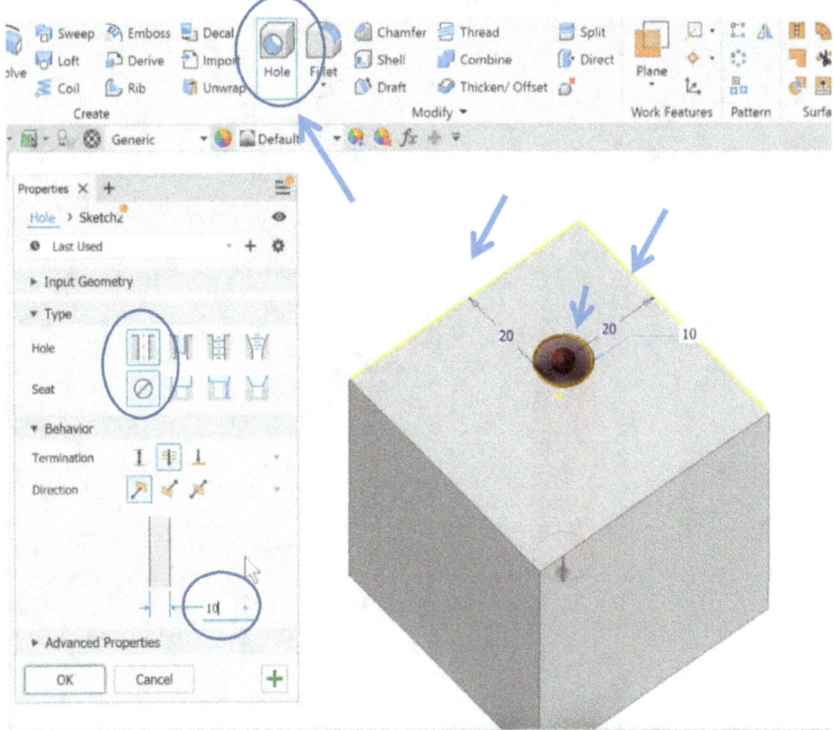

Figure 52: Create a hole with the "Hole" command; first select edges for dimensioning to the edges and enter dimension (without "Enter"); then select 10 mm as diameter

In the options window that appears, you can then select the type of hole, the dimension of the hole and the specific hole parameters. For example, we select a simple, so-called through-hole bore with a diameter of 10 mm. We could also create threads here, but more about that later.

For the cutout, we first need to create a 2D sketch of the geometry again. To do this, click on "Start 2D Sketch" / "Create 2D Sketch" and select, for example, the upper surface of the cuboid, since we want to bring the section into the cuboid from top to bottom.

Place a rectangle on the surface in the area of the cube with a click and enter a dimension of 10 mm each. Confirm with "Enter". Then we define the position of the rectangle on the surface using the "Sketch Dimension" or "Dimension" function. Since we are in two-dimensional space, i.e. sketching on a parallel of the x-z plane, we need an x and a z dimension to finally define the sketch, i.e. the rectangle, completely, i.e. to define the position and geometry. Enter the desired dimensions, e.g. 5 mm each from the left and upper edge of the cuboid.

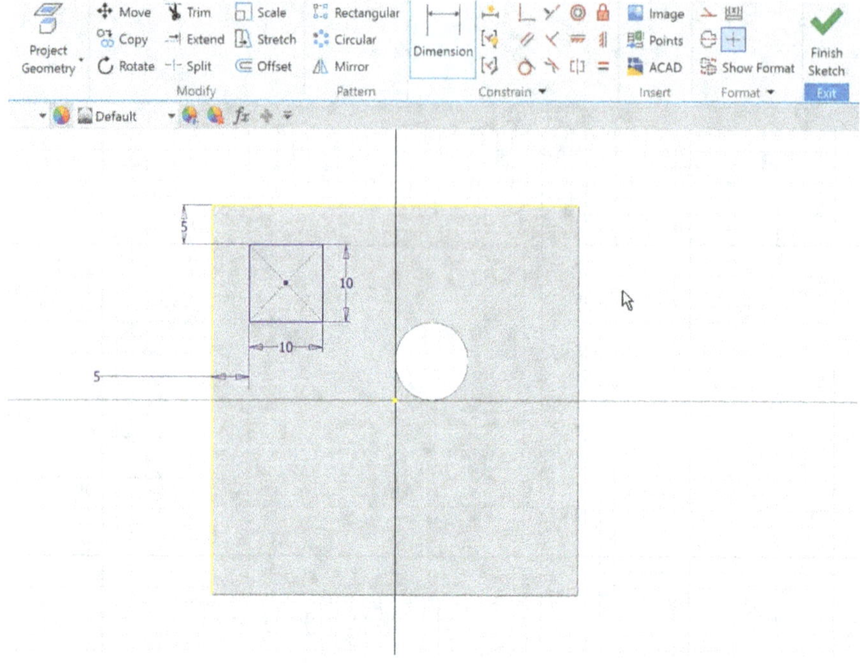

Figure 53: Draw a 10x10 mm rectangle on the top face of the cube with "2D Sketch"

Now the rectangle is completely dimensioned. As you may have noticed, the profile has turned blue. This indicates that all degrees of freedom are fully constrained, i.e. the position of the profile in the plane is fully defined by dimensions and dependencies, the "constraints", and cannot simply move by itself in later editing steps. A complete dimensioning and a fully defined sketch are very important for good results, always pay attention to them. After we have finished the sketch, we can create the section using the "Extrude" function. For example, the cutout should go completely through the part.

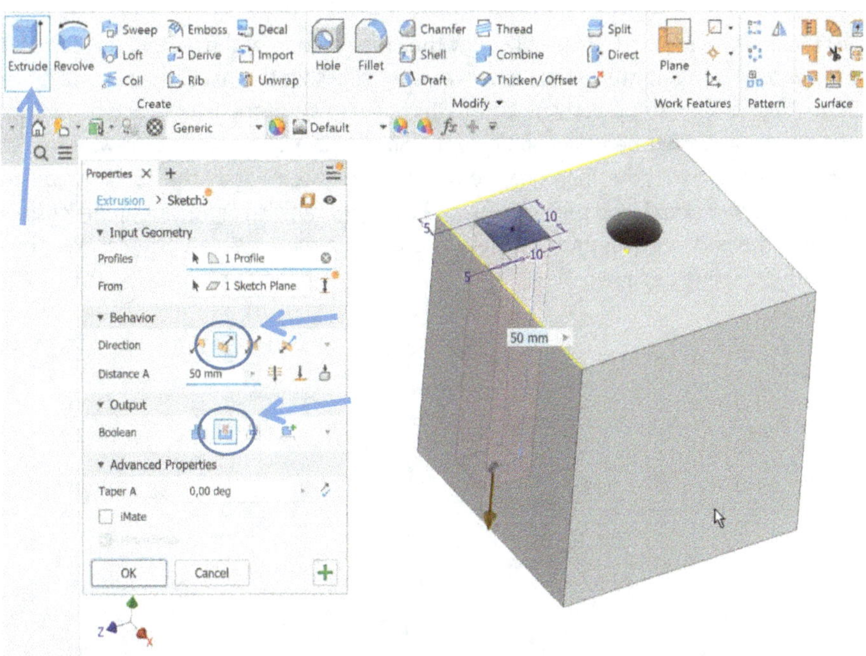

Figure 54: Insert the section as a rectangle with "Extrude"; for "Direction": select "Flipped"

The "Extrude" / "Extrusion" function can now be used to both remove and add material from the created sketch. So you can use "Extrude" in the design for a subtractive approach but also for the additive way of working.

To make the difference between the two working methods clear, we will now construct our first very simple part, which could serve as an assembly component for a machine, for example. First with additive working method and then with subtractive working method. By the way, it doesn't matter which method you choose, they both lead to the goal, the only difference here is in terms of effort and time required.

Figure 55: We would like to construct this fictitious assembly component in two ways

For the additive method, we simply draw the cross-section of the part. In this case, we can even do it in one step. Of course, we could also split the part into its rectangular bodies and line them up body by body, which would be more like the actual additive way. But that would be very cumbersome. So, in 2D mode, we first draw the cross section of the part on a plane of the coordinate system. Start the construction by selecting a new sketch and the plane. By the way, you can also right-click on the desired plane in the part browser and then select "Create Sketch" / "Create Sketch". We then draw the first line as shown.

Figure 56: First draw a vertical line of 50 mm on the x-z plane; start at the origin

Complete the profile with the following lines and dimensions. Simply trace them!

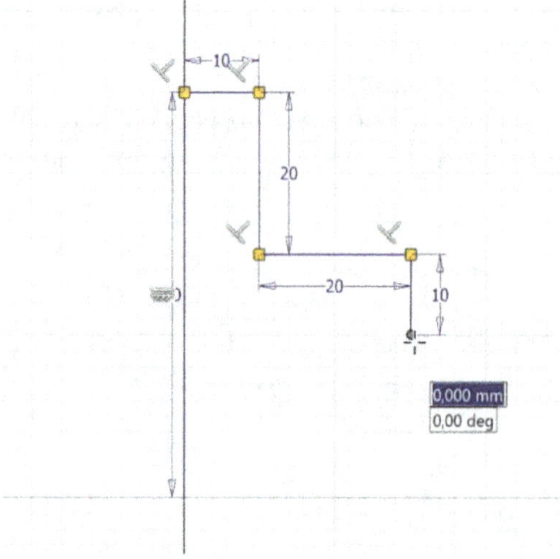

Figure 57: Draw additional 10 mm and 20 mm long vertical and horizontal lines

Then complete the cross-section profile with additional lines as follows.

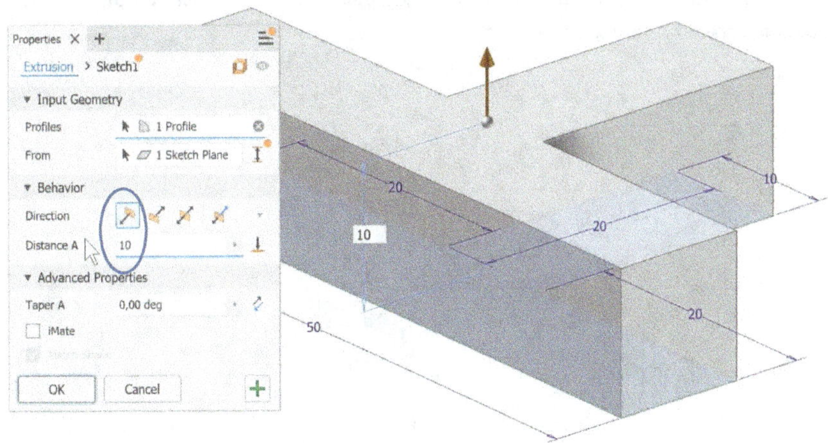

Figure 58: The complete profile of the component on the x-z plane

Then you can leave the 2D sketching environment and thus switch to 3D mode. Select the "Extrude" function and create a three-dimensional body from the 2D cross-section, using a dragging movement in the direction of the displayed arrow. Enter a dimension of 10 mm with the help of the keyboard. That's it!

Figure 59: Using the Extrude function to create the 3D body

Finally, we create three holes for mounting. For this we use the "Hole" command.

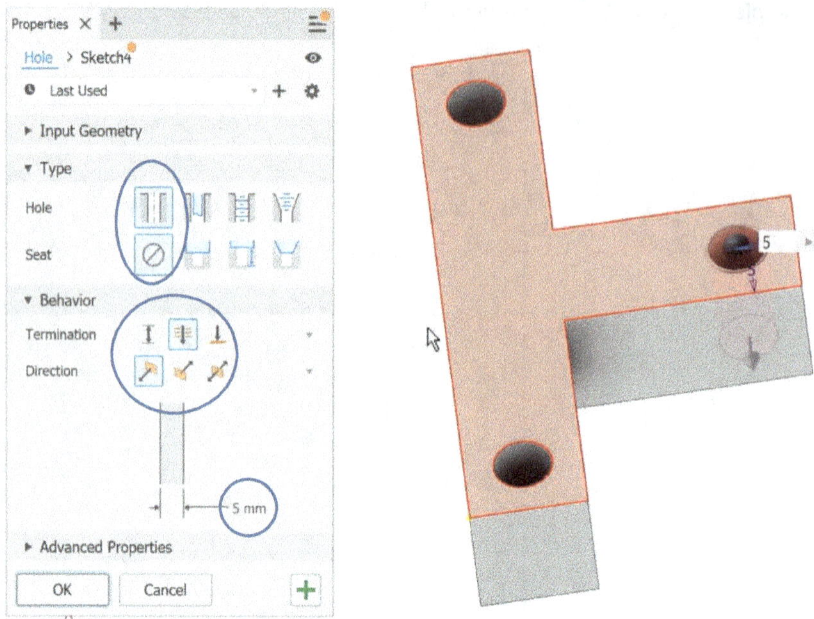

Figure 60: The three holes, each 5 mm from the edges and 5 mm in diameter

Now we would like to use the subtractive construction method for the same part for illustration. To do this, we draw a rectangle with the dimensions 50 mm and 30 mm in 2D sketch mode in a new document and create a cuboid with 20 mm using the "Extrude" / "Extrusion" function. We thus virtually first create the starting material, the so-called semi-finished product, from which the part would be punched out, cut out or milled out in reality, for example.

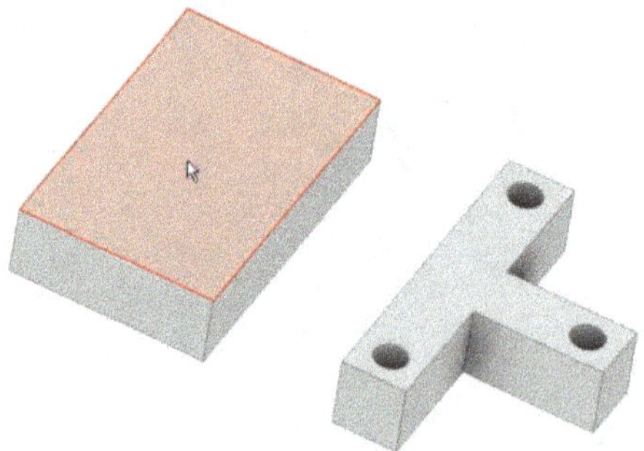

Figure 61: Creating a cuboid (left) with 50 x 30 x 20 mm for the second working method

Then we draw the cutouts in the solid material. To do this, we first create a 2D sketch on the upper - alternatively, of course, the lower - surface. First sketch the upper half

44

of the cutout for the geometry of the part using lines. Make sure that surfaces are created, that is, that you also connect the profiles at the edges.

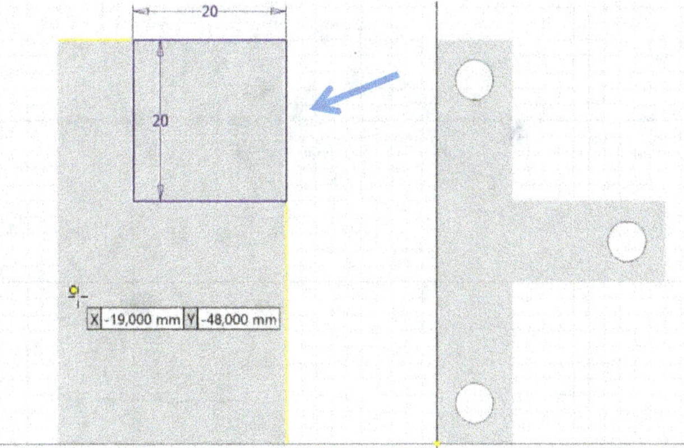

Figure 62: Drawing the upper half of the cutout on the cover surface in a 2D sketch

And then the bottom half. We can also simply create a rectangle for this instead of using lines. We draw the negative of the part into the solid, so to speak. We can also draw the geometries for the holes in this sketch at the same time, to execute them as a cutout instead of using the "Hole" command, and save ourselves a step this way.

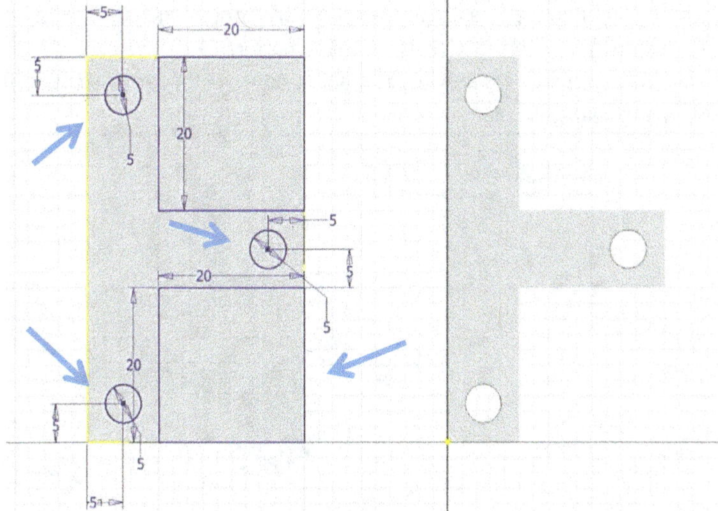

Figure 63: The complete profile for the section

Then you can again use the Extrude function to cut out the two drawn faces from the solid.

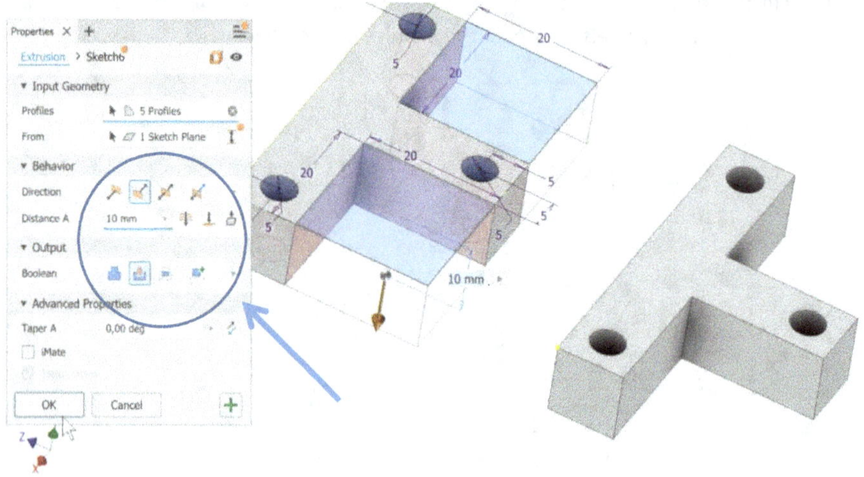

Figure 64: Use the "Extrude" function to create the section; select the rectangular profiles and the three circles and make settings

Two approaches for an identical solution. One quite simple, the other a bit more elaborate.

Now let's look at a few more possible ways of working with the construction. In addition to the "Extrude" function, there are a few other functions in the "Create" section that we would like to take a brief look at in this chapter. First, there is the "Revolve" command. You can use this whenever you want to construct a part with a rotation axis, e.g. a part that in reality would be machined by "turning".

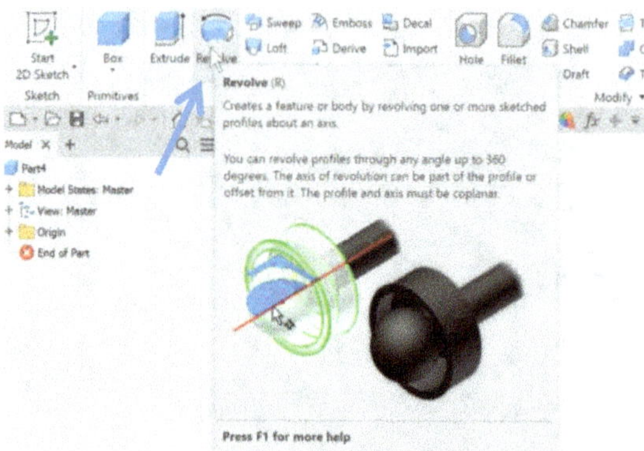

Figure 65: The "Revolve" command from the "Create" section of "3D Model"

To do this, simply draw a cross-section on one of the planes, e.g. on the x-z plane or x-y plane. Why these planes? Because we want to use "x" as our axis of rotation. But you could also use the y-z plane and then use "y" or "z" as your axis of rotation. Let's take a closer look. Feel free to draw along with it. For example, we will create the following basic profile of a bolt in the 2D environment.

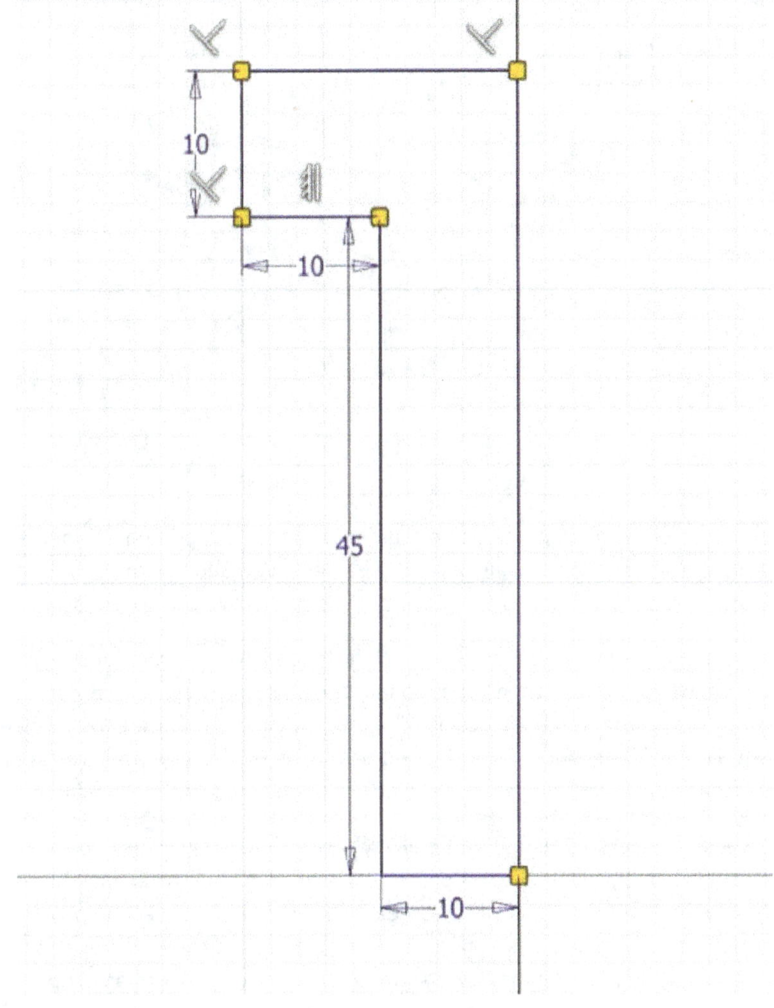

Figure 66: Half of the cross section of a bolt; it is best to start with the bottom 10 mm line and then draw the 45 mm line and so on

We need to draw one half of the cross section of the 3D body. After finishing the sketch and selecting the "Revolve" / "Rotate" command, we must first define our rotation axis, in our case the x-axis. As you can see, the software then creates the solid.

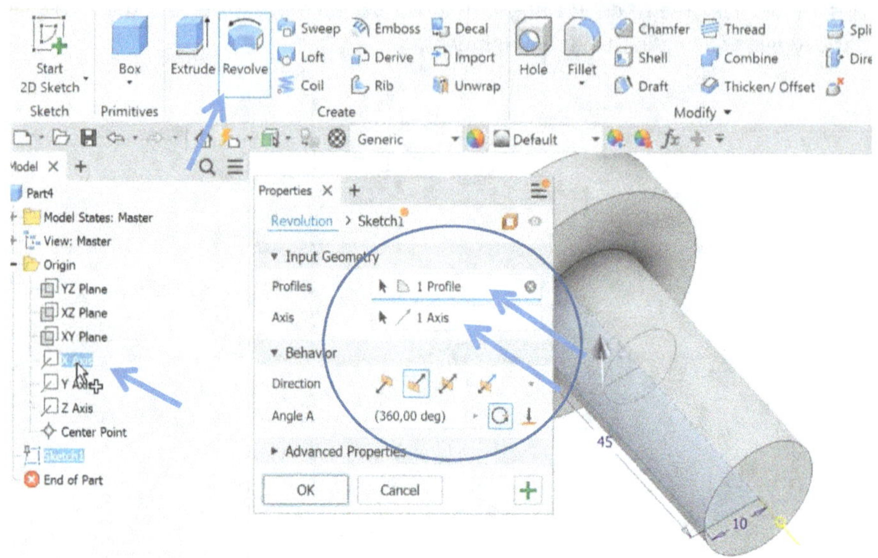

By entering a number of degrees, you can define the range of rotation. Of course, such a bolt could also be created using several sketches, in an additive manner, using the "Extrude" function. Just think for a moment how that would work in this case.

However, the way via rotation is usually much faster and more elegant for such a rotary part. This is what I meant when I mentioned that there are several ways of working even for one and the same part. Depending on the part, these are faster, slower or simple or cumbersome, but usually all lead to the goal. By the way, the thread of bolts is then added in mass production by rolling between two rollers.

The "Sweep" / "Sweeping" command is always useful when you want to create a part that follows a slightly more complex path. Let's take a look at how to understand this. For the "Sweep" command, you always need a 2D sketched cross-section profile and a path, that is, simply a line, or an arc or "spline" or freeform curve. For example, let's create a "spline" by selecting the command in a 2D sketch on the x-y plane and drawing several points as you like. But make sure that the end point or start point is the coordinate center. The more points, the more detailed the contour will be.

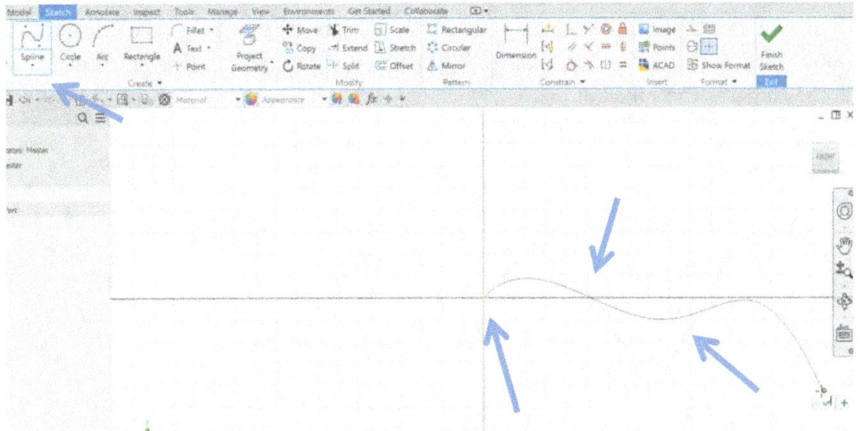

Figure 67: Creating a "spline" by starting at the origin of the coordinate system and then setting points several times at intervals ("Spline" can be found at "Line" in the drop-down menu); geometry freely selectable on the x-y plane

For the cross-section profile we now have to change the plane. To do this, we close the sketch and start a new sketch on the y-z plane. We draw e.g. a circle or a rectangle and select the end point of the previously drawn deposited profile in the x-y plane.

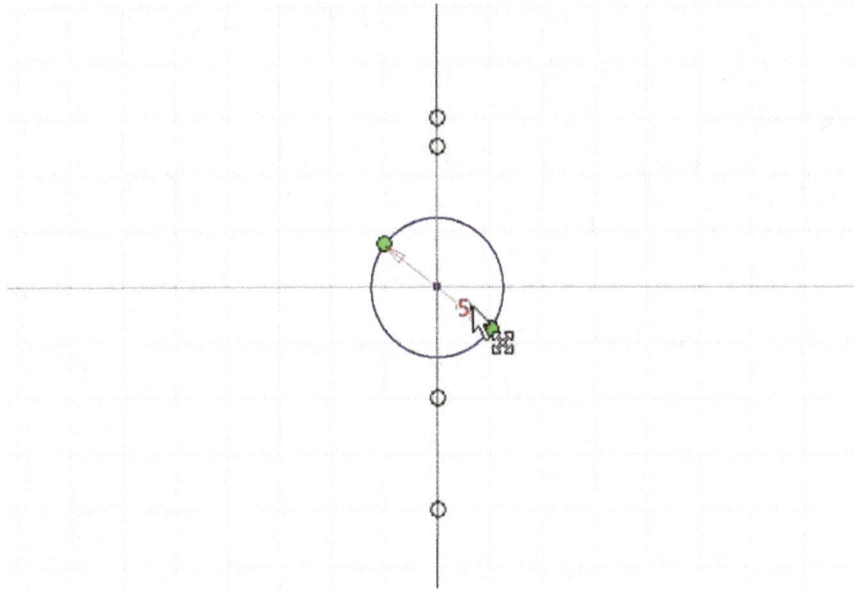

Figure 68: Draw a 5 mm circle at the origin of the x-y plane (the small circles represent components of the "spline" in the other plane, you do not need to draw them)

Then, when we finish the sketch, in 3D mode, we can run the "Sweep" command and would normally have to select the profile first and then the path. However, the program already creates the solid automatically.

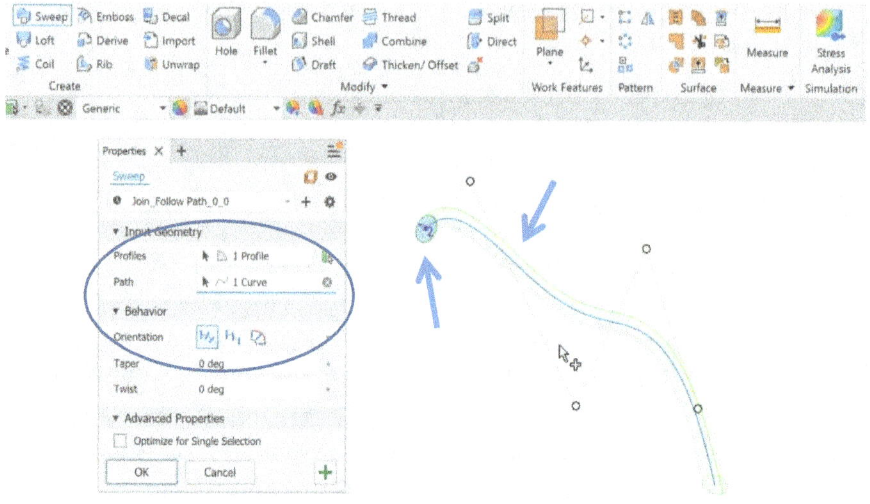

Figure 69: Select the "Sweep" command in 3D mode; select profile and path if necessary

In the "Properties" window we could still make various settings, e.g. change the alignment.

The last important command from this section and for this chapter is "Loft" / "Elevation". With "Loft", simply put, you can have two surfaces connected to each other in 3D space. Let's try it out! We will draw a profile in the x-y plane, e.g. a rectangle or any other shape.

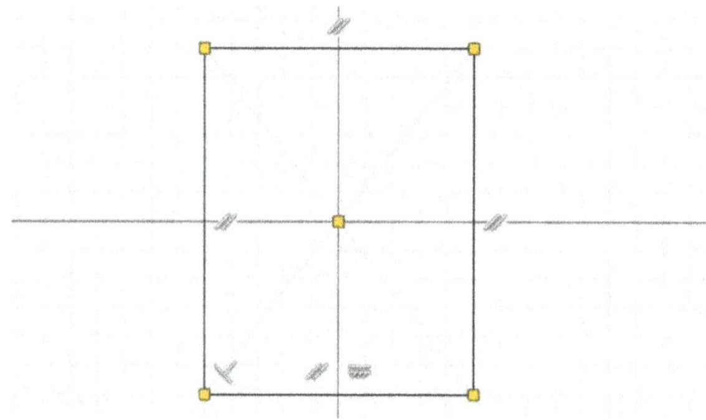

Figure 70: Draw rectangle on x-y plane; dimensions freely selectable

Then we first create a new plane parallel to the x-y plane with an offset or offset to it. Right-clicking on the x-y plane and selecting "Offset Plane" / "Offset Plane" makes this very easy.

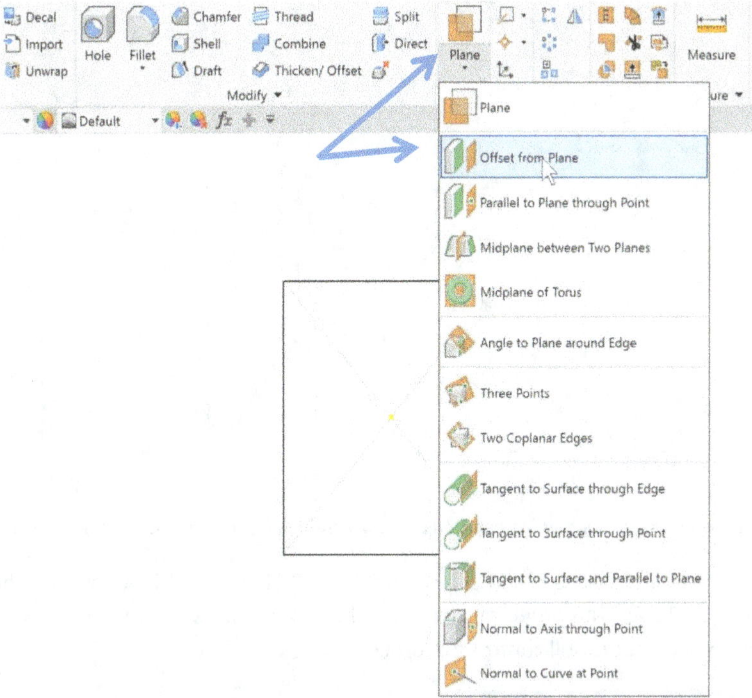

Figure 71: An offset plane can also be created in the "Plane" drop-down menu; first select command and then parallel plane (here e.g. the x-y plane)

We then drag the arrow or enter a dimension with the keyboard.

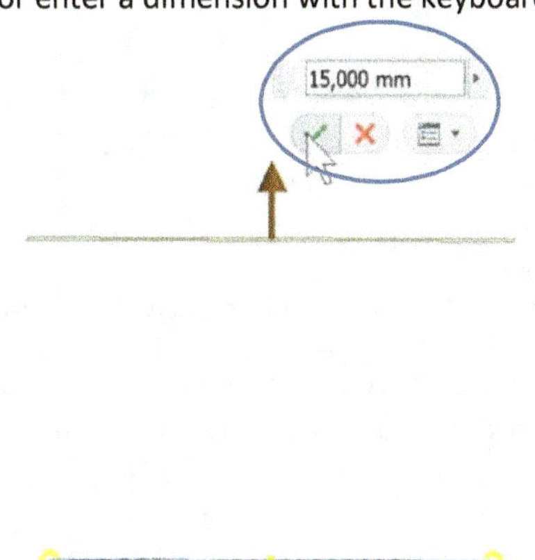

Figure 72: Selecting 15 mm as the distance for the parallel plane to the x-y plane

On this new layer we draw the second surface for our project in the next step. E.g. a slightly larger rectangle. The centers should be congruent.

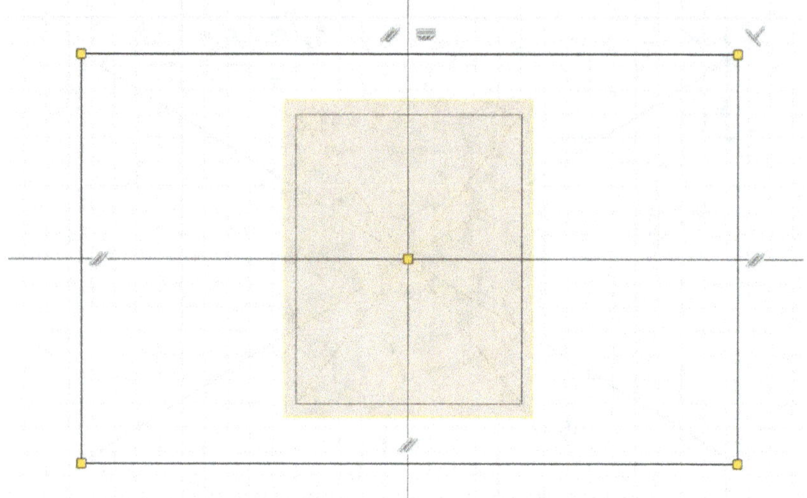

Figure 73: Create another rectangle on the newly created layer; dimensions freely selectable

Then we finish the sketch and select the "Loft" / "Elevation" function and the two sketched surfaces. The program then joins the two surfaces to form a 3D solid. With the settings we could still control this process in detail.

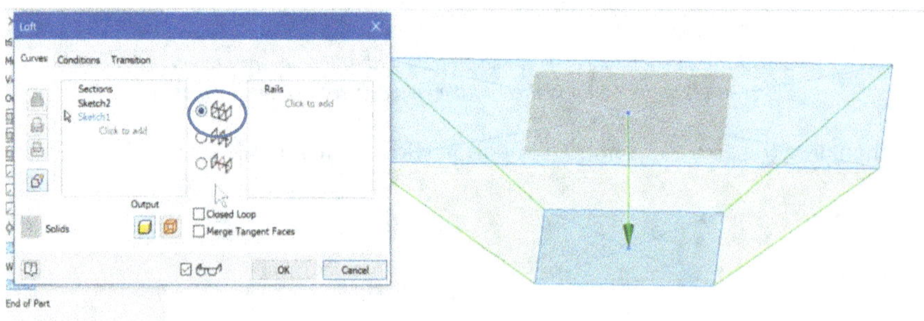

Figure 74: Select "Loft" command in 3D mode and then select both rectangles

Very good! So much for the approach and working methods in CAD design. We can successfully check off this chapter and move on to the next one. In the following, we will take a closer look at the difference between a single part and an assembly.

3.4 Individual parts vs. assemblies

As in the real world, you can also virtually assemble a component or assembly from several individual parts in the CAD environment. To design a complex machine or other complex assembly, one first designs the individual parts of this complex part and then virtually assembles these individual parts in the software. To do this, you use mates, connections or relationships. In "Inventor" there is also the possibility to create "Joints". But more about that later.

In Inventor, you create the parts and the assembly in a separate environment. When you have finished creating the individual parts, you insert all the individual parts of an assembly into the file of the assembly and then connect them in the assembly environment, e.g. to a machine or simply said: to an assembly. Each individual part has its own origin and its own folder in the part browser of the assembly. The assembly itself also has its own origin. Other CAD programs are structured somewhat differently here and, for example, everything can be created and joined together in one program environment; this is the case, for example, with "Fusion 360", also from Autodesk.

So how does this work? For an assembly, you must first create all the parts in the "Part" environment. When you have finished designing a first part, e.g. such a simple turned part, which you can create yourself using the following dimensions, you simply create a second new part in a new file.

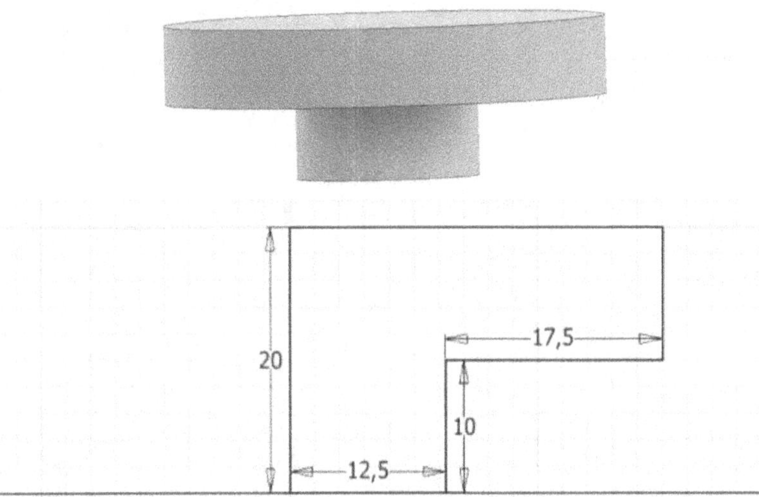

Figure 75: Create the first turned part (top) using the profile (bottom) and Revolve

We could, for example, draw another such profile for a second turned part, which we then create again using the "Revolve" / "Turn" function.

Figure 76: The second turned part as a counterpart to the first turned part;
try to determine the profile and dimensions for it yourself

Then you create an assembly file. The two individual parts are then inserted into this assembly using "Place".

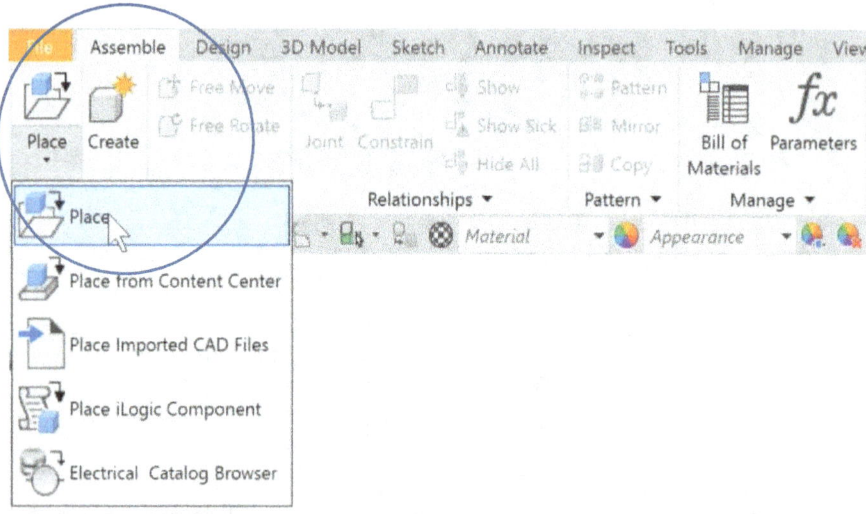

Figure 77: Using the "Place" command to insert a single part into an assembly
(we are in the "Assembly" environment in this picture, for this you have to create an assembly)

Click on the drawing layer to insert the part. If you want to insert it again, simply click a second time, if not, end the process with the "ESC" key. Alternatively, you can create a new part directly in an assembly. To do this, use the "Create" command from the "Assemble" menu in an assembly.

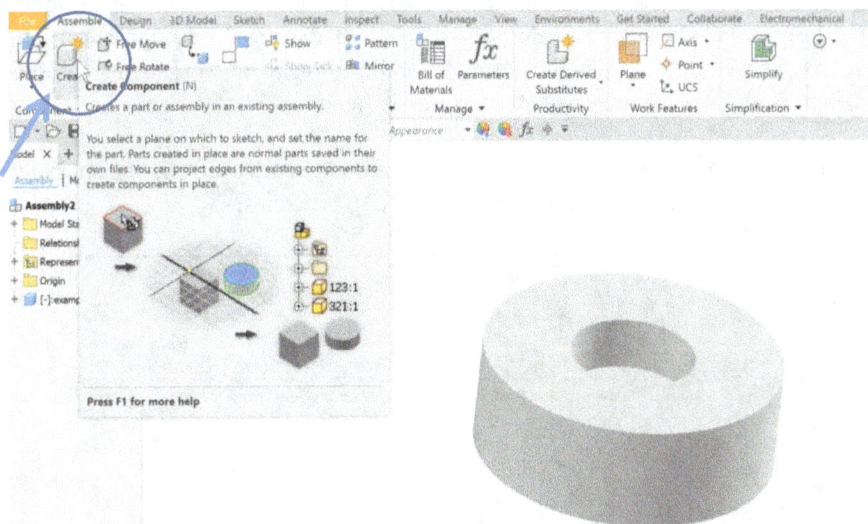

Figure 78: Using the "Create" command; creating a single part directly in the assembly

This is often very helpful, since the first component remains as a reference and thus the dimensions for the new part can be very easily drawn or determined to fit exactly. This would then work as follows for our second single part:

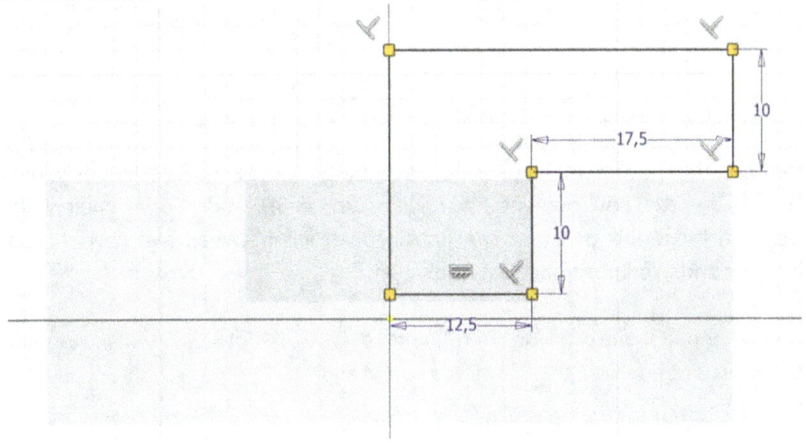

Figure 79: Draw the sketch for the other part on the y-z plane in the assembly

By the way, whether you want to create the new single part directly in the assembly or whether you create it in the single part environment is a matter of taste and varies depending on the user and the way of working.

Let's now take a look at the assembly of these two individual parts. We can move the two inserted individual parts freely in space, so we need to link the two individual parts in the next step to define the positions and the range of movement in three-dimensional space. Here we need the "Assemble" menu.

In "Inventor" you have two possibilities to link parts with each other. On the one hand, you can work with constraints as in many other CAD programs.

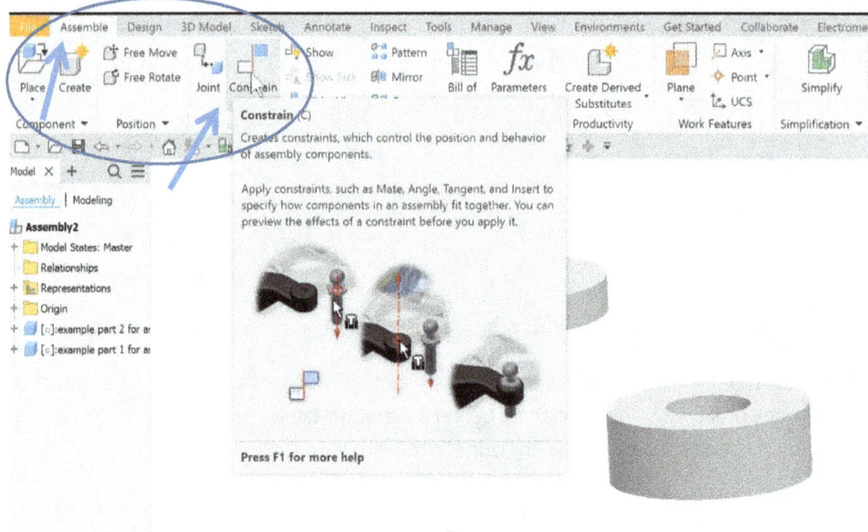

Figure 80: "Constrain" in the "Relationships" area of the "Assemble" tab in an assembly

With these, the movement range of individual parts is restricted. We already know this from the 2D sketch environment. It works similarly in 3D mode. For example, you can create a distance link or e.g. a concentric constraint between two parts to get an assembled and fixed positioned assembly.

On the other hand, one can work with "joints" or "articulations". Instead of restrictions, one creates a defined range of motion through a joint.

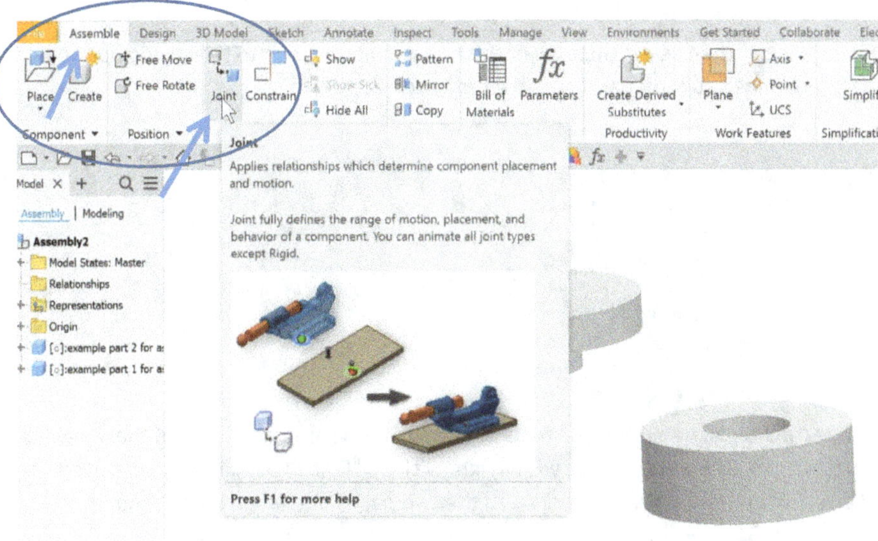

Figure 81: "Joint" in the "Relationships" area of the "Assemble" tab in an assembly

An example: In a hinge joint of a garden gate, for example, only one rotation around one axis is allowed, all other so-called degrees of freedom are blocked. Thus, no other movement can be executed.

First the method of "constraints" / "restrictions". This is also used by default in other CAD programs and is therefore generally a bit more common. To link our two example parts we choose a concentric constraint, which in this case is called "Insert".

Figure 82: Select the "Constrain" command and then select "Insert" for "Type"

Simply select, then select the axes of the two individual parts to be linked and the two parts are joined together and are now firmly connected.

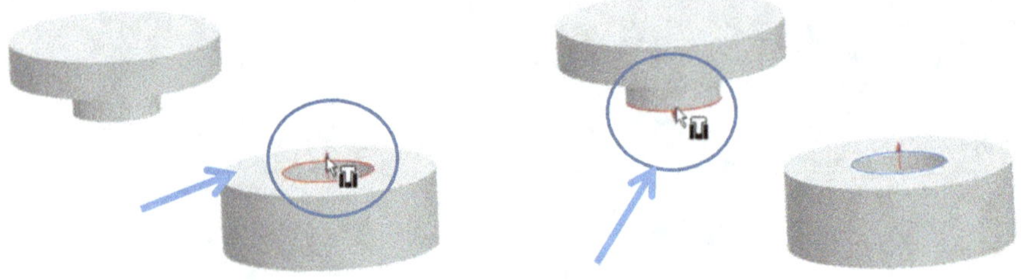

The restriction is then displayed to us in the part browser in the folder of the individual part. We can also edit this here with a right click on "Edit". For example, we can add an "Offset" if we want a distance between the two parts, or change the alignment.

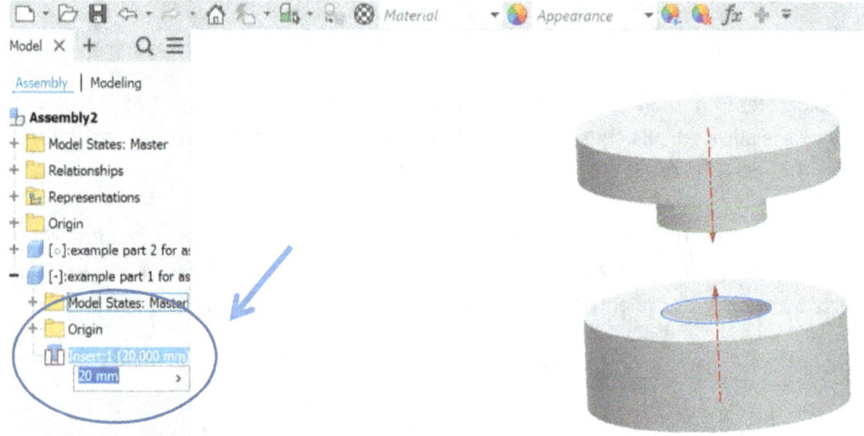

Figure 83: The two linked individual parts with an offset of 20 mm

There are also other constraints available, namely: "Mate", "Angle", "Tangent" and "Symmetry". With "Mate" you can make two surfaces congruent with each other. Simply select one face of the first part and one face of the second part. These two surfaces will then be congruent with each other. A movement in the plane is still possible. With "Tangent" you can connect two elements tangentially and with "Angle" you can create an angular relationship between two elements. Based on the name, you can already derive the function very well.

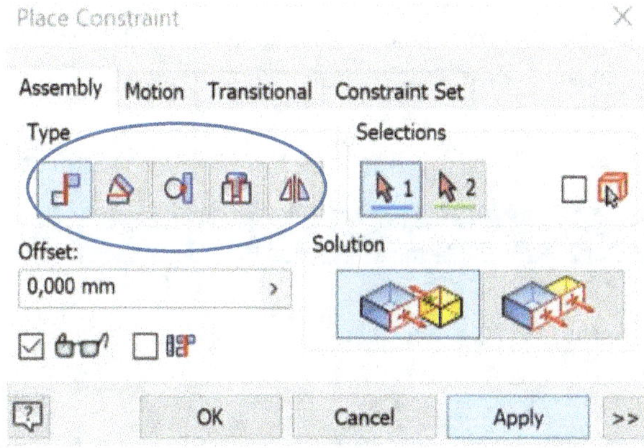

Figure 84: The other available constrain types

The goal is to link the individual parts realistically, i.e. to link a bolt, for example, concentrically and rigidly with a borehole of an assembly part. Or, for example, to link a piston of a lifting cylinder so that it is guided linearly and has two stop points.

However, our two joined individual parts can now still be moved freely in the assembly, since the reference to the origin of the assembly is still missing. The easiest way is to fix one of the two individual parts at the origin. We do this with the "Ground and Root" command from the "Assemble" menu section in the "Productivity" area.

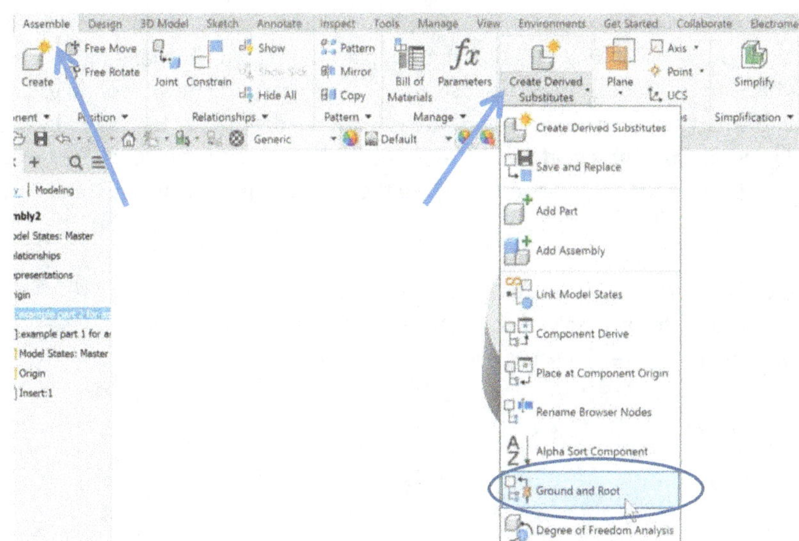

Figure 85: The Ground and Root command in the Productivity drop-down menu

Simply select the item and command, then enable "Ground at origin" and optionally "Create origin flush constraints".

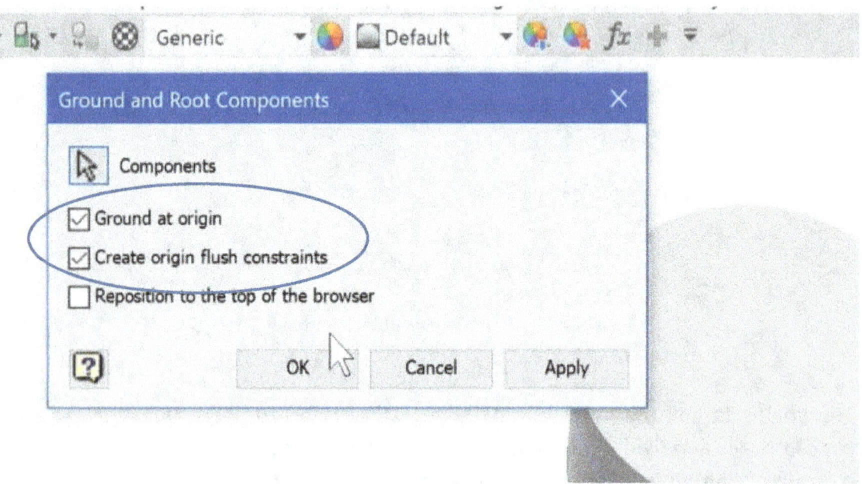

Figure 86: The options of the "Ground and Root" command

Then the part is moved to the origin of the assembly and fixed there. If the option "Create origin flush constraints" is activated, three constraints are created for the fixation, if not, the part is fixed without constraints. The advantage of the constraints is that you can edit them later if you want. For example, you could set an "offset". Another advantage is that you can animate "Constraints" in the animation environment "Inventor Studio" with one click, i.e. you can play and record a movement. This is not possible with Joints. By the way, you can also drag a single part into an assembly. Simply select the part and drag it into the assembly. If it is the first part of the assembly, it will be aligned and fixed based on the origin, so you don't have to use the "Ground at origin" command. The next part that you drag into the assembly is then initially free to move again.

As already mentioned, "Inventor" also offers the possibility to use "Joints" for these connections or the assembly of single parts to an assembly. In the menu "Assemble" / "Zusammenfügen" we first select the command "Joint" / "Gelenk".

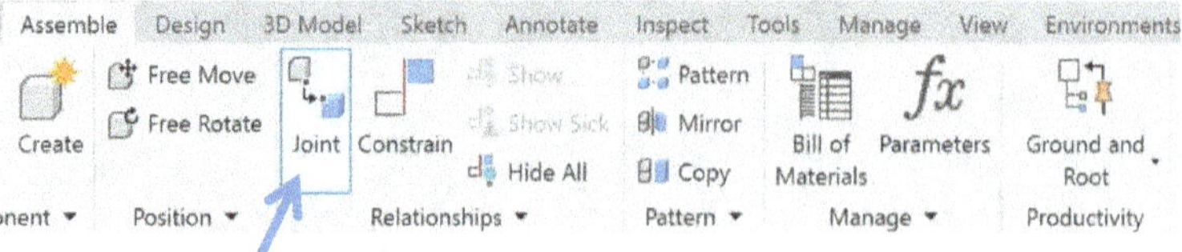

Figure 87: Selecting the "Joint" command in the assembly

Then we have to perform two steps. On the one hand, define the positions of the joint origins, e.g. select the points on the surfaces we want to link, and on the other hand, define the range of motion using the joint. Let's try a few possibilities. On the one hand, we could select these two joint origins on these surfaces and create, for example, a rigid link with "Rigid" / "Rigid".

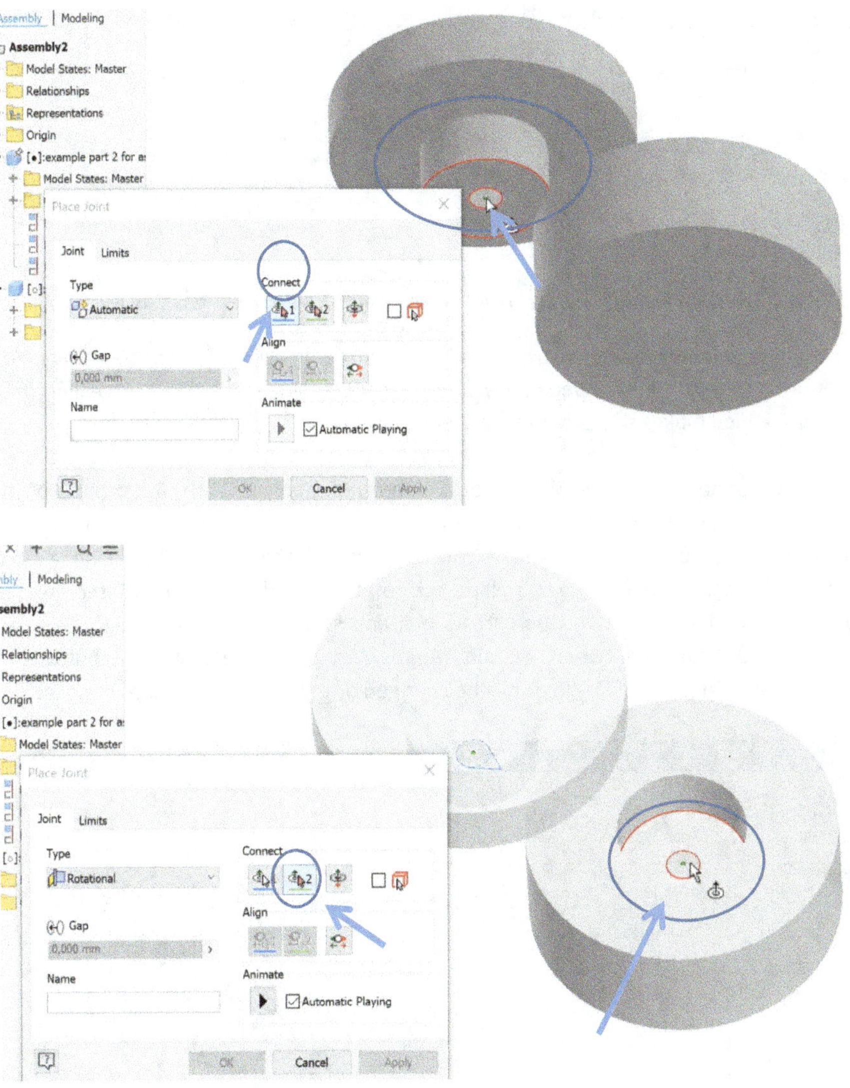

Figure 88: Selecting the two points shown as joint origins

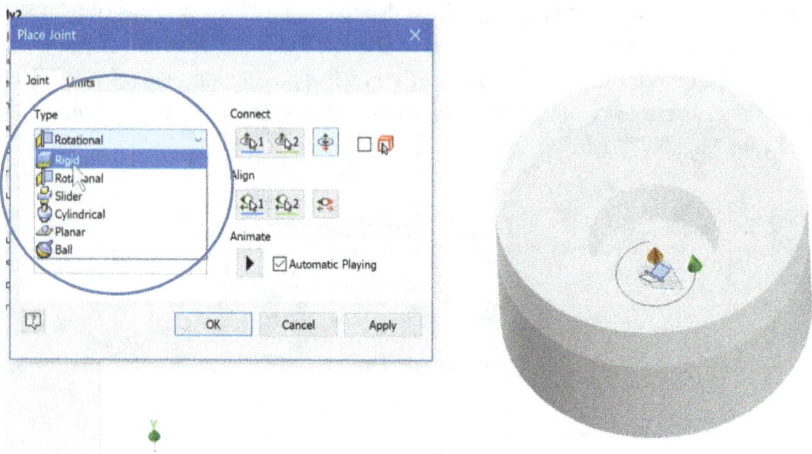

Figure 89: In the options for "Type" : select "Rigid"; Try the other "Types" as well

By the way, when selecting the relationship, a short animation of the possible range of motion is played, which I personally find very successful and helpful. A really great feature, which makes this program very descriptive.

On the other hand, we could allow a rotation around the y-axis with "Rotational". With "Slider" we can allow a movement along the x-axis and with "Cylindrical" both a movement along the y-axis and a rotation around this axis. With "Planar" the component can move linearly in a plane and rotate around an axis. Very interesting is also the function "Ball", which creates a ball and socket joint. In the field "Gap" an offset, i.e. a distance between the joint origins, can be selected. With the buttons at "Align" the alignment of the joint can be changed or mirrored at the mate surface.

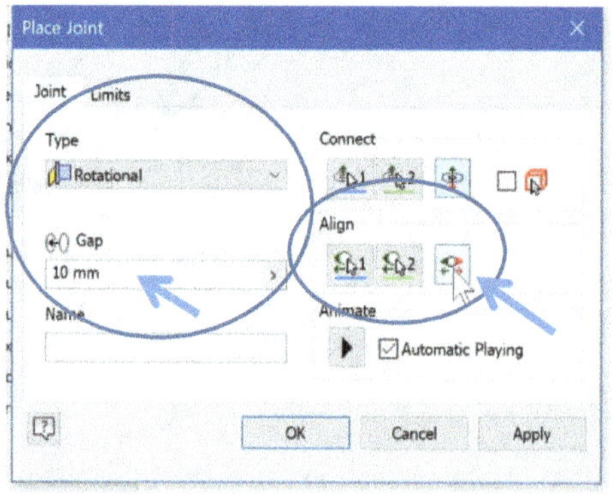

Figure 90: "Gap" when "Rotational" is selected; Align buttons for alignment

If we switch to the "Limits" tab, further settings can be made, such as determining a start and end position.

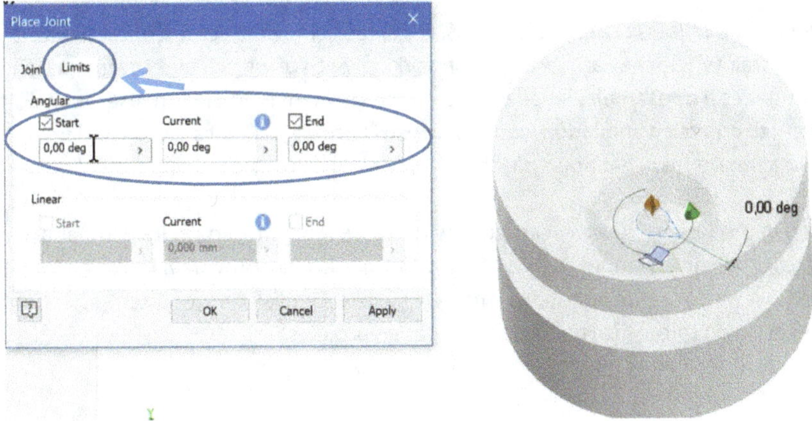

Figure 91: The "Limits" tab in the joint settings

If we now select the motion type "Cylindrical" / "Cylindrical", for example, we see that we can only move the component in the defined degrees of freedom. The joint also appears in the folder of the linked component in the part browser and can be deleted, suppressed or otherwise edited by right-clicking on it.

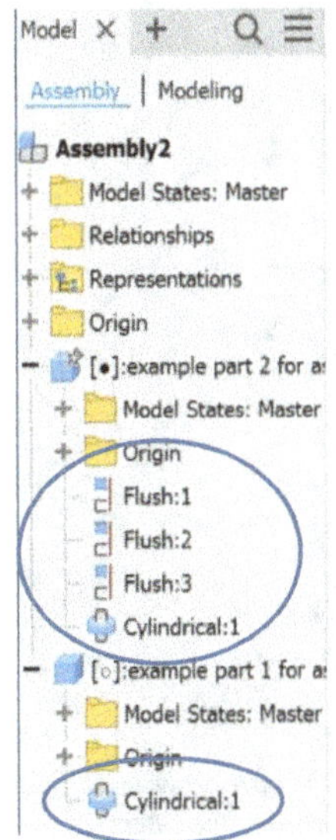

Figure 92: The joints and links appear in the part browser

By the way, if no range of motion is desired, the relationship "Rigid" / "Rigid" can usually simply be selected.

The advantage of joins is that often the same can be achieved with fewer clicks as with the "constraints". So they are two ways of working, both of which have advantages and disadvantages. For example, if you plan to create a dynamic simulation, use "Joints". If you want to create an animation, you should use "Constraints" because, unlike "Joints", you can animate them with one click.

Perfect! In this lesson we have learned how to create multiple parts in Inventor and link them together or assemble them virtually. In the next lesson we will take a look at different views and representations. Then we have learned all the important basics and finally get down to the great and practical design projects!

3.5 Views and representations (basic views, sectional view, etc.)

In this lesson we will briefly look at the possible views and representations in "Inventor". The basic views can be found on the left in the part browser in the folder "View: ... ". In this folder we can choose between "Top", "Front", "Right" and "Isometric", i.e. top, front, right, isometric.

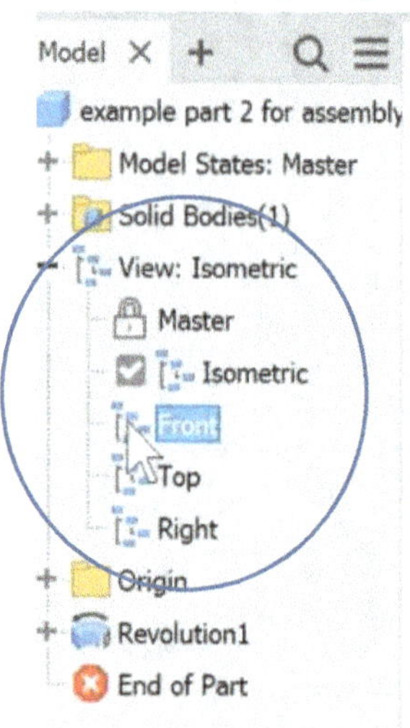

Figure 93: The selection of the basic views in the part browser at "View: ..."; We are again in the single part environment ("Part")

If we want to look at a specific surface, we can select a surface in the small menu bar on the right side with the function "Look at" / "Align to". This surface will then be displayed vertically from above.

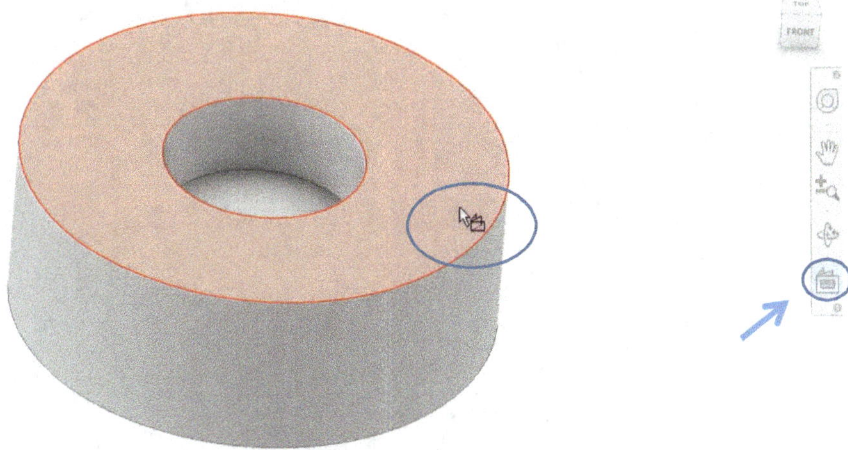

Figure 94: Select "Look at" command and choose surface to look at vertically

With the function "Zoom Window", also from this bar, we can enlarge a defined area. To do this, we simply drag a small window around the desired area.

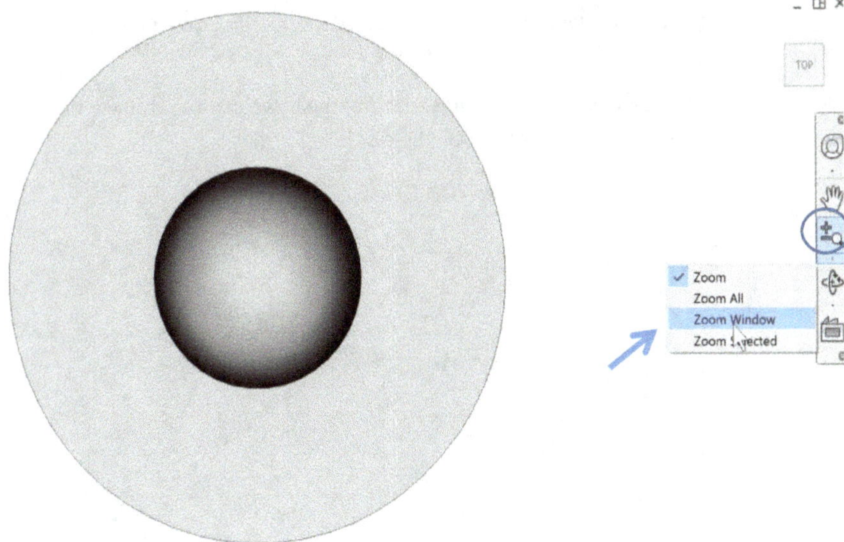

Figure 95: Select the "Zoom Window" command and simply zoom in on an area with the mouse

In the menu tab "View" in the upper area there is the selection menu "Visual Style", with which we can change the display of our components.

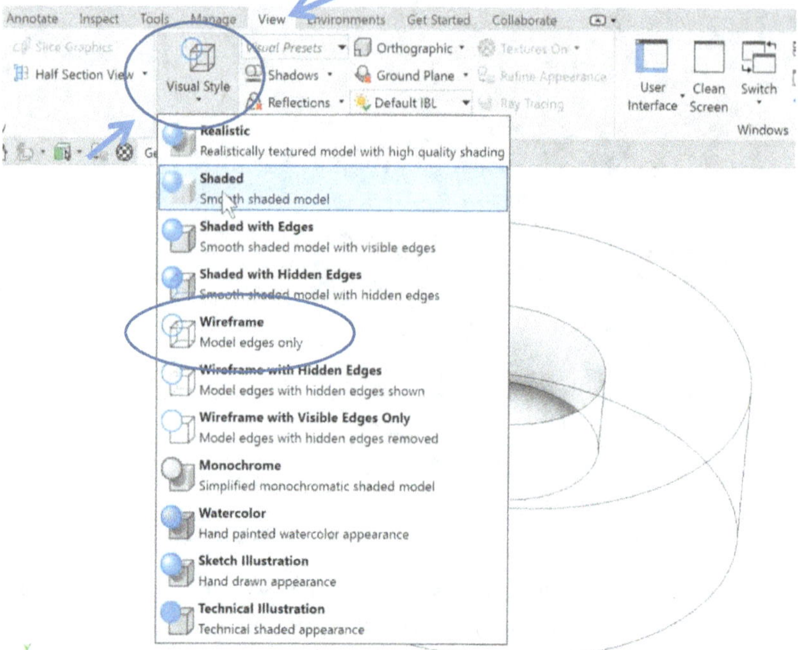

Figure 96: Changing the "Visual Style" of an object (in the image, the object is displayed as a "wireframe")

On the far left at "Object Visibility" / "Objektsichtbarkeit" we can generally define which elements, such as layers and axes, should be displayed or not.

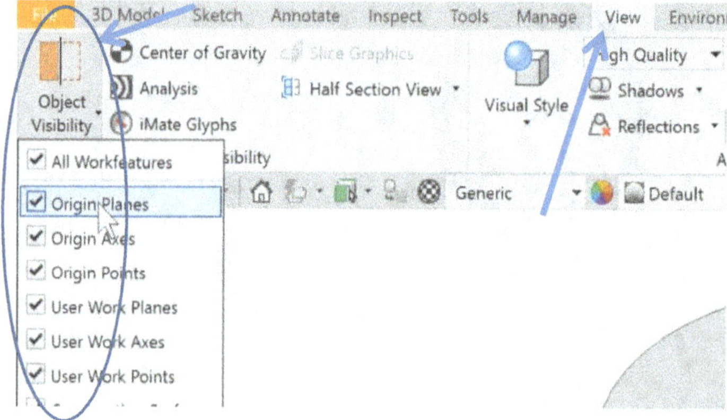

Figure 97: Edit display settings of layers, points, etc. with "Object Visibility"

Here we can also create a section view. We do this with the command "Section view" from the section "Visibility" at "View".

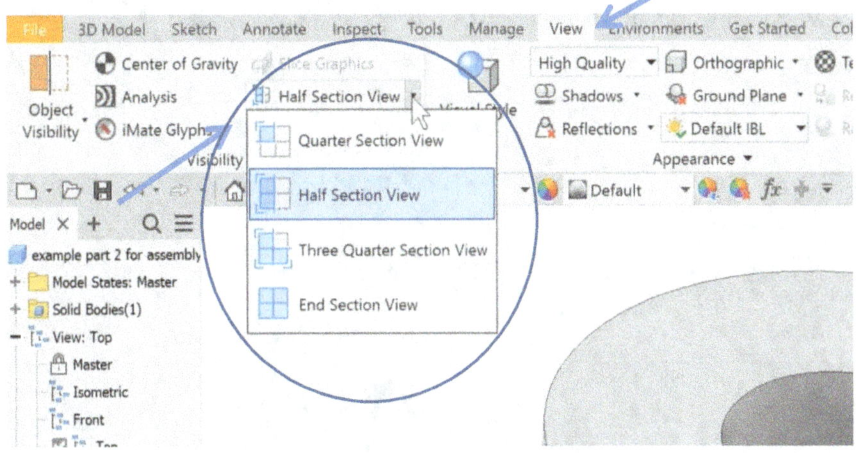

Figure 98: Create a section view to look inside the part

We can display a half, a quarter, or three quarters of the part and thereby look inside. Just think of it as cutting a cake and looking inside. For a quarter view we select the command and a first plane e.g. the y-z plane, then click on the small arrow and select a second plane e.g. the x-y plane.

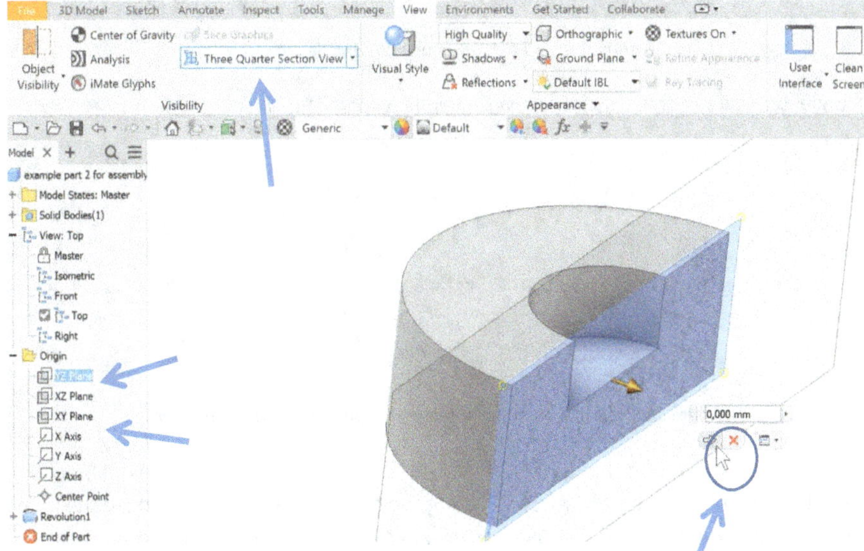

Figure 99: Creating a three-quarter view: 1) select command and y-z plane; 2) click the small circled arrow; 3) select x-y plane

Now the section view is created. By the way, for a half cut you only need to select one layer. You can also set an offset using the arrow or the keyboard. With "End Section View" from the drop-down menu you can end the section view again.

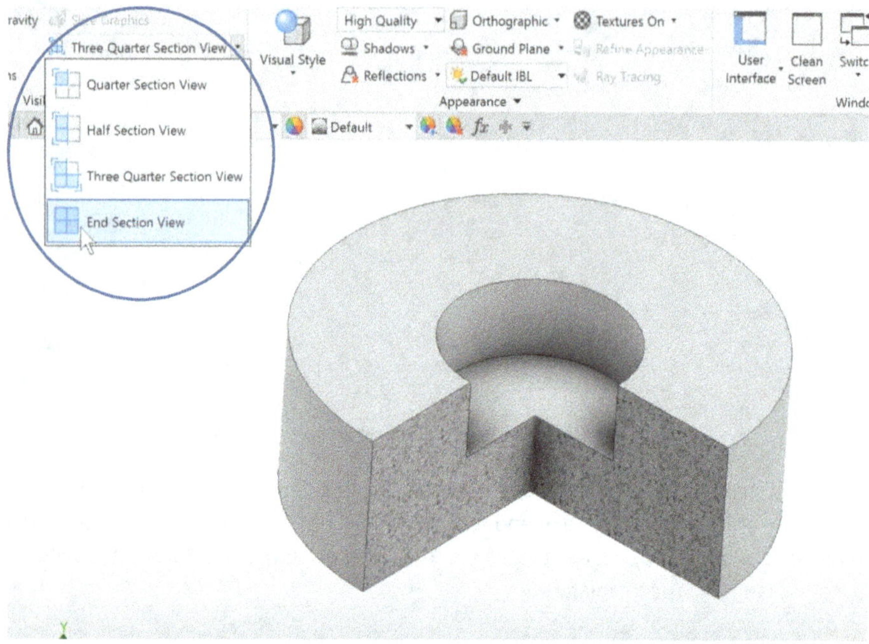

Figure 100: End section view with "End Section View"

Finally, we will get to know a few useful displays from the "Inspect" menu.

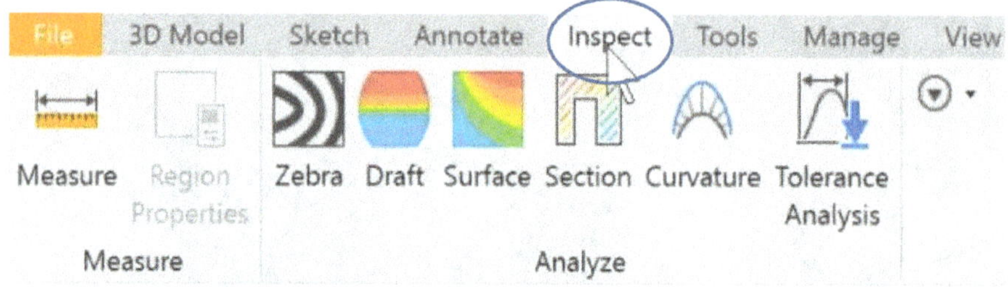

Figure 101: The "Inspect" menu tab with numerous analysis functions

Using the "Section" command, we can also display and even analyze the cross-section of a component or assembly. After selecting the function, we have to choose the plane in which we want to cut the part. Alternatively, we can also select a surface. For example, we select the y-z plane. The part will then be cut in this plane. We can now either confirm, or move the cut surface using the arrow or by entering a dimension.

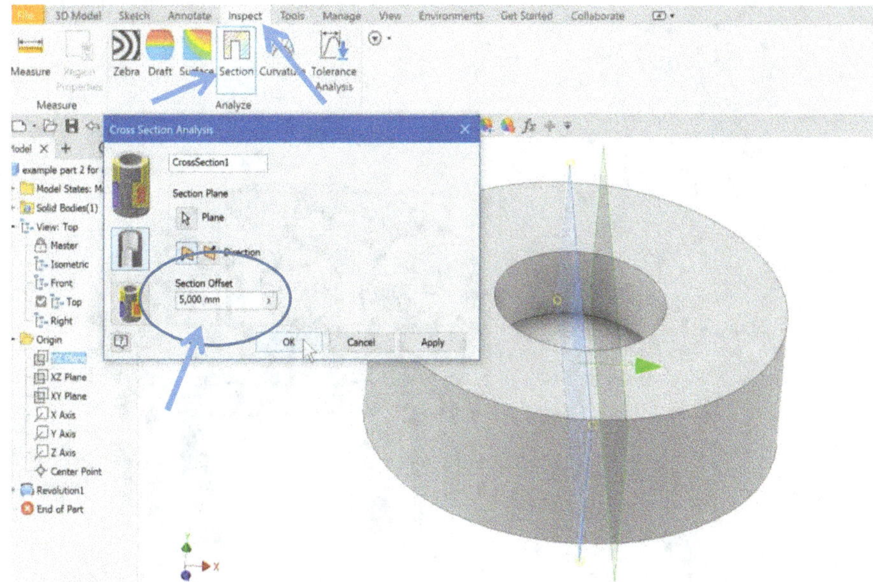

Figure 102: Analyzing the cross section of a part

After confirming, the section view appears in the "Analysis" / "Analysis" menu folder on the left of the part browser, where we can edit or delete it with a right click.

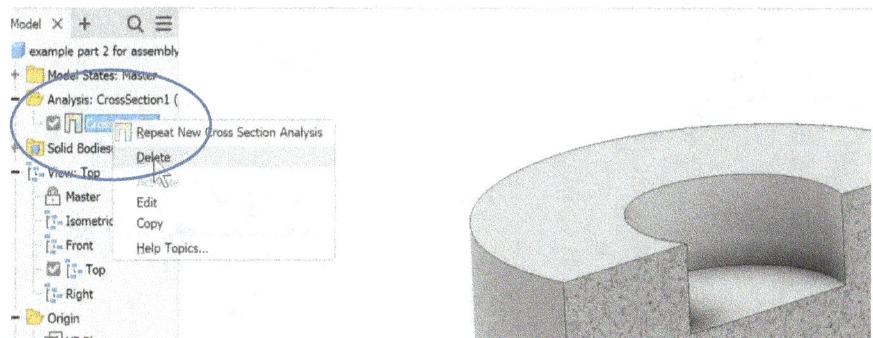

Figure 103: Section analysis is displayed in the "Analysis" folder

In the "Inspect" menu you will also find analysis functions such as the zebra analysis. With the help of this you can check transitions between surfaces by means of black and white stripes projected onto the surface and, for example, examine the surface of an aircraft wing for its surface continuity or smoothness. This is of importance for the flow resistance, for example.

Figure 104: Zebra analysis in the "Inspect" tab

To conclude this chapter, let's take a look at the part browser on the left. Here, the individual construction steps are shown in chronological order and we find the generated features, such as "Sketch", "Extrusion", etc., one after the other, depending on the construction.

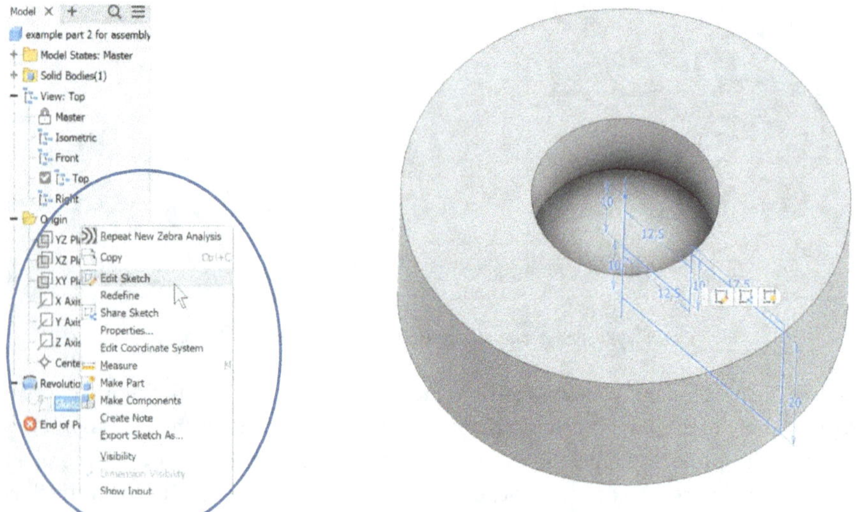

Figure 105: The part browser can be used to edit the individual features and sketches

The great thing now is that with this part browser the construction can be reproduced relatively easily.

You can also return to a specific point in the construction by simply placing the branch with the red dot called "End of Part" in front of a specific construction feature.

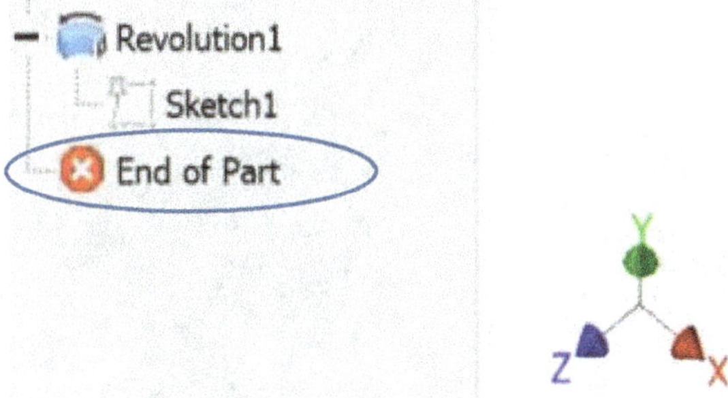

Figure 106: Placing the "End of Part" button in front of a specific feature

The program then shows the part with all design steps only up to this point. By right-clicking on the individual design steps, you can also edit the respective steps, e.g. a 2D sketch, or change the properties of an extrusion. This bar is also very helpful in order not to lose the overall view, especially with more complex constructions. Especially if you are used to assigning a name to each construction step. This is done with a very slow double click on the element in the part browser.

Class! Now we have learned all the relevant and important basics and the general handling of the CAD section of the program, so that we will deal with the construction of example projects in the following. In the first project, we'll get right into the swing of things, learning the design procedure based on a very simple carabiner. This is followed by a model of an exhaust manifold, which is already a bit more difficult to implement, then a simplified model of a truck front end and finally a simplified model of a 4-cylinder car engine, where things do get a bit more complex.

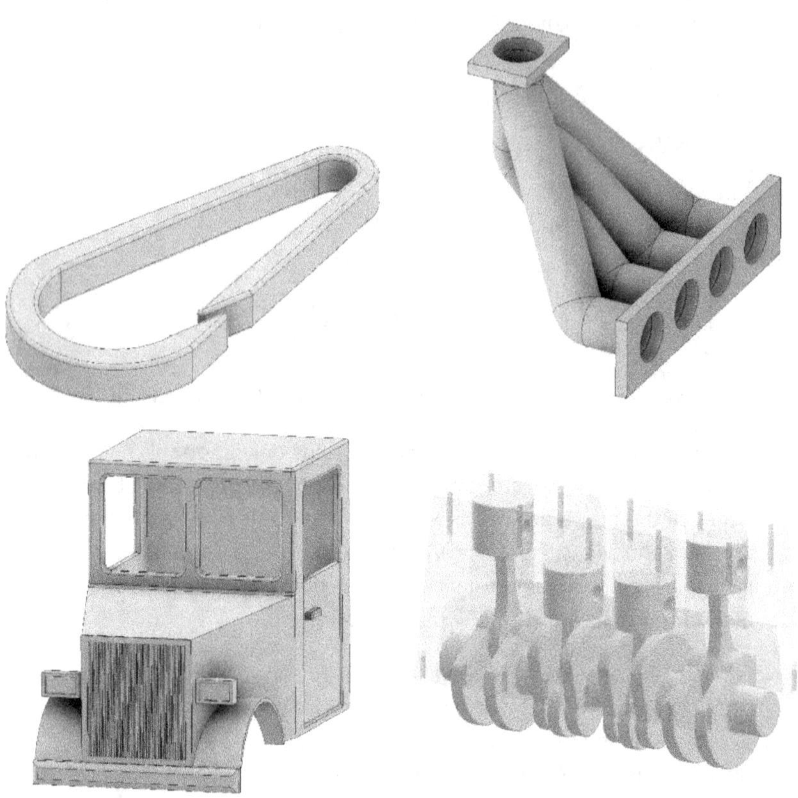

Figure 107: The design projects that are still waiting for you in the following chapters

But don't worry, we will go step by step. By the way, by working practically we will get to know even more new functions and commands, as well as consolidate the basics. So learning by doing! Stay with us, it will be exciting!

4 Practical CAD application: construction projects

4.1 Design project I: Simple snap hook

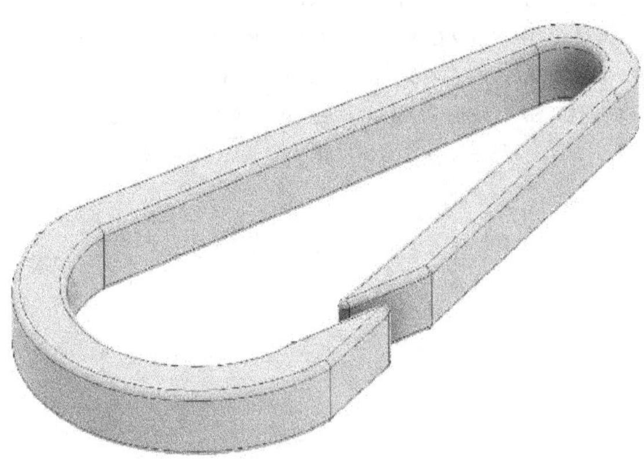

Figure 108: A simple snap hook becomes our first design project

For the carabiner we start in a new single part: "Part" with the button "Start 2D Sketch" / "Create 2D Sketch" and the selection of a plane, e.g. the x-z plane. Let's first consider how the carabiner is constructed and how we could best construct it. If we look at the carabiner a little closer, we notice that you can put a circular shape in each of the left and right areas, and the struts of the carabiner represent tangential connections between these circles.

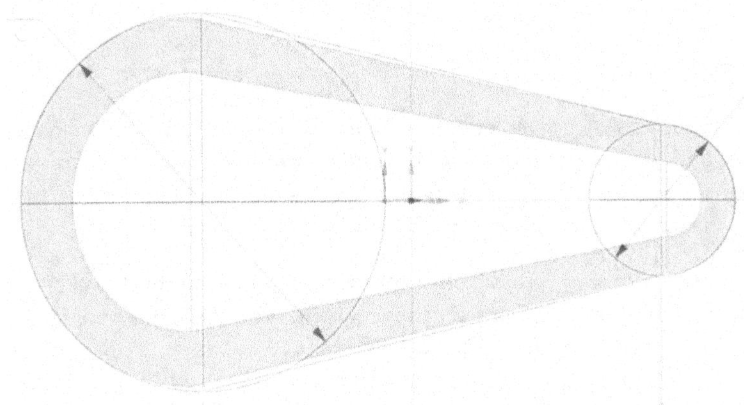

Figure 109:
We construct the carabiner using two circles and lines

Let's construct the carabiner in this way. So let's first draw the first circle with a starting point on the horizontal line, which in this case, is the z-axis. For example, we choose a diameter of 50 mm.

Then create another circle with a diameter of 20 mm a little further to the right. We then dimension the distance between the two circles as 70 mm. To completely define the previous sketch, which you will see by the blue coloring, we now need a reference in the direction of the x-axis and the z-axis to the origin. We define the position of our sketch in z-direction for example by another dimension of 35 mm from the center of the first circle to the origin. The x-position simply with the dependency or "constraint": "vertical".

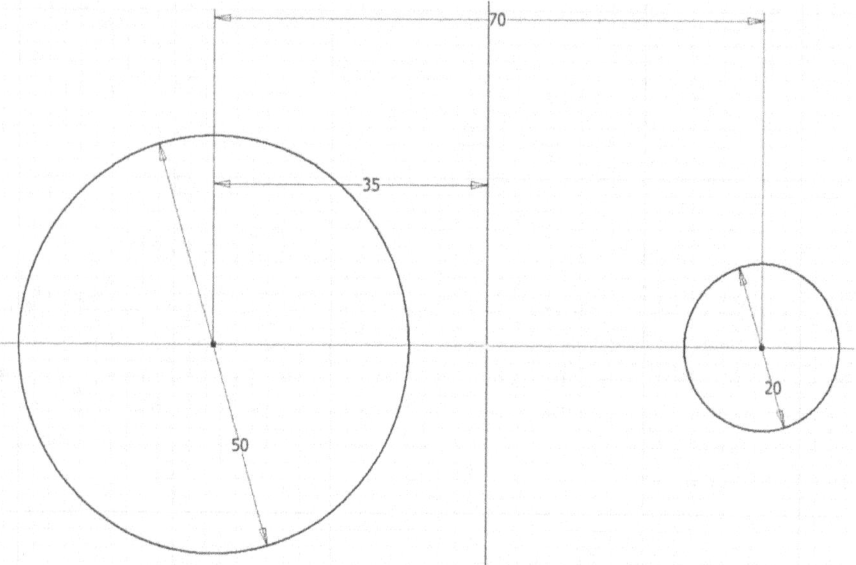

Figure 110: Two circles form the beginning of the sketch for the carabiner

You can either define a sketch completely by dimensions only, or choose a combination of dimensions and conditions, as here. For the condition we choose the center of each of the two circles and then the origin. Now the sketch is blue and fully defined, i.e. it can no longer be moved in the plane without further ado.

Then we draw horizontal and vertical guides through the centers of the two circles to make it easier to apply the dimensions and tangent lines. Draw the lines and right-click on them to select the "Construction" command.

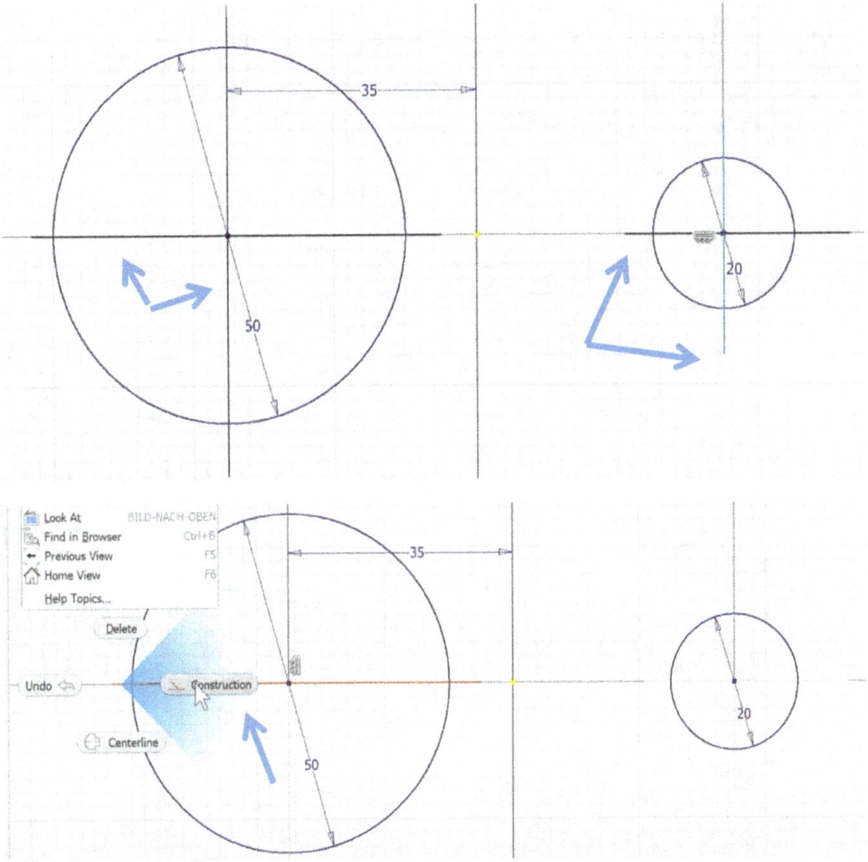

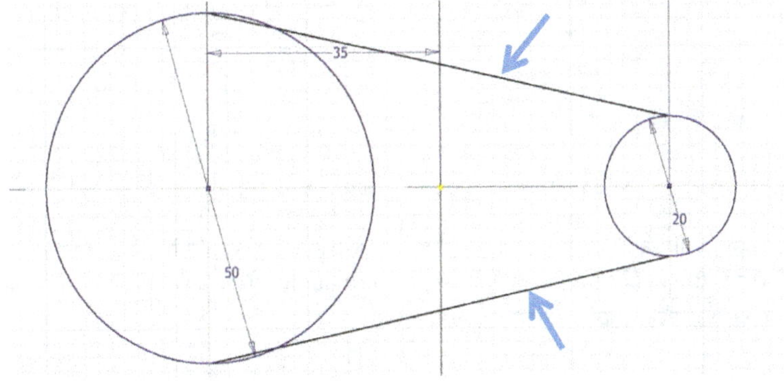

Figure 111: The auxiliary lines through the centers of the two circles

In the next step we connect the intersection points of the vertical guides with the circles by two lines.

Figure 112: Drawing two tangential connecting lines

To get a self-contained shape, we need only the outer contour, so we use the "Trim" tool.

Use the tool to remove all superfluous line segments as follows:

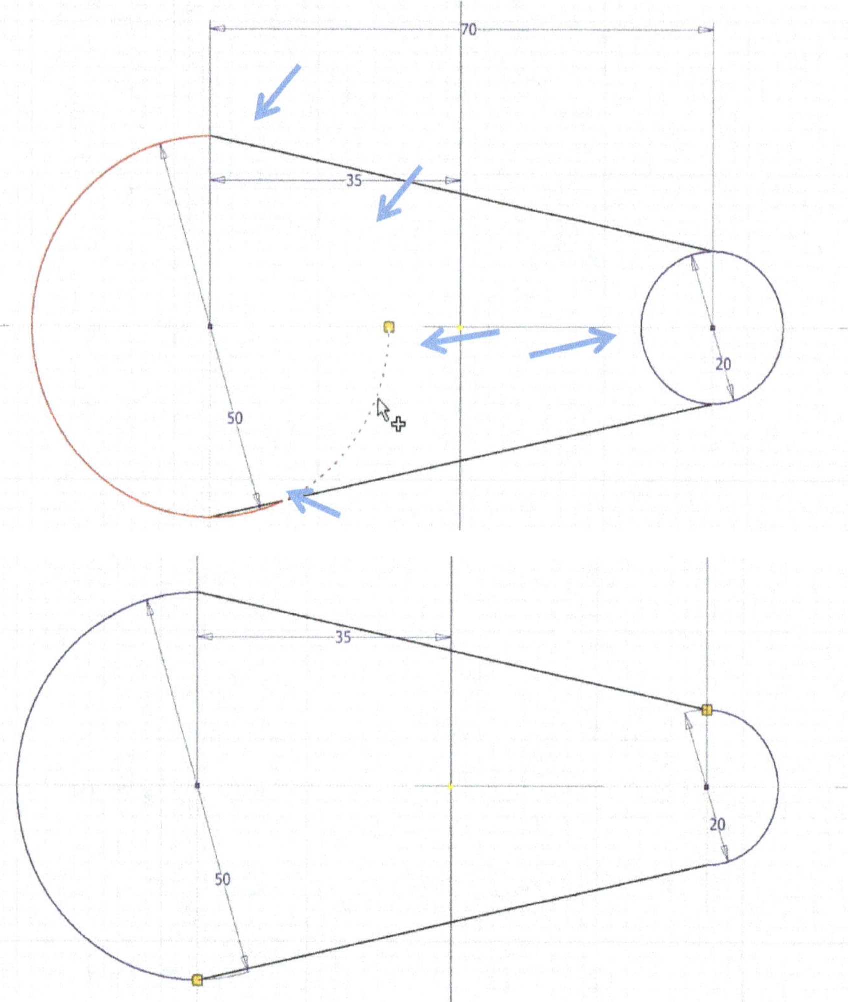

Figure 113: Remove superfluous sections of the circle

Now we could already extrude the surface. But then we would have to make another cutout to get the final carabiner. But we can also apply a faster solution right away and draw the cross section of the carabiner in one step.

To do this, add two additional circles of 35 and 10 mm diameter in the inner area of the carabiner and, analogous to the previous steps, again draw two lines from the intersections of the circles with the auxiliary lines.

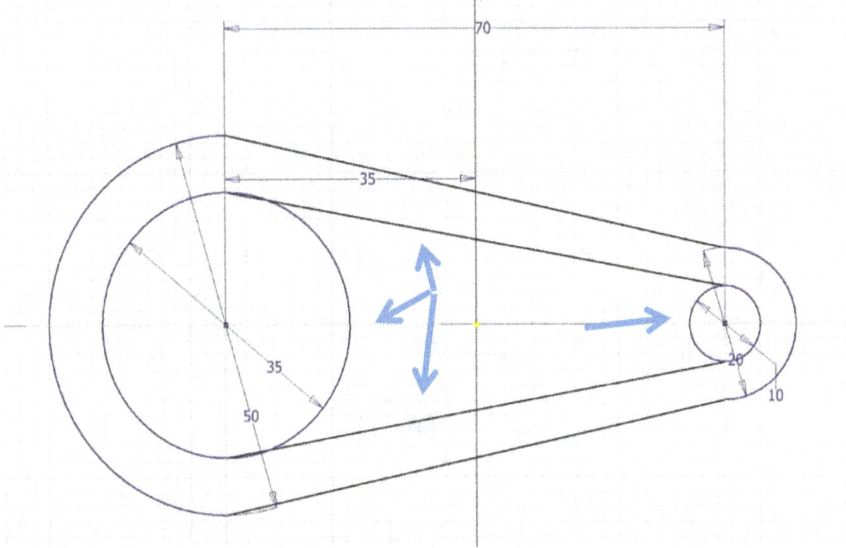

Figure 114: Draw circles and tangential lines again (inside; see arrows)

Then remove all superfluous line segments by using the "Trim" feature again.

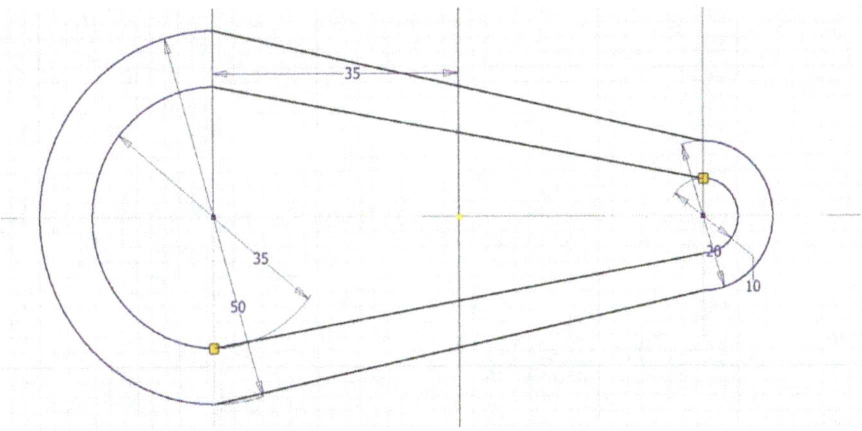

Figure 115: All superfluous sections of the two circles have been removed again with "Trim

To create the cutout for the opening of the carabiner at the same time, we draw a line at 100° from the base of the inner tangential connecting line to the outer connecting line of the carabiner. The dimension is automatically obtained by specifying the angle and the end points. You can switch between dimension and angle input with the tab key.

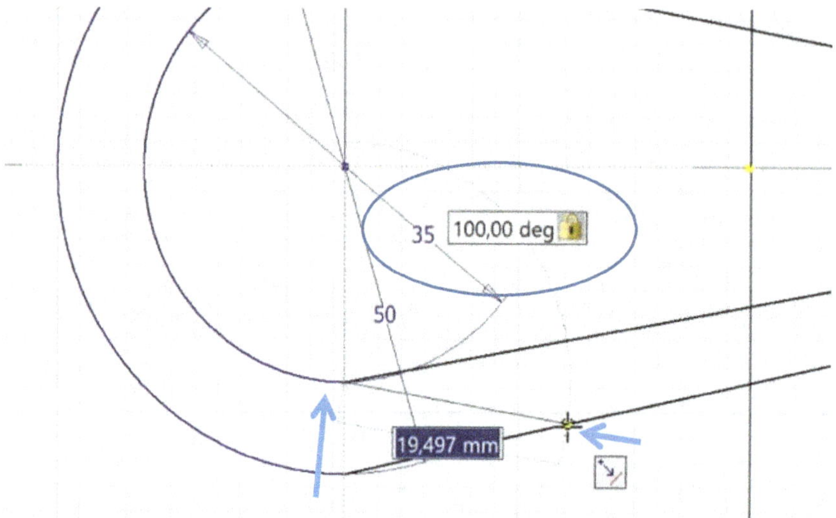

Then draw a second parallel line and dimension a 2 mm distance. If the parallelism is not created automatically - pay attention to the small background characters - you will have to create it yourself.

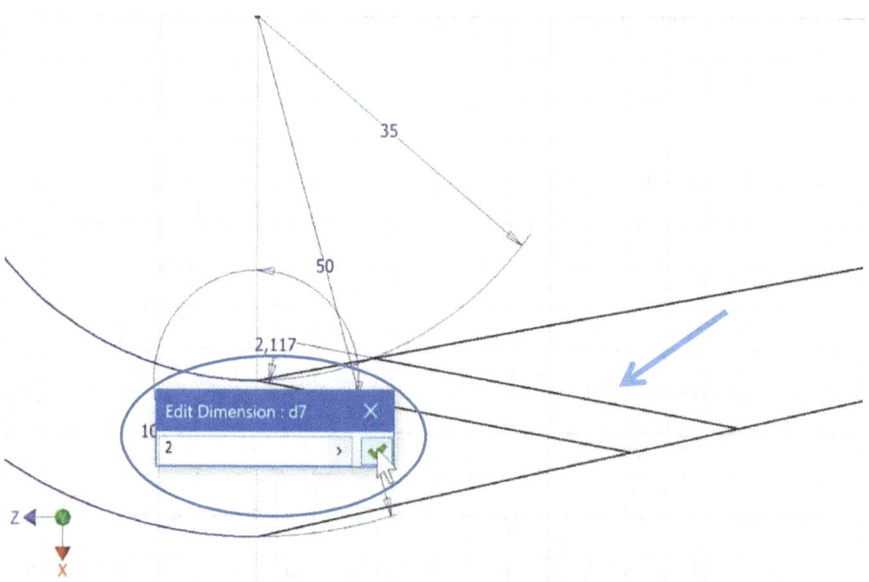

Figure 116: Creating a second parallel line at a distance of 2 mm

With the "Trim" function we again remove the superfluous line segments.

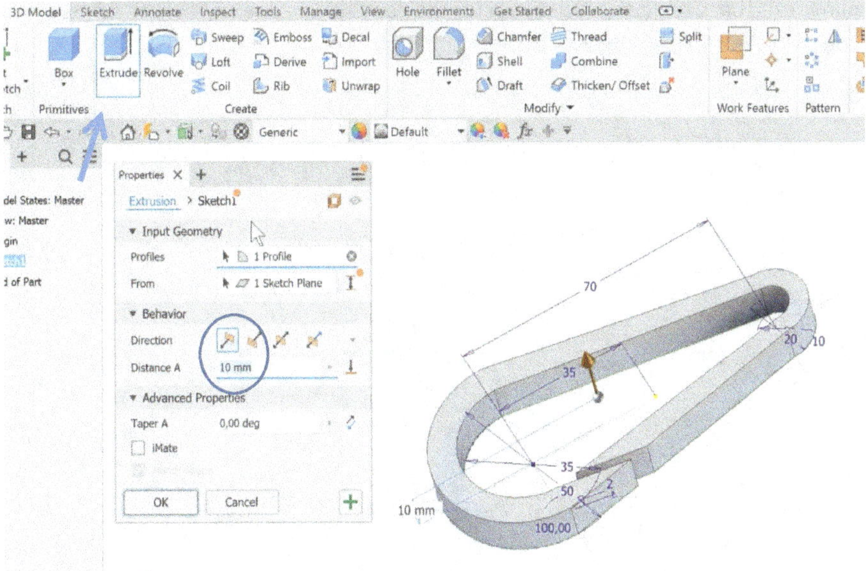

Figure 117: Remove superfluous lines with "Trim" so that an opening is created

As you can now see, we have saved ourselves a few machining steps and can now extrude the finished basic shape of the carabiner right away.

To turn the 2D surface into a 3D body now, we switch to 3D mode with "Finish Sketch" / "Finish Sketch" and use the "Extrude" function. To do this, select only the outer surface as the profile for extrusion in the options and enter a value of 10 mm.

Figure 118: Extrude the carabiner with "Extrude" in 3D mode

You can either extrude in one direction only, or symmetrically or independently in two directions. You select this at "Direction" / "Richtung". If you want to have a conical shape, you could also specify an angle at "Taper Angle" / "Taper Angle". But we do not need that here.

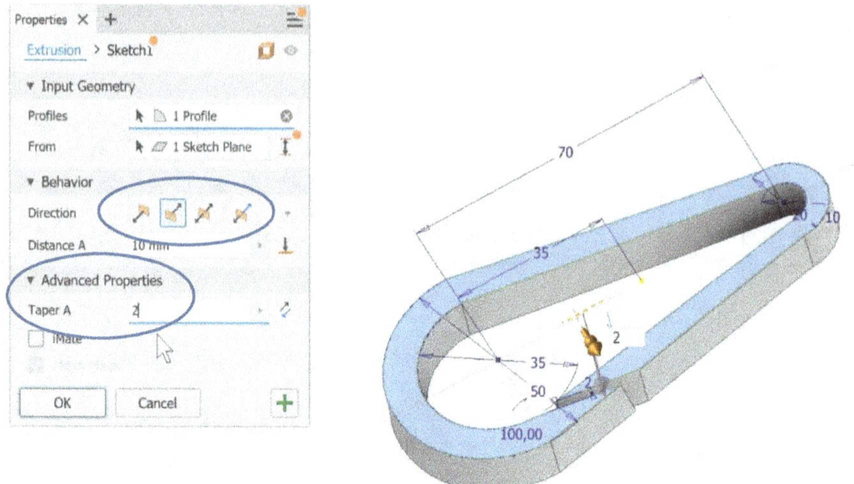

Figure 119: Select direction of extrusion and enter taper angle if desired

Finally, we round a few edges using the Fillet command from the Modify section. 20 mm for the back top edge. And 1 mm for the edges of the opening as well as the sides. You can select several edges one after the other.

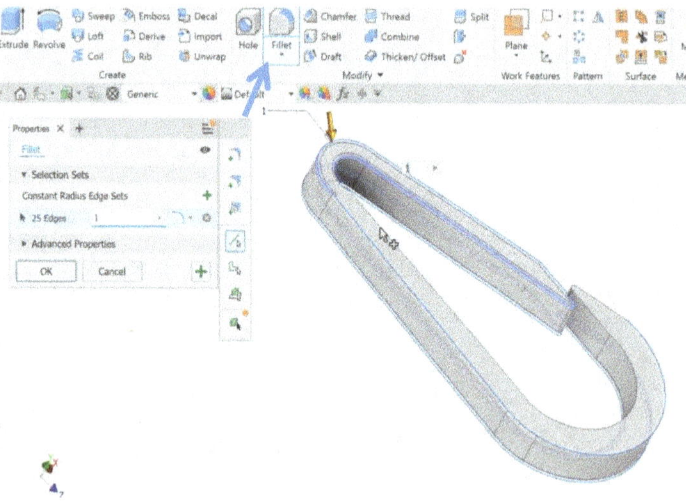

Figure 120: Apply edge fillet with "Fillet" to taste; e.g. 1 mm

Flawless! Before we move on to the next design project, let's save the part. If we want a different file format, e.g. for 3D printing or another program, we can create this file using "Export" and selecting "CAD Format", specifying the desired file format and location. For example, the "CATIA" and the "PRO/Engineer" formats are available, as well as commonly known "stl" and "step" file formats.

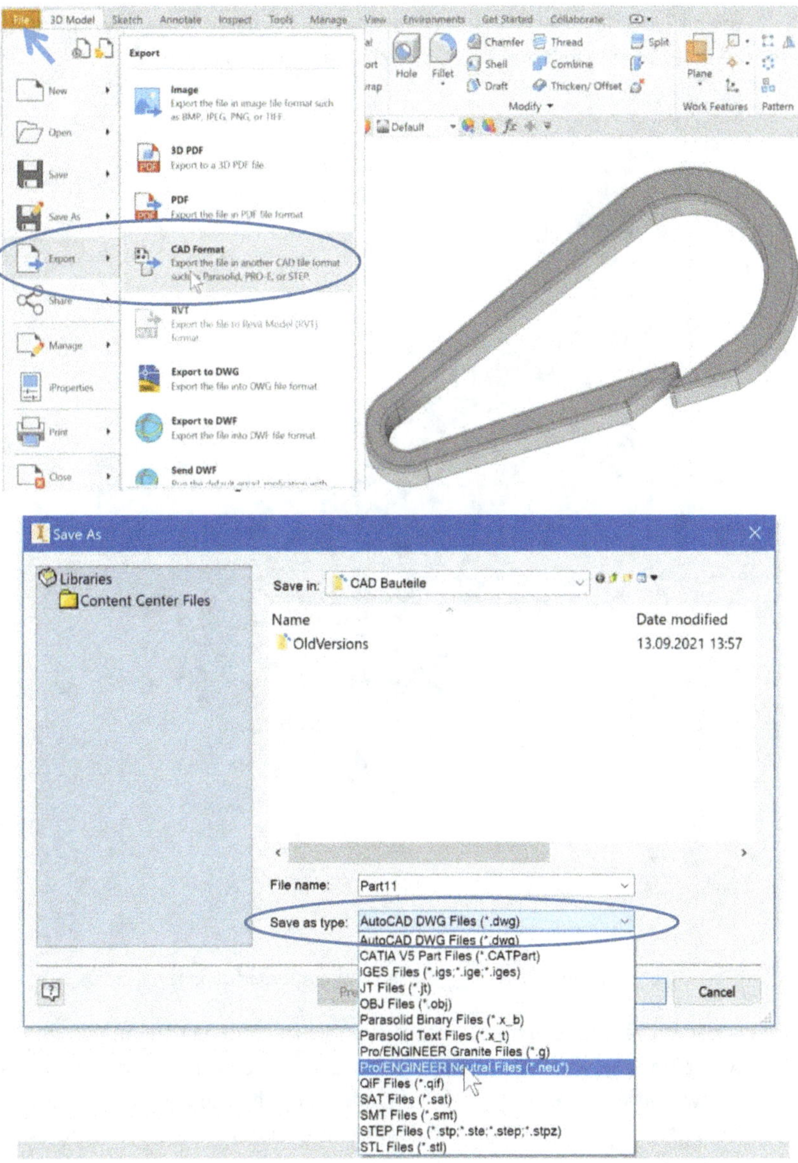

Figure 121: File in another format using "File" →"Export" →"CAD Format"

4.2 Design project II: Exhaust manifold

Welcome back! In this chapter we will implement the design of an exhaust manifold to increase the difficulty level a bit. In this chapter we will work with the "Sweep" function and for the first time we will make a 3D sketch in addition to the 2D sketches.

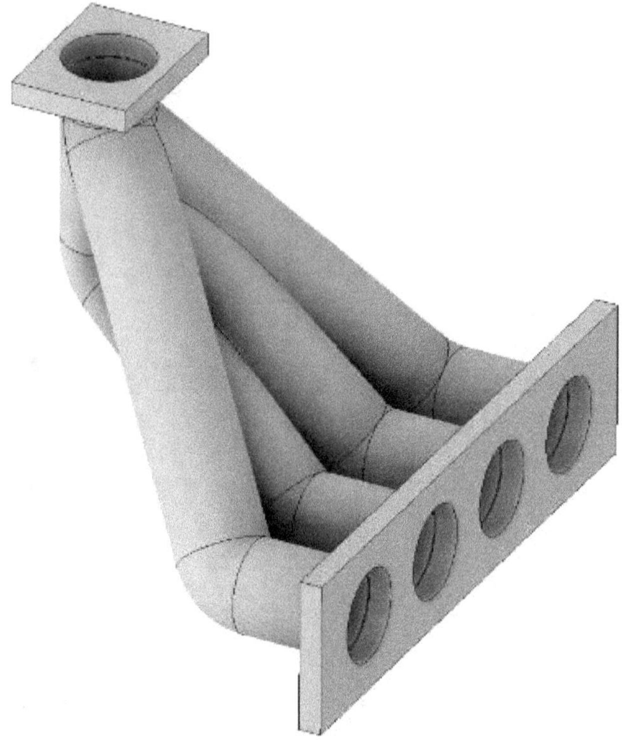

Figure 122: An exhaust manifold becomes our second design project

Before we get started, let's first consider again how to construct the manifold. When we first look at it, we see that in this single part we have two basic rectangular elements that are on two different and non-parallel planes. Between these rectangular bodies then sit the curved tubes for the individual cylinder ports of an engine. So we can construct the manifold in these three steps. Let's go!

We start again in the "Part" environment with a new single part. For the rectangular element that would later sit on the motor, we start a sketch on the x-z plane and draw a rectangle with the dimensions 100 mm and 400 mm. We select the coordinate origin as the starting point.

Then we add four circles for the openings. The circles should all be the same size - we achieve this with the relationship "Equal" - and have a diameter of 60 mm. The distance to each other should be e.g. 90 mm. Now we need a dimensioning in x- and in z-position on this plane, so that our sketch is fully defined. At the moment the circles are movable, which is not desired. For the z-position we dimension one of the circles to the center with 45 mm distance. And for the x-position we use the relation "horizontal", with which we link the circles horizontally with the origin.

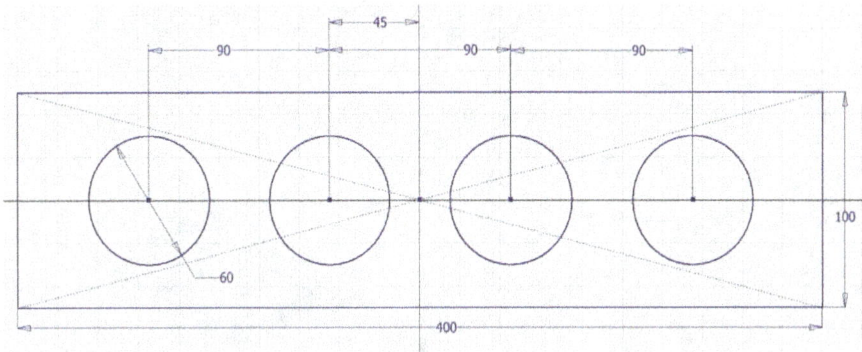

Figure 123: Sketching the rectangular profile with the four circles on the x-z plane

Then we finish the sketch and extrude the area 15 mm. To do this, select the area between the circles and the rectangle.

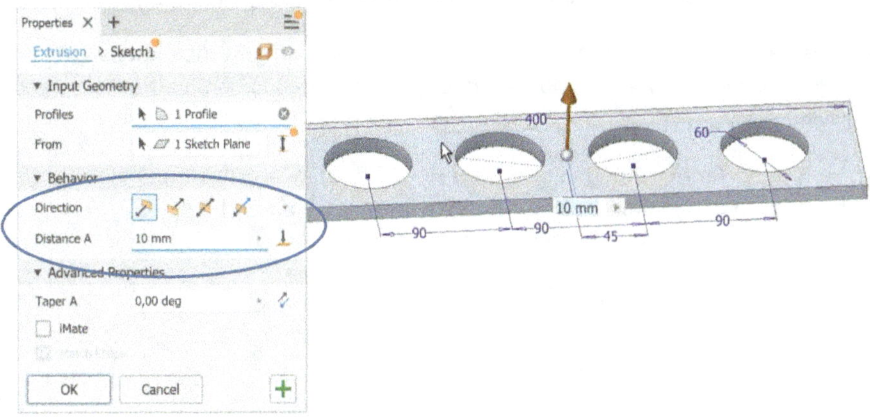

Figure 124: Extrude the profile with "Extrude" 10 mm

In the next step, we create the rectangular element that would be mounted on the center muffler or catalytic converter of the exhaust system. To do this, we need a sketch on a plane that - in this case - is parallel to the x-y plane.

So, to do this, we create a parallel plane or "offset" plane using the "Offset from Plane" command from the "Work Features" and "Plane" section in "3D Model". Select the command and the x-y plane and enter a distance. In our case -250 mm. We need the minus for the correct direction, which here is the negative z-direction.

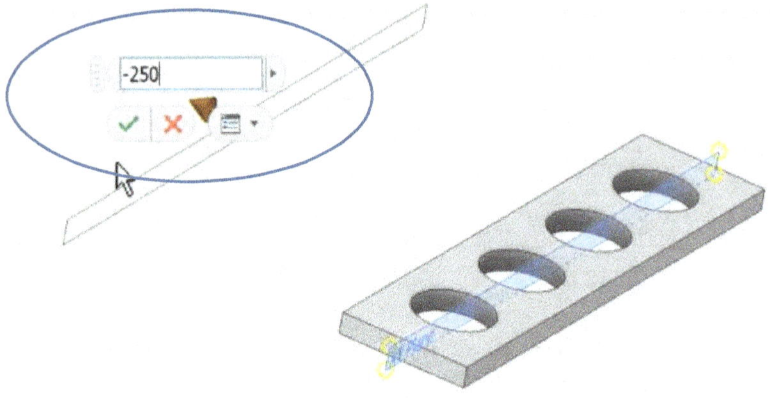

Figure 125:Create a parallel plane to the x-y plane; select an offset of -250 mm

On this plane we start a new sketch and draw a rectangle with the dimensions 110 mm and 80 mm. We get a fixed position in x-direction with the condition "vertical" between the center of the rectangle and the coordinate origin.

A fixed position in y-direction using a dimension of 250 mm from the center of the circle to the origin. We also draw a circle with a diameter of 60 mm.

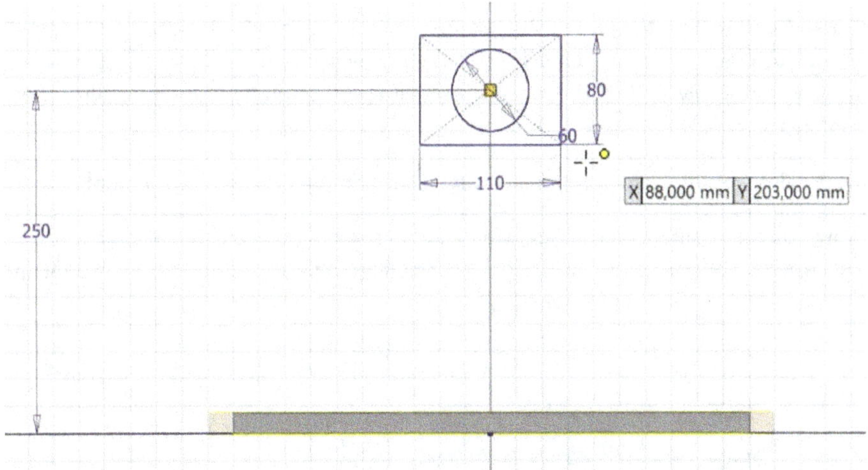

Figure 126: Sketch the second profile of the part on the created parallel plane

Then this sketch is ready and can be closed. We extrude the area between the rectangle and circle again 15 mm.

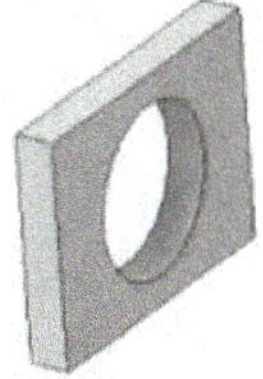

Figure 127: The result after 15 mm extrusion

Great! Now we have the two rectangular geometries and can turn to the exhaust pipes. We will use the "Sweep" function in this chapter, because we can create the geometries quickly and easily with this function. As you may remember, this function always requires a profile and a path.

As profiles we simply draw four congruent circles on the first created element.

Now, to create the desired shape, we need to create a path, e.g. a line, across the 3D space from the respective circle of the first rectangle to the circle of the second rectangle. This works easiest with a 3D sketch.

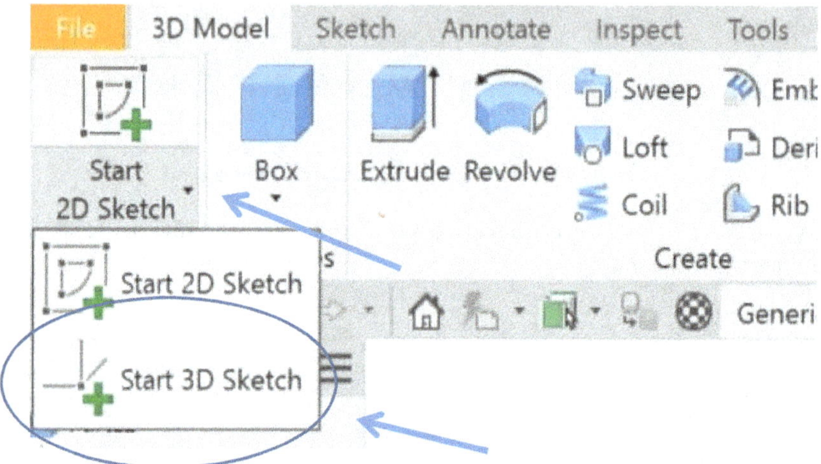

Figure 128: Starting a 3D sketch is almost the same as starting a 2D sketch, but in 3D.

So far, we have always drawn a 2D sketch on a plane when we created an element. But you can also sketch in 3D space. This is actually relatively easy, it just takes a little more imagination. You'll also get a better idea if you just rotate the drawing plane a lot, giving you multiple perspectives.

So we select the "Start 3D Sketch" command and then we are taken to the 3D sketching area.

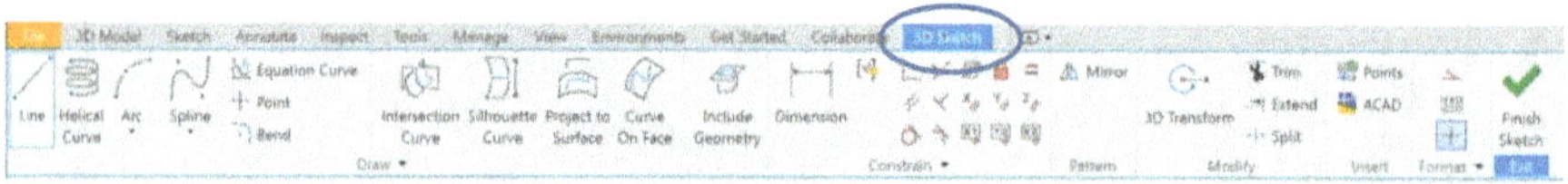

Figure 129: The "3D Sketch" toolbar; appears automatically after selecting the command

If we select the "Line" command normally, we can build our path from individual lines. We start by clicking on the center of the first circle. Now we are shown a coordinate system with the three colored axes "x", "y", and "z". The orientation matches the coordinate system of the single part. Depending on which axis direction you now move with the mouse, you can draw a line on one of the axes. We first need to move in the y-direction, i.e. upwards. Move your mouse up and sideways so that a green line, the extension of the y-axis, appears. Then you can enter a dimension, for example 80 mm.

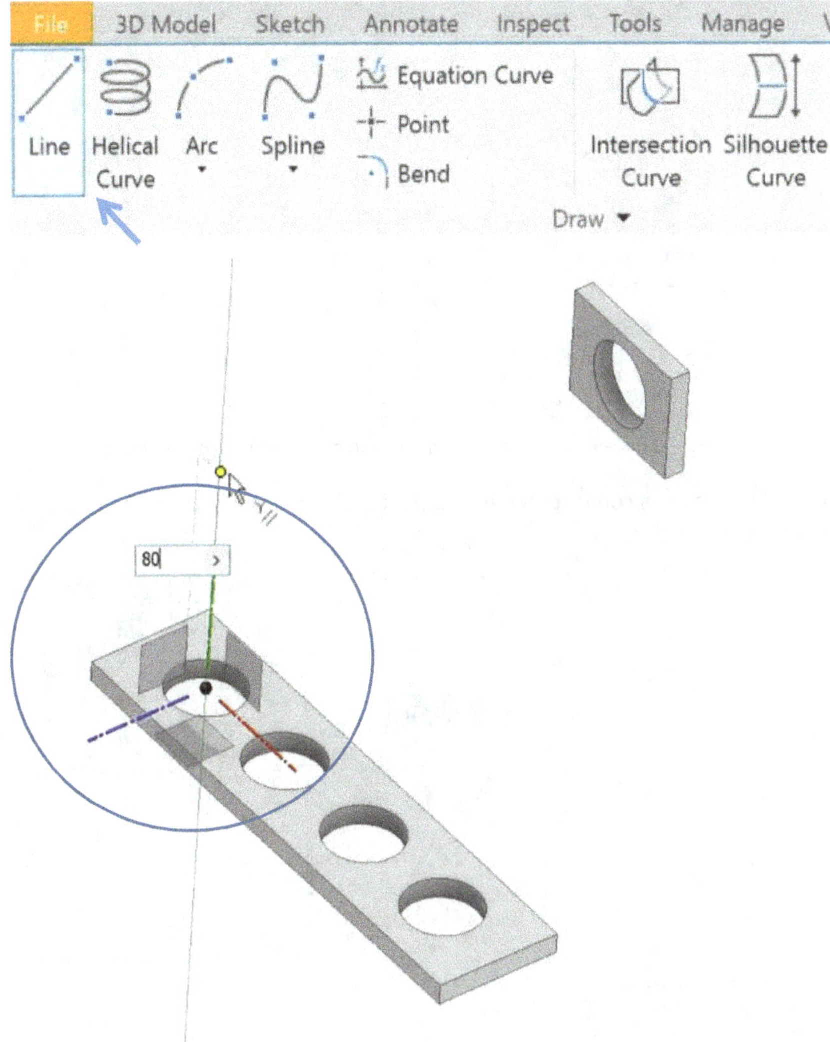

Figure 130: Draw a line in 3D space; start at the center of the circle and move in the direction of the green line; enter the dimension and press "Enter"

Now we have a line of 80 mm in y-direction, as if we had drawn on the x-y plane. Next we draw a line of 30 mm in the z-direction, i.e. the blue line must appear. To do this, we start at the center of the second element created.

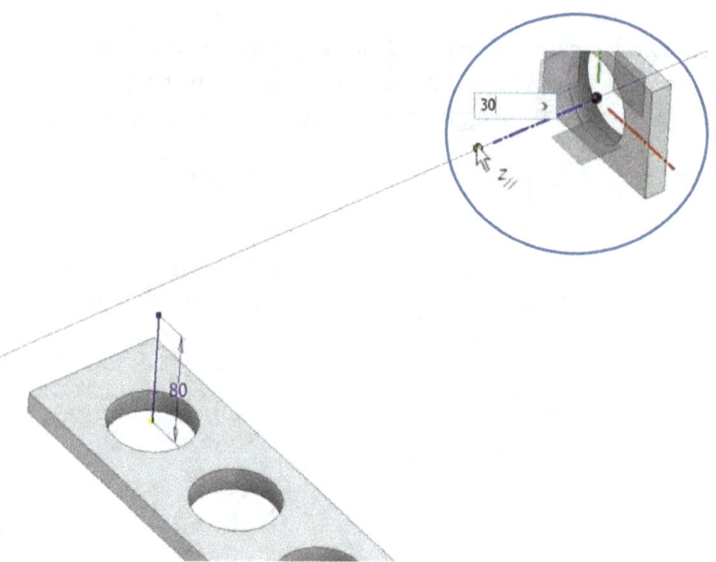

Figure 131: Creating a 30 mm line in the z-direction for the second element

And lastly, we simply connect the two endpoints of these two lines in 3D space so that we get a diagonal line.

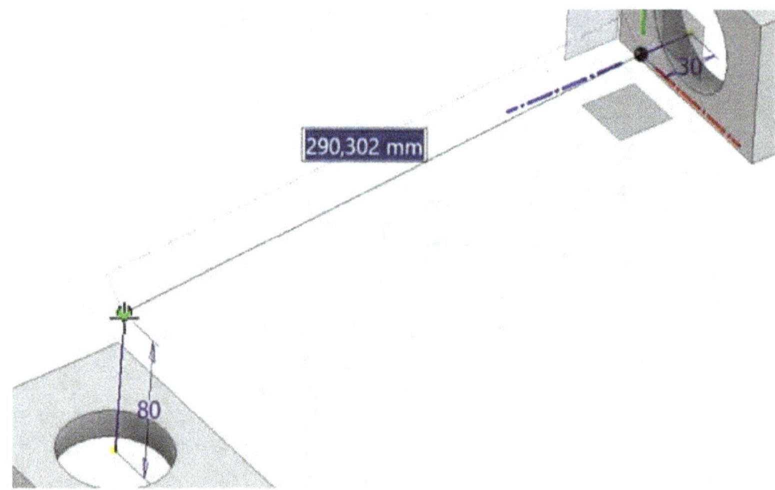

Figure 132: Creating a link line in 3D space; simply select the vertices

With the "Bend" command we can still round off the two sharp corner points with e.g. 30 mm.

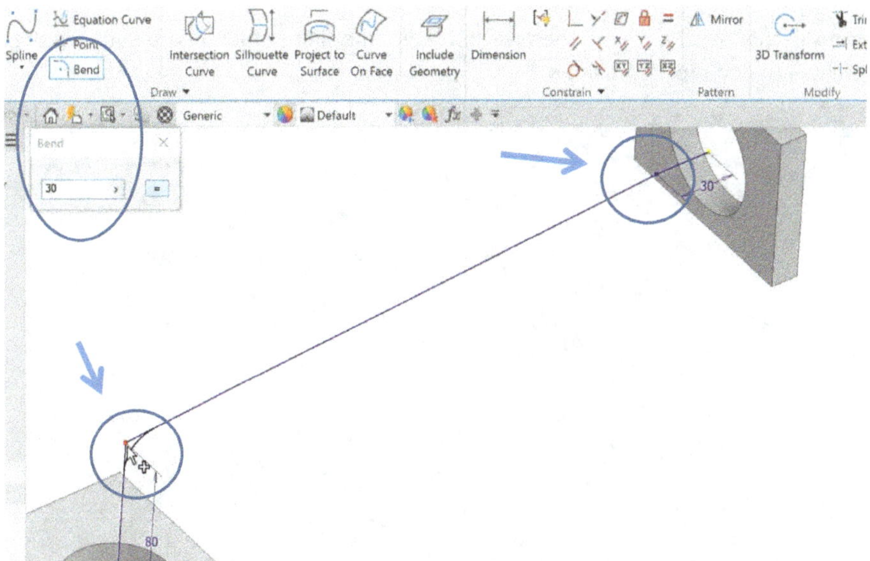

Figure 133: Using the "Bend" command to round the corners (see arrows); select 30 mm as the radius

The first path for the "Sweep" command is ready. As a profile, we simply draw a congruent circle in a new sketch on the rectangular element.

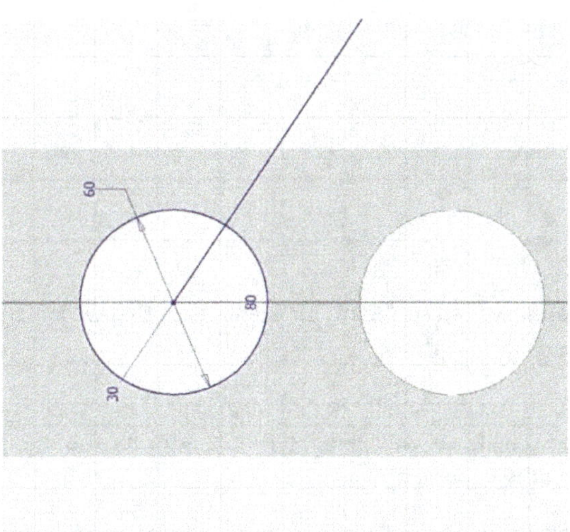

Figure 134: Drawing a congruent circle on the upper side of the rectangle

When starting the command, we must first activate the "Profile" selection in the "Properties" window, then we can select the first circle profile. Then we have to change the selection to "Path" and then we can select the first path. The program will then create our first pipe segment.

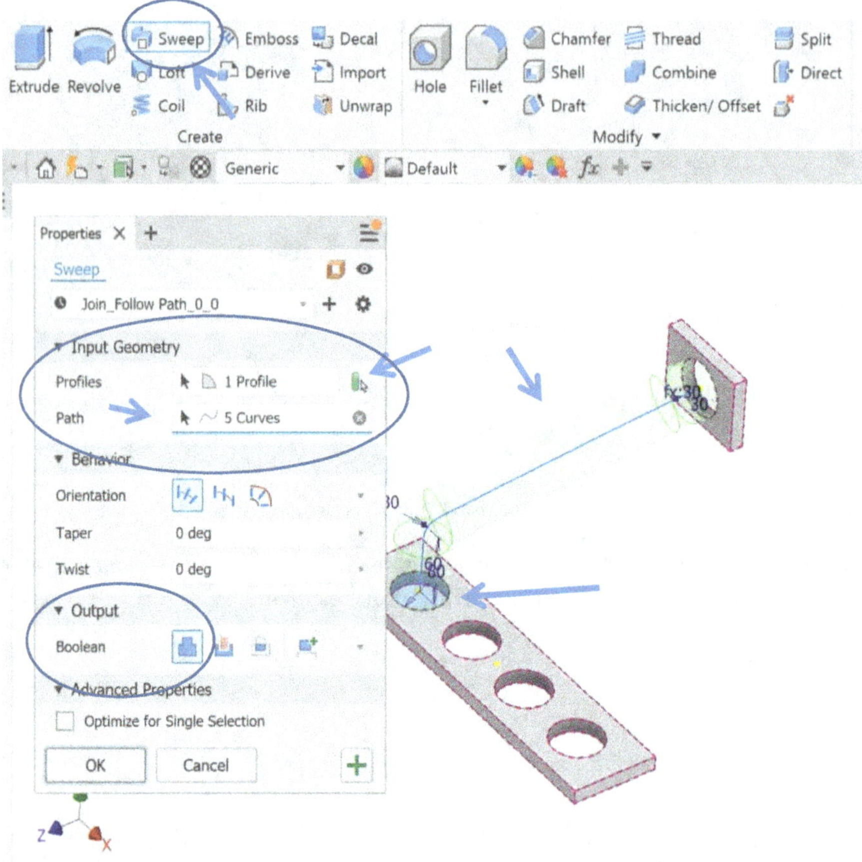

In the "Output" area, we can set "Join", for example, so that we join the created bodies together. Finally, confirm with "OK".

The procedure for the remaining three pipe segments is identical. The only difference is in drawing the 3D path, i.e. we need different lengths for the lines in the z-direction for the element in the upper area.

We had at the first path: 30 mm. For the second path we need 60 mm, for the third 120 mm and for the fourth again 30 mm. Try it!

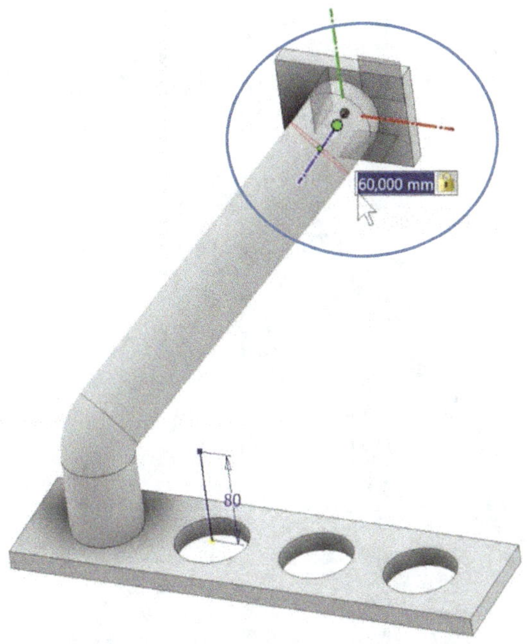

Figure 135: For the second pipe segment we need a 60 mm line in z-direction

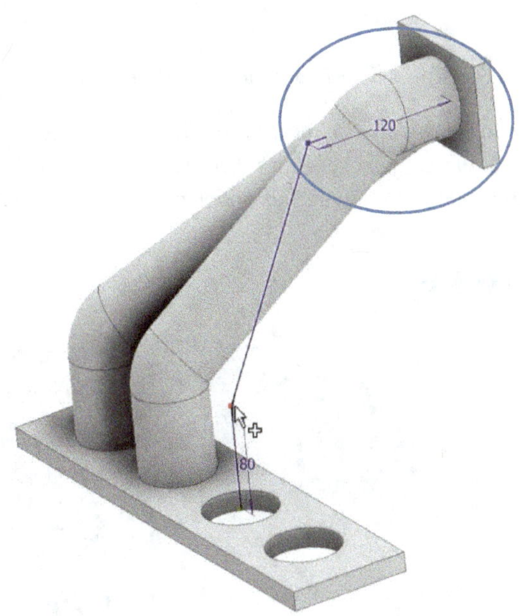

Figure 136: For the drite tube segment we need a 120 mm long line in z-direction

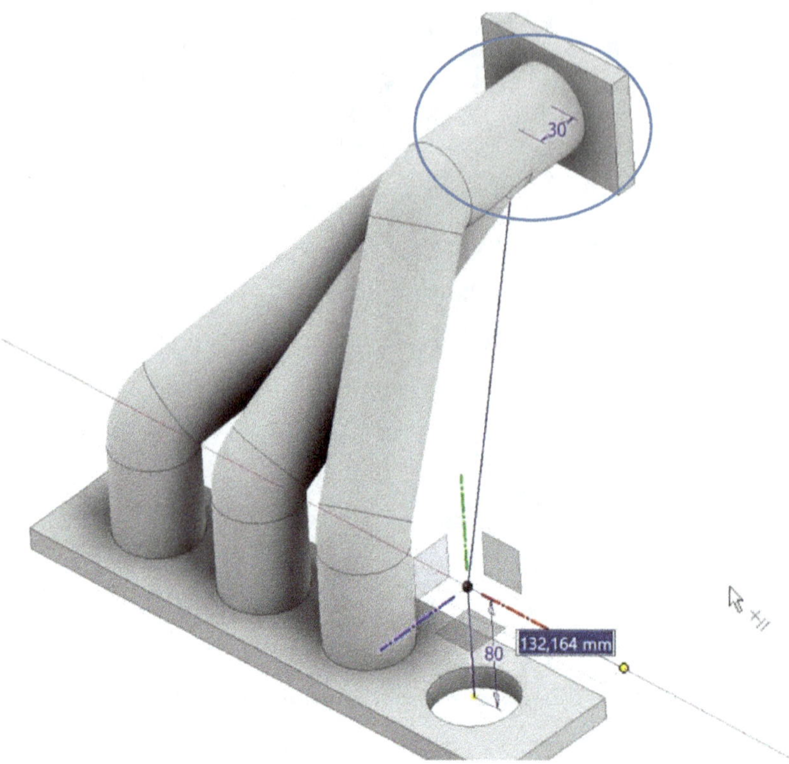

Figure 137fourth tube segment, we again need a 30 mm line in the z direction

Very good! The exhaust manifold is almost finished! We now need to hollow out the created solids so that we actually get pipes. We do this with the "Shell" command. Select the command, select the lower and upper circular surfaces and enter a wall thickness of e.g. 2 mm.

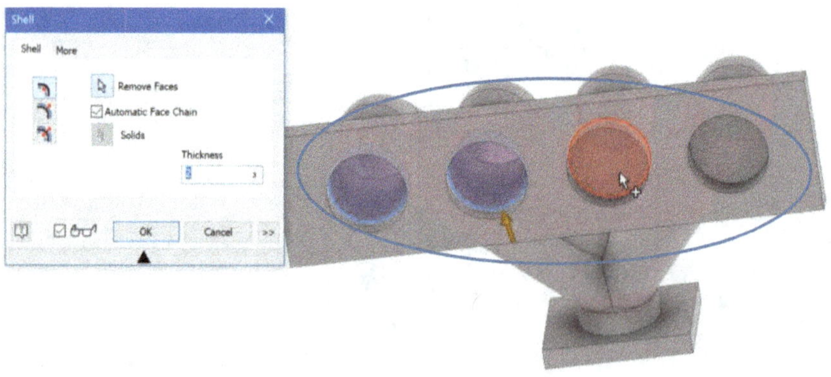

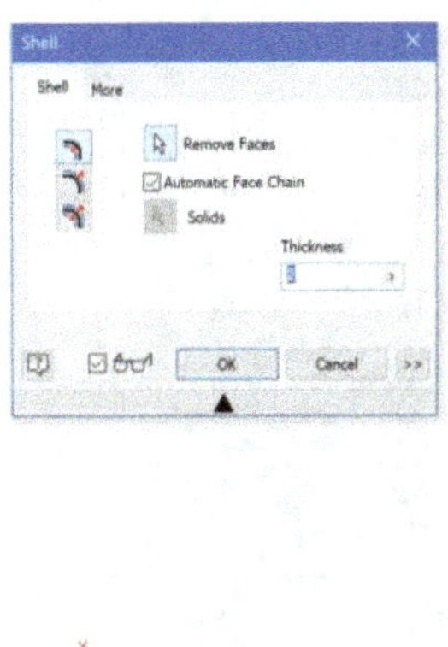

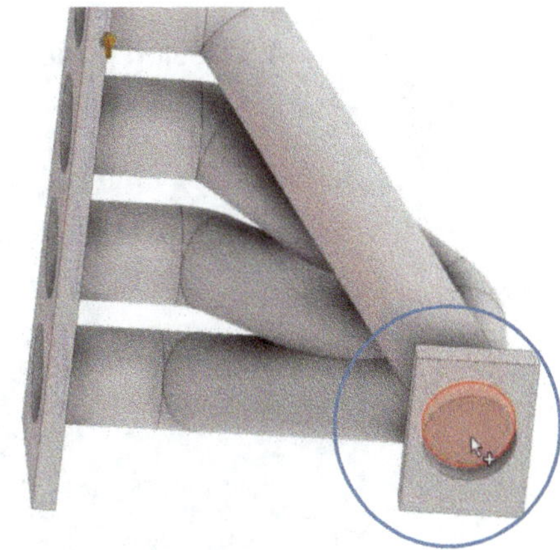

Figure 138: Hollowing out the exhaust manifold; select circular areas at the top and bottom and enter a 2 mm wall thickness in "Thickness" in the options

Super! In this lesson we learned quite a bit. The creation of a 3D sketch, an "offset" layer and the practical use of the "sweep" and "shell" commands.

As the penultimate design project, we will construct the front end of a truck with passenger cell or driver's cab in the following chapter. This will be a bit more challenging, but together it is no problem!

We will go step by step again! Stay with it and please continue, it gets more and more exciting!

4.3 Design project III: Truck front end

Figure 139: A truck front end becomes our third design project

For the front part of the truck we start a new single part. First, let's think about how best to build the model. We need a trapezoidal section for the hood, a cuboid for the actual cab, and add-on parts like fenders, headlights, grille, and bumper. This means we could start once with the section for the engine hood, for example. To do this, we start a sketch on the x-y plane and draw a simple rectangle. The starting point should be the center point and the dimensions should be 140 mm in width and 90 mm in height. Then we create a parallel plane to the x-y plane with 120 mm distance.

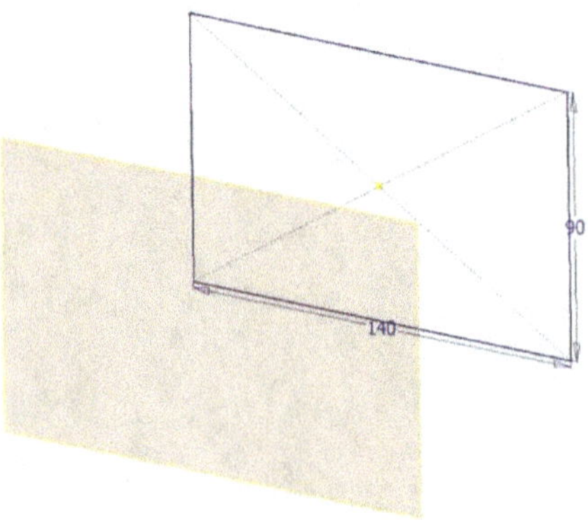

Figure 140: The rectangle on the x-y plane with the parallel plane at 120 mm distance

On this plane we will now sketch another rectangle which will be somewhat smaller, 75 mm wide and 80 mm high to be more precise. The distance of the center should be 5 mm to the coordinate origin, so that the two lower edges of the rectangles are congruent.

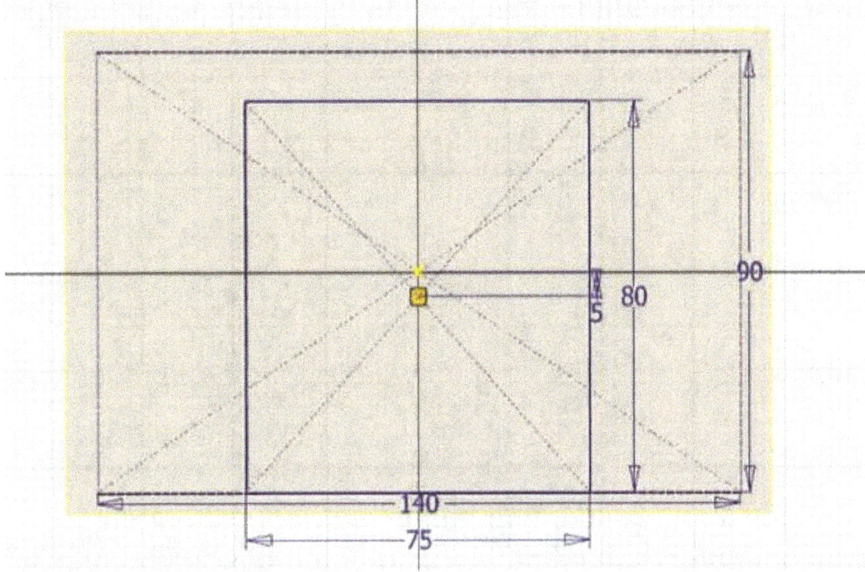

Figure 141: Sketch the second rectangle on the parallel plane

With the "Loft" function, we can now have the two rectangles connected in 3D mode to form a solid.

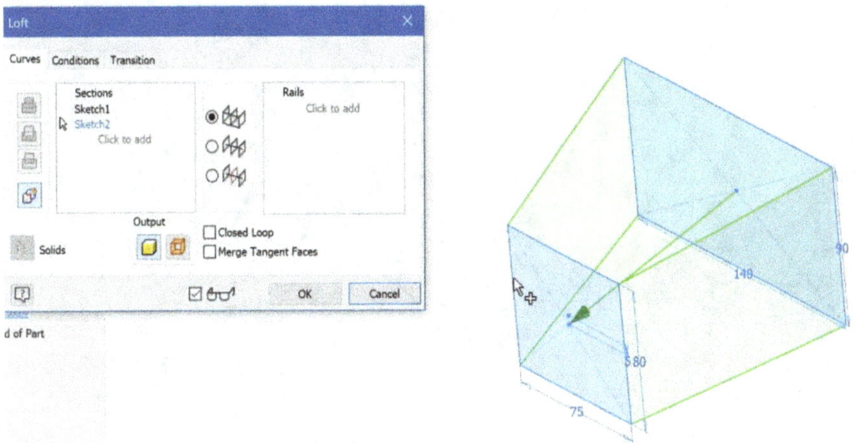

Figure 142: Apply142"Loft" function to obtain a solid

For the driver's cab, we then draw a new sketch with a 140 mm wide and 170 mm high rectangle on the rear plane of this solid.

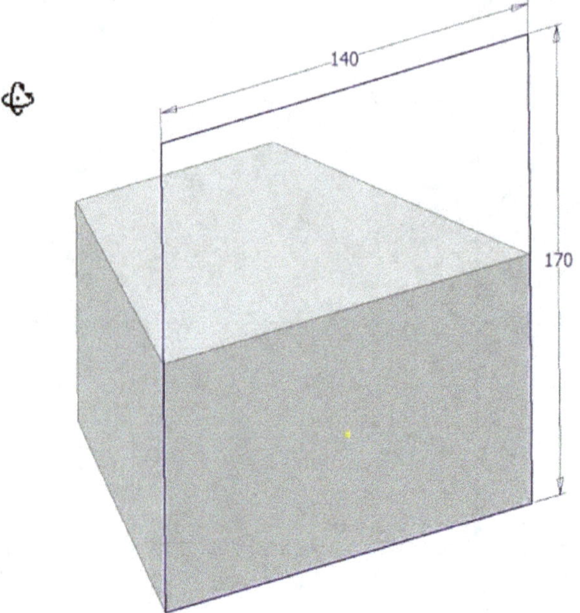

Figure 143: Sketching the rectangle on the rear face of the base body (view rotated here)

We then extrude this rectangle 120 mm.

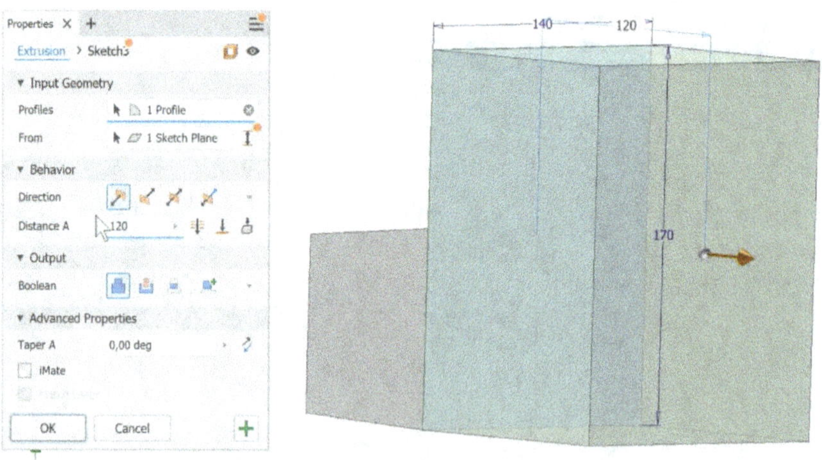

Figure 144: Extrude the rectangle 120 mm

Now we already have the two basic shapes for our object. For the two fenders or wheel arches, we draw a sketch on the y-z plane in the next step, since we want to extrude them symmetrically from the center. After starting a sketch, we first draw a 3-point arc with 50 mm radius and 72 mm distance in horizontal direction to the origin. We set the two remaining points coincident i.e. congruent with the left corner and once with the bottom line of the engine compartment.

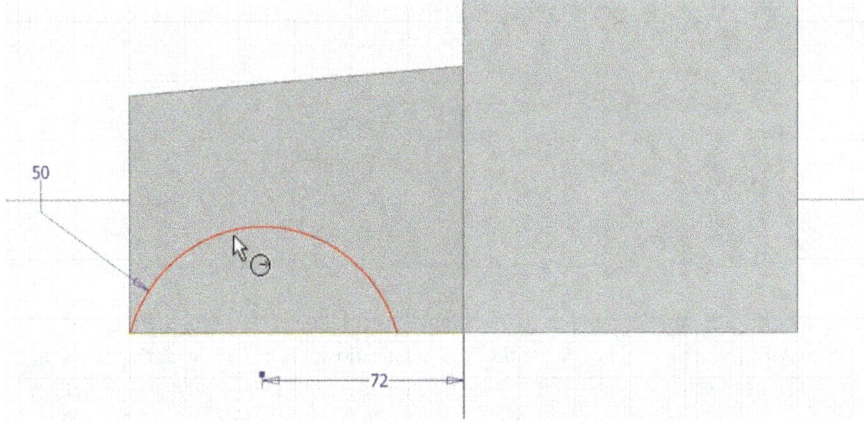

Figure 145: Sketching a 3-point arc on the y-z plane; Mark for visibility

Then we need another 3-point arc, which we set concentric to the first arc, and two horizontal lines, each 2.5 mm long, which connect the two corner points of the arcs.

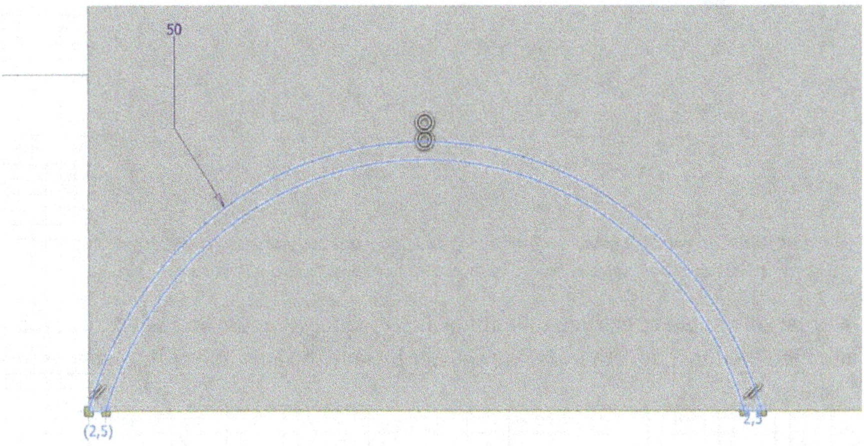

Figure 146: Sketch the second arc concentrically to the first one; add 2.5 mm long connecting lines; mark for visibility with the mouse

Dimension them with 2.5 mm each. To select a specific element, stay a little longer with your mouse at a position. Then a small drop-down menu will appear, with which you can choose which congruent element you want to select.

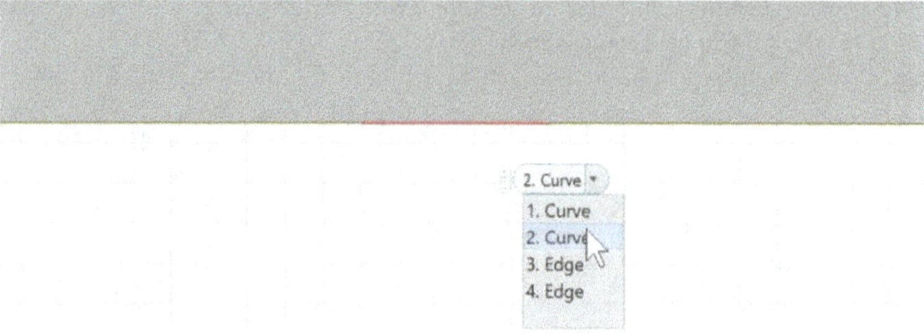

Figure 147: The small drop-down menu for selecting congruent elements

The second 2.5 mm dimension is no longer necessary. This results from the other dimensions and the concentric condition. This dimension would overdefine the sketch, so we can only use a controlled dimension here, which is then placed in brackets. A controlled dimension is not fixed, but changes when we change another dimension. So it just shows a value. We could also just omit them.

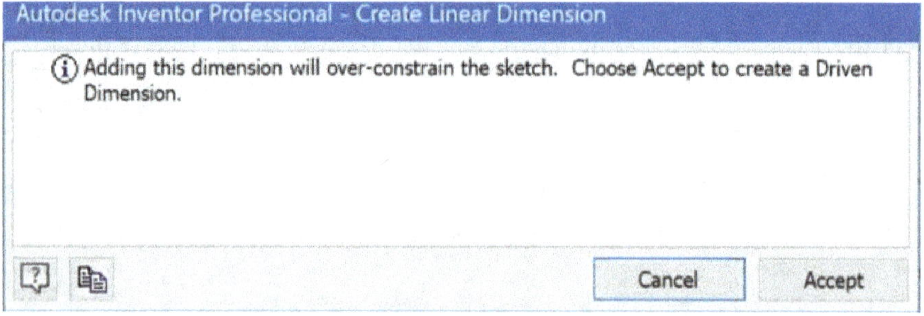

Figure 148: The warning when a dimension overdefines a sketch; press "Accept" for a controlled dimensioning

In order to be able to extrude the profile in 3D mode, we must first select the profile and then the function, otherwise we will not be able to select the profile because it is inside.

We take a dimension of 140 mm with symmetrical direction or "Direction": "Symmetric". If we want to create an independent body for the volume element, we select "New Solid" for "Output", otherwise simply "Join", then it will simply be merged with the previous body. In this case we choose "Join" because we still want these fenders to be part of our basic body.

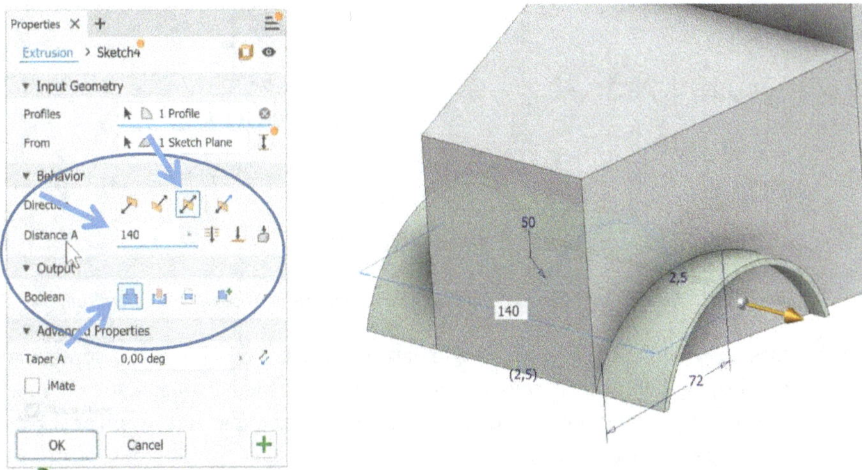

Figure 149: First select the sketch in the part browser, then start the "Extrude" command

In this chapter we only want to create a new body for each add-on part such as the radiator grille, headlights and bumper, but not a separate individual part as we would do in a normal assembly. We have already briefly touched on how to deal with individual parts in an assembly and how to link them to joints in an assembly in a previous chapter and we will learn about this in more detail in the next chapter.

Note that in this context, body and component are different terms. Confused by bodies, parts and assemblies? Let's make a short digression about body vs. single part: the difference between body and single part is that each assembly consists of single parts and each single part in turn consists of bodies. So it's a kind of hierarchical detailing. For example, in a car, the parts of the chassis, the doors, the wheels, and all other parts, down to the smallest bolts, are designed as individual parts. Each of these individual parts of a main assembly, can in turn be divided into several bodies or even solids. But you don't necessarily have to do that, you can also build a single part from just one body, especially if it is very simple in design.

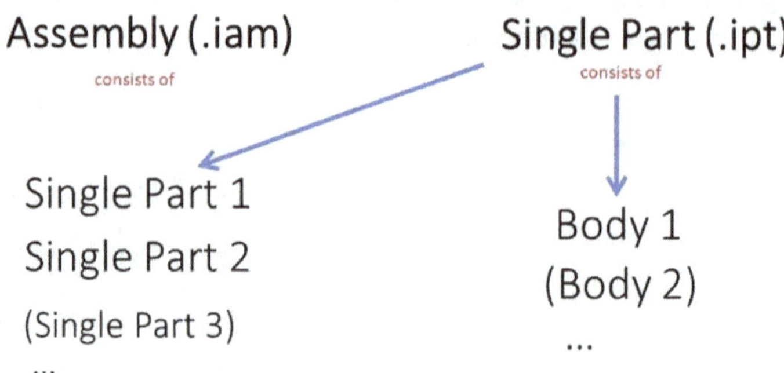

Figure 150: Difference between body, individual part and assembly; shown schematically

In this case, we build our model as a single part, but since the single part is somewhat more complex, we build it from several bodies. This offers the advantage, for example, that we can clearly delimit the individual bodies and, for example, hide them or slightly change the appearance of these bodies.

To summarize briefly in conclusion: A body is, so to speak, a more detailed demarcation within a single part, which in turn can belong to an assembly. A body is primarily a component of a single part, whereas a single part can move freely within the parent assembly and is linked by joints within an assembly. Don't worry if you don't understand it right away, you will understand it even better during the course based on practical implementation.

Back to our truck. In the next step we want to hollow out our solid, we do this with the command "Shell", a click on the lower surface and the input of a 5 mm wall.

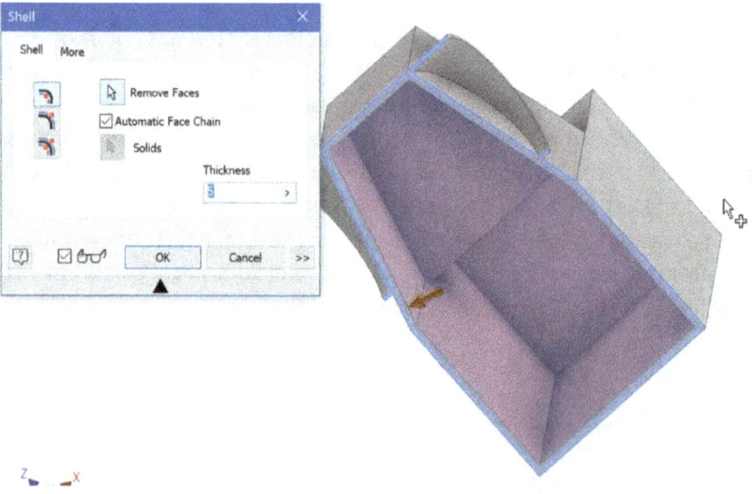

Figure 151: Hollowing out the previous body with "Shell" and a 5 mm wall

We would also like to remove the surfaces inside the wheel housings. On the one hand, we could start an extrusion, as we know it. On the other hand, in this case we can also simply remove the face, using the "Delete Face" command from the "Modify" section. Please note that you have to check the option "Heal remaining Faces", otherwise it will not work as desired.

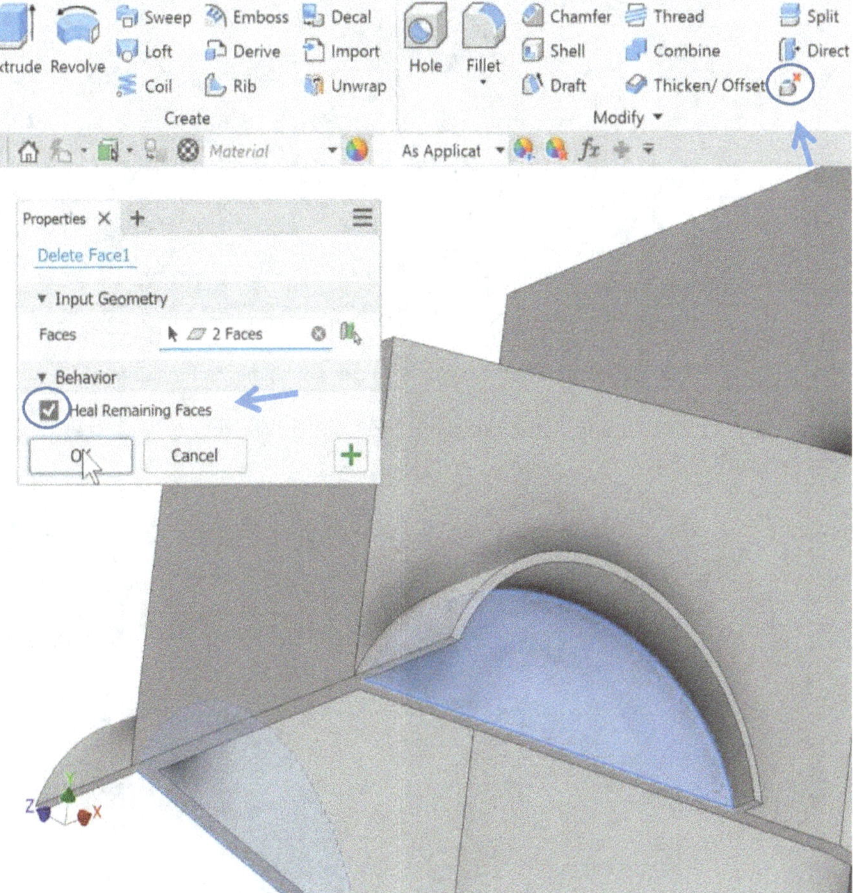

Figure 152: The Delete Face command from the Modify section

We will then take care of the two-part windshield. We want to build this from two simple rectangles. Take the dimensions from the following profile:

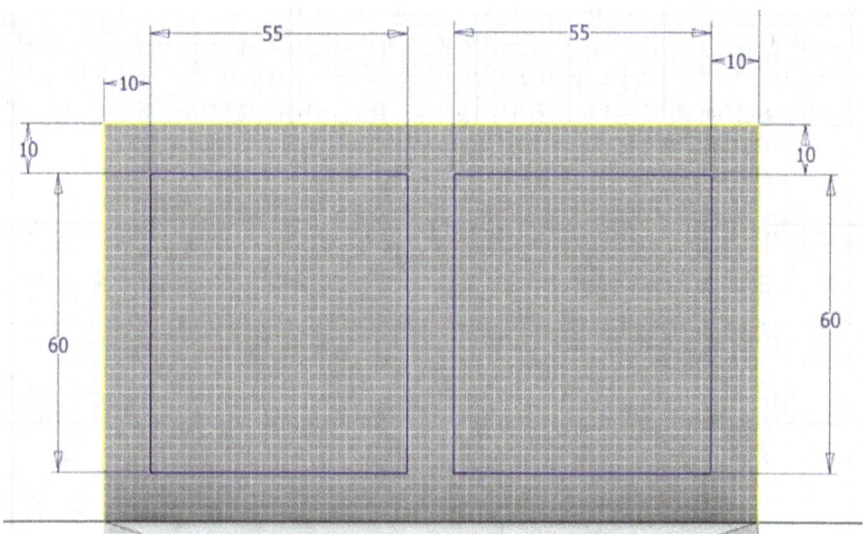

Figure 153: Sketching the profile of the two rectangles on the front top surface

Then finish the sketch and cut it out with "Extrusion". We round the edges of the windows with 5 mm.

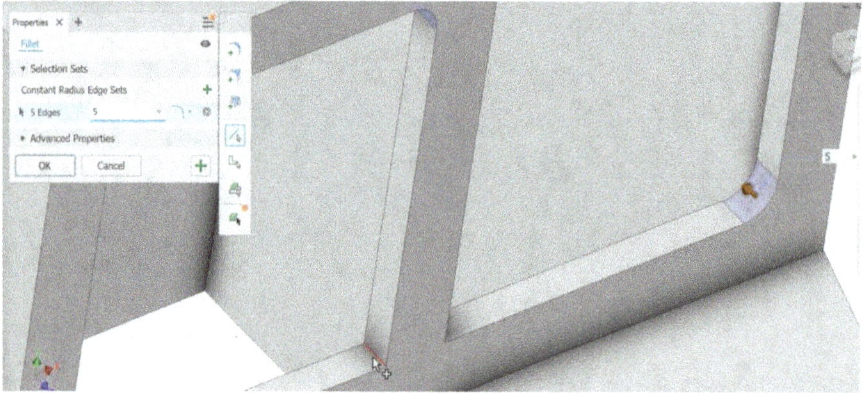

Figure 154: Rounding the edges of the windows with 5 mm

We proceed similarly for the side windows. For this, however, we draw only a rectangle on one side and then simply cut through the entire width, since the cabin is hollow anyway. The dimensions and position of the rectangle should be as follows:

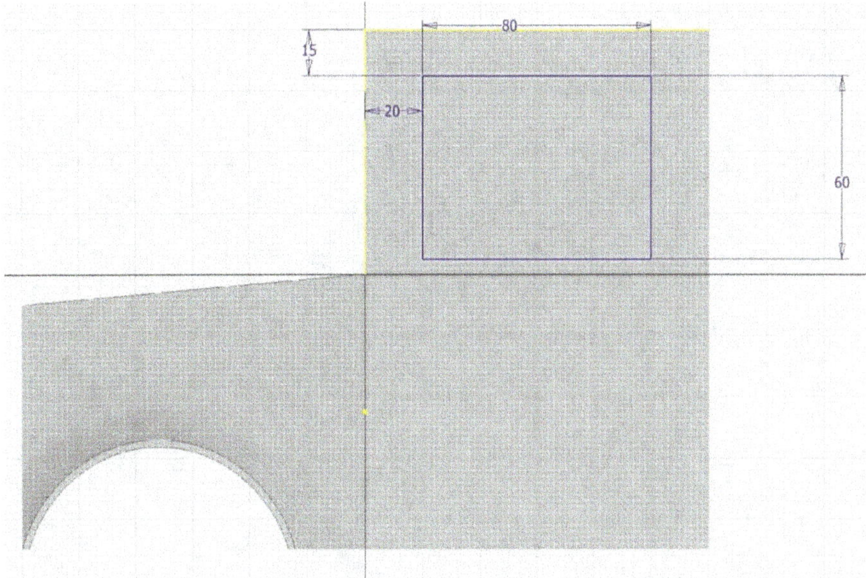

Figure 155: The profile for the cutout for the side windows

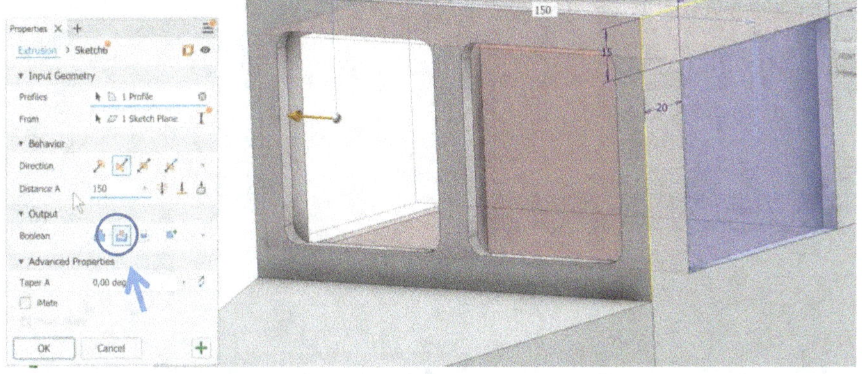

Figure 156: Cutting out the windows from one side; for output: "Cut

To give our model also at least the appearance of a door, we will get to know a new function, the command "Emboss" or "Emboss".

For this command we first need a sketch, so we draw a rectangle for embossing the door on the side surface of the driver's cab. The starting point should be in the lower left corner of the window and the rectangle should be 90 mm high and as wide as the window.

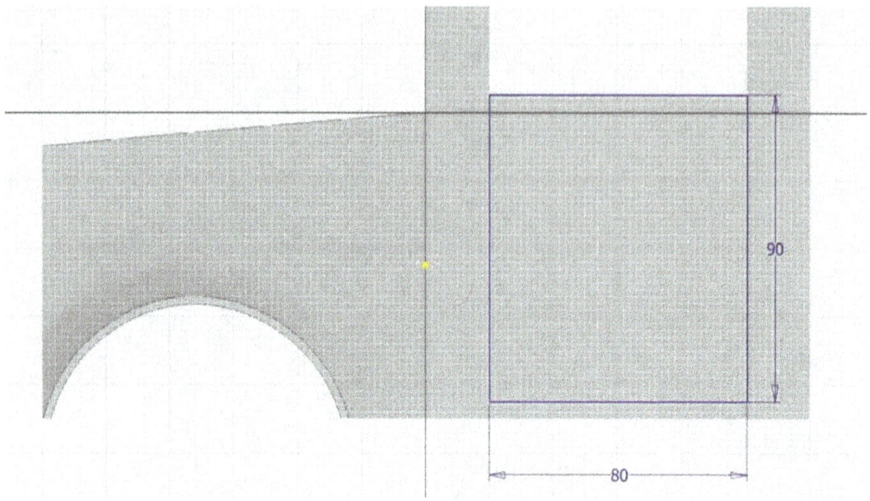

Figure 157: The profile for embossing the side door

Then we select the command "Emboss" / "Emboss", the sketched profile and select as effect "Engrave from Face" / "Einstanz", because we do not want an elevation but a depression and specify 1 mm as depth.

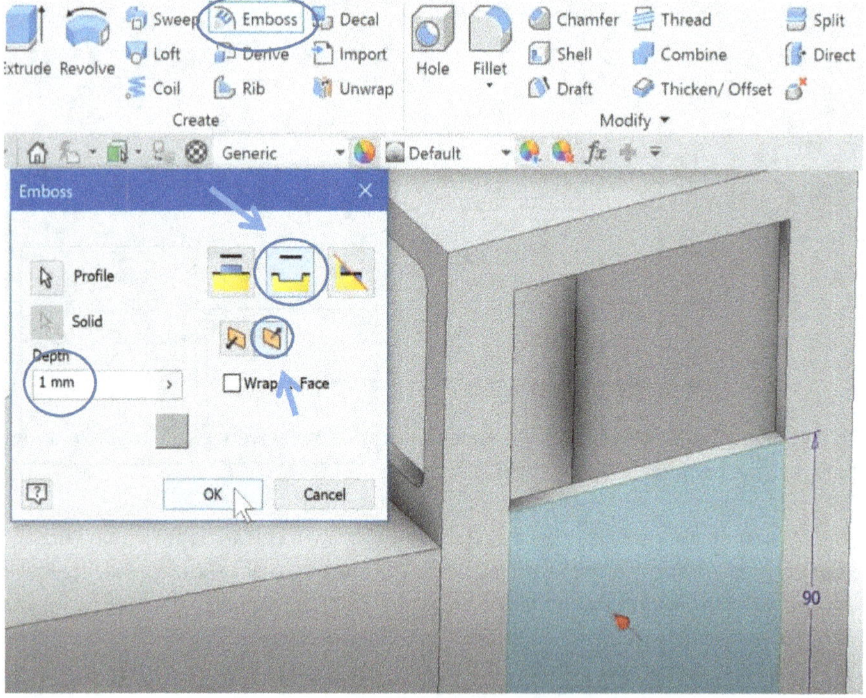

Figure 158: The Emboss command from the Create section

As you may have recognized, this step would also have been possible with "Extrude". For the door handle we now draw a rectangle on this surface again. This time with the following dimensions:

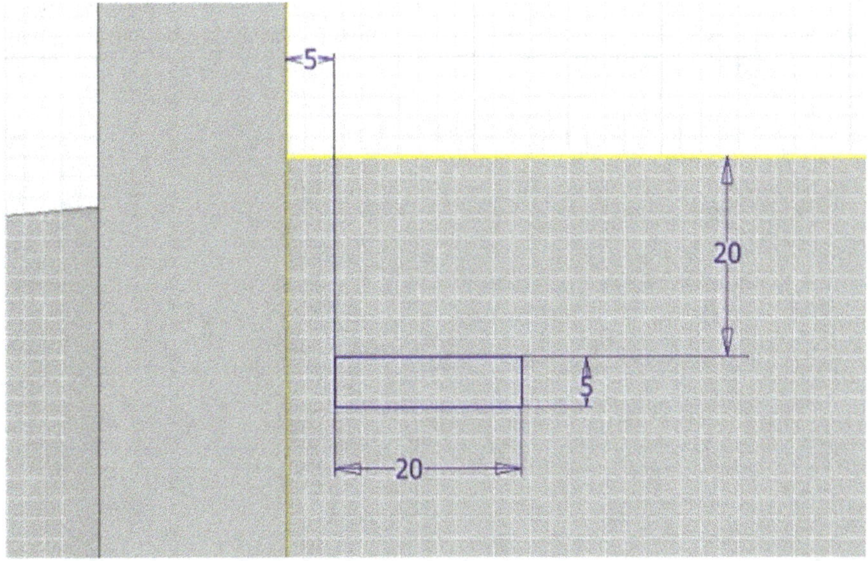

Figure 159: The 2D sketch for one of the two door handles on the side surface of the truck

Then we extrude the profile 5 mm and select "New Solid" in Operation, because we want to create a new body for this.

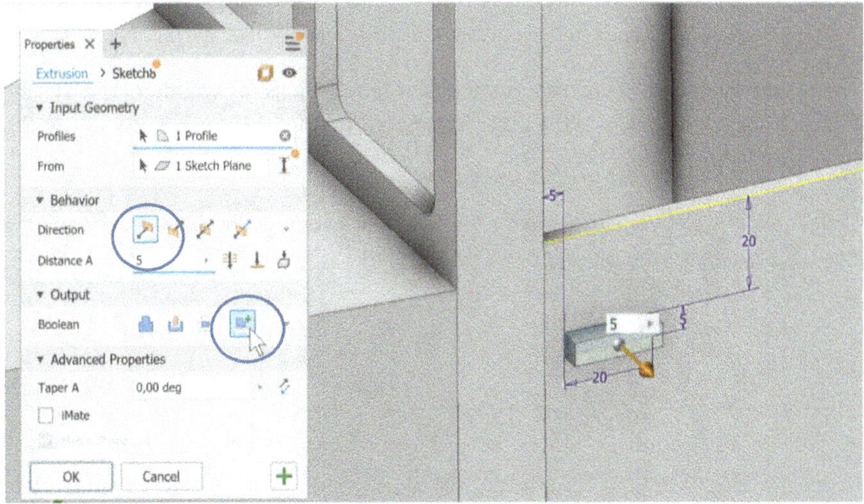

Figure 160: Extrusion of the handle (5 mm; select "New Solid" in "Output")

To make it easier for us, we simply mirror these two features to the other side. To do this, we select the "Mirror" command and in the "Type" options: "Features" or "Elements". We now simply select the embossing and the door handle in the part browser and then switch to "Mirror Plane" / "Mirror Plane" in the options and select the y-z plane as the mirror plane. Just try it one after the other in case mirroring both features at once doesn't work.

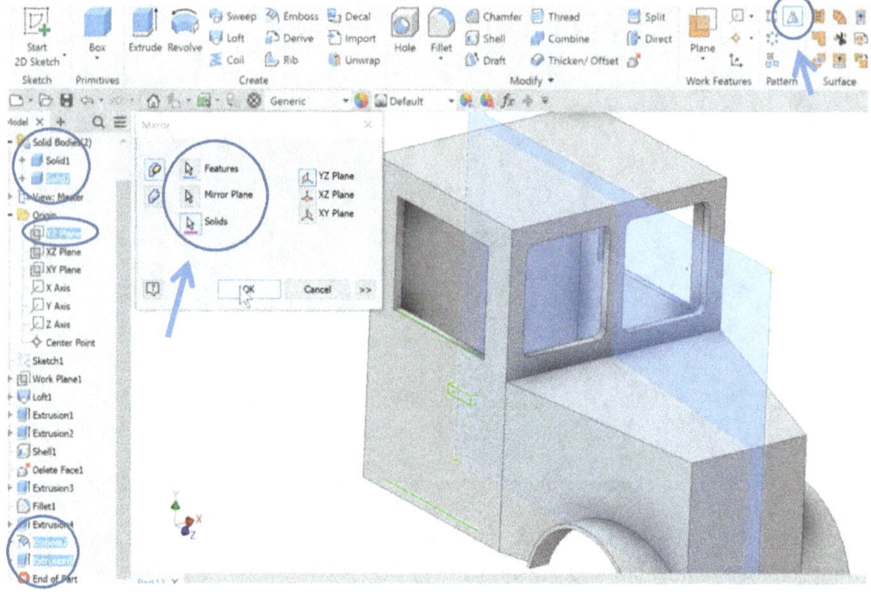

Figure 161: Using the "Mirror" function; first select body, then mirror plane

The Mirror function usually creates significant time savings for symmetrical parts and features, incidentally also in the 2D sketching environment. Therefore, try to use this function as often as possible.

We continue with two fillets, one for the two door handles with 1.5 mm each and the two upper edges of the side windows with 5 mm each.

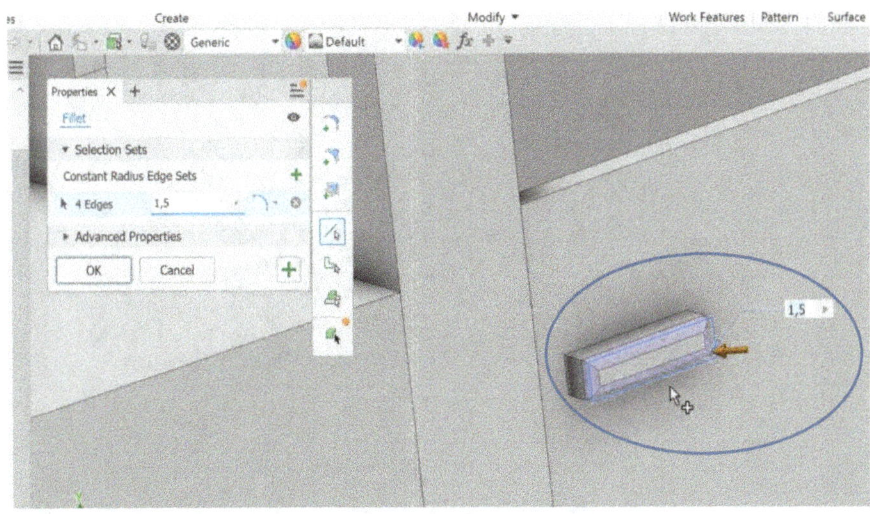

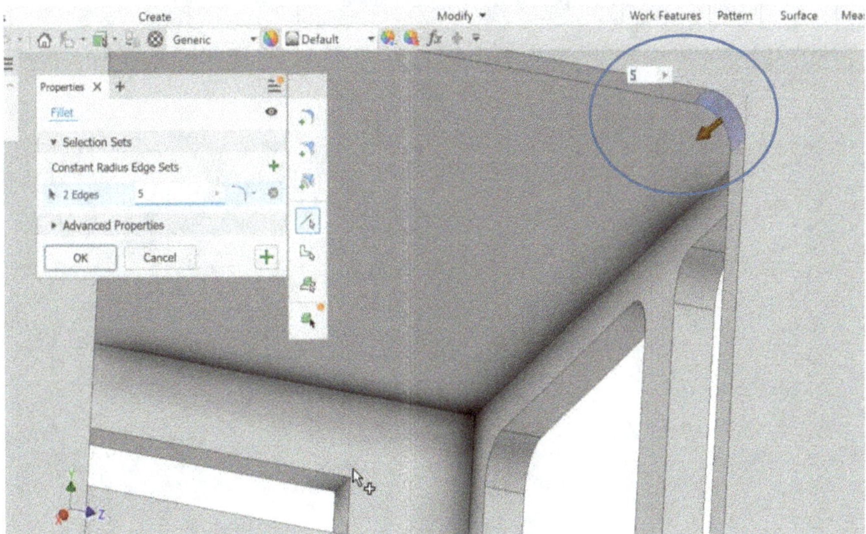

Figure 162: The fillets for the door handles (1.5 mm) and side windows (5mm; upper edges only)

Now we draw the bumper. This should sit at the front with the dimensions 140 mm and 15 mm. To do this, we again use the dependency collinear for the upper horizontal line that we link to the truck front and, for example, the left vertical line that we link to the side of the truck to fully define the sketch.

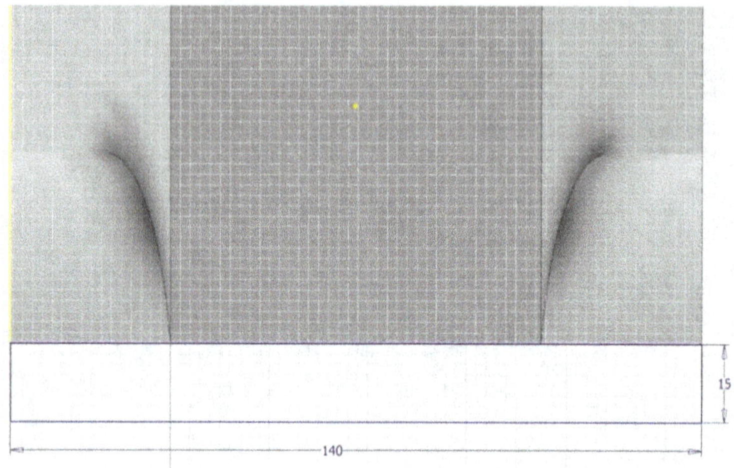

Figure 163: The rectangular profile for the bumper (sketch on the front surface)

Then we can extrude the profile 8 mm, we again create a new body for it, and still round off with 4 mm.

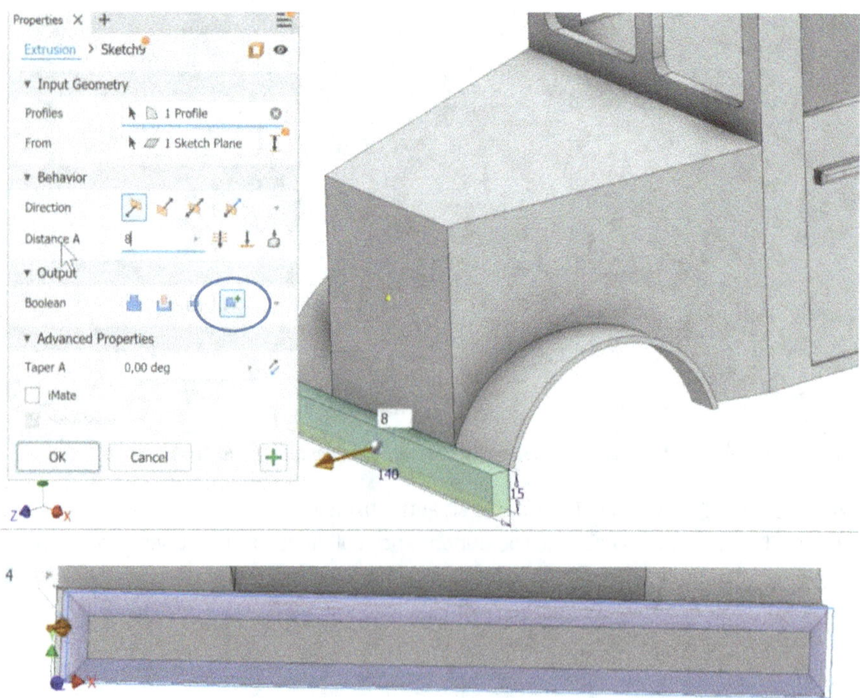

Figure 164: The extrusion of the profile (8 mm) and the filleting of the edges (4 mm)

For the headlights, we first draw one of the two needed on the front surface and then mirror it.

For example, the profile should have the following dimensions:

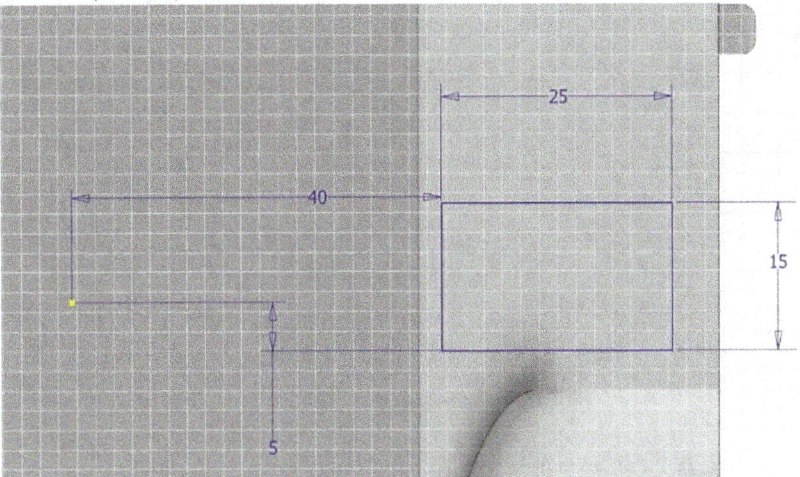

Figure 165: The profile for the headlight housing (sketch on the front surface)

We then extrude it with 10 mm.

In addition, we draw another 2 mm cutout with 2 mm distance to the headlight body to improve the design a bit.

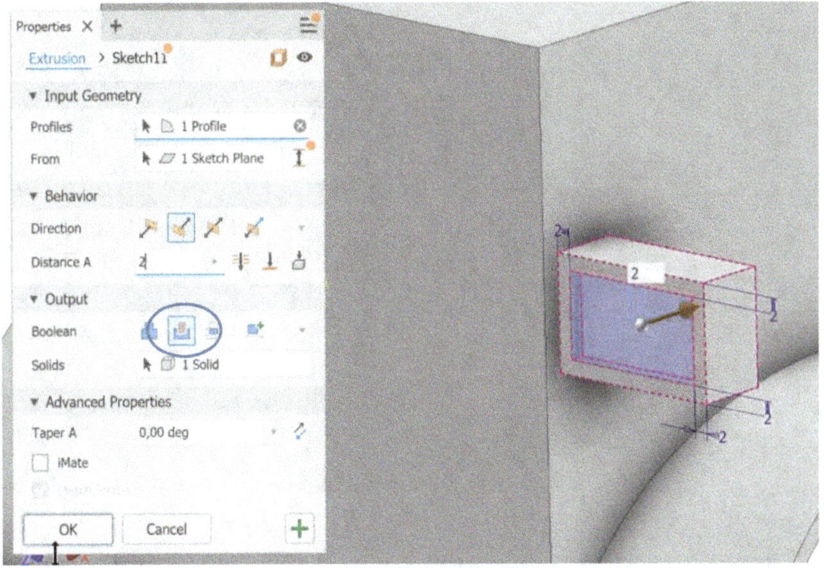

Figure 166: Draw a profile with 2 mm distance to the edge on the extruded housing and then cut out 2 mm ("Cut" at "Output")

And a connecting strut to suggest a little more stability. For this connecting strut we need a circular geometry on the front side surface of the truck with 6 mm diameter at a distance of 83 mm and horizontal to the origin.

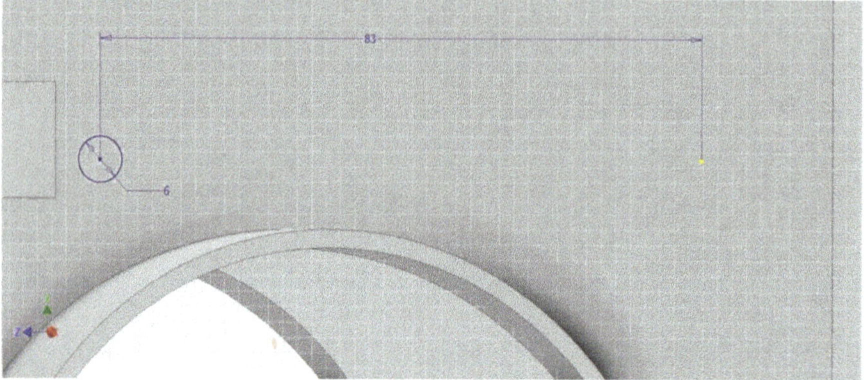

Figure 167: Draw a 6 mm diameter circle on the front side surface of the truck

In addition, another circular geometry on the back of the headlight, also 6 mm in diameter, which we simply dimensioned from the top and side edges at 8 mm and 12 mm.

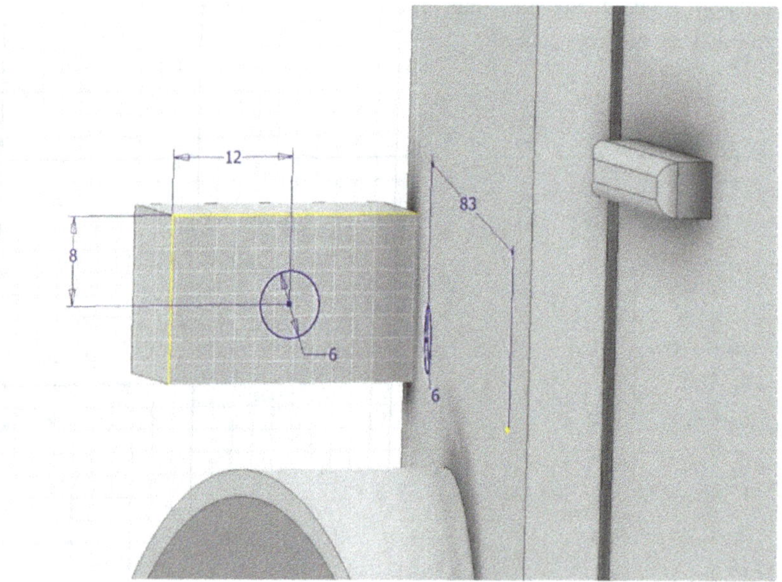

Figure 168: Sketch the second circle on the back of the headlight (rotated in the view image)

Then we use the "Loft" command and connect the two circular surfaces to form a three-dimensional connecting strut.

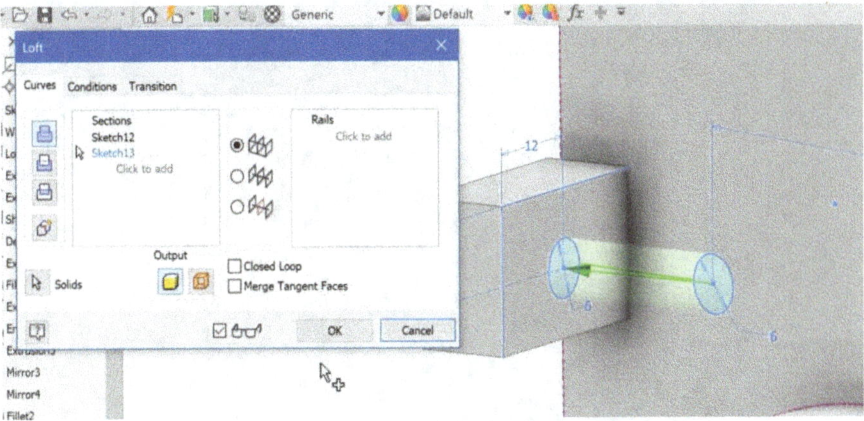

Figure 169: Using the "Loft" command to create a connecting strut

Now we can mirror the headlight and the strut to the other side.

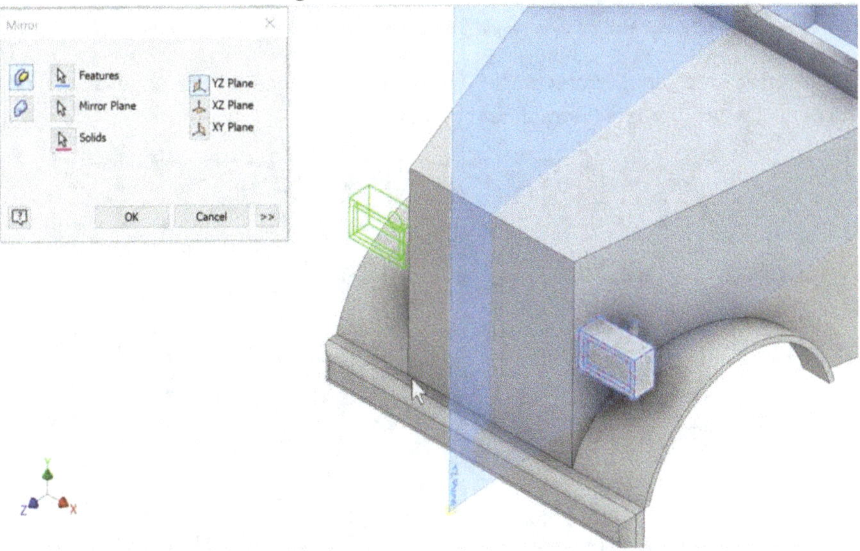

Figure 170: Mirror the spotlight and the strut with "Mirror" in the y-z plane

As a last detail of our truck front we would like to draw a radiator grill. For this, we first start a new sketch on the front surface.

Then we first draw a rectangle with 75 mm width and 80 mm height. The side line and the top line should each be collinear with the lines of the front face.

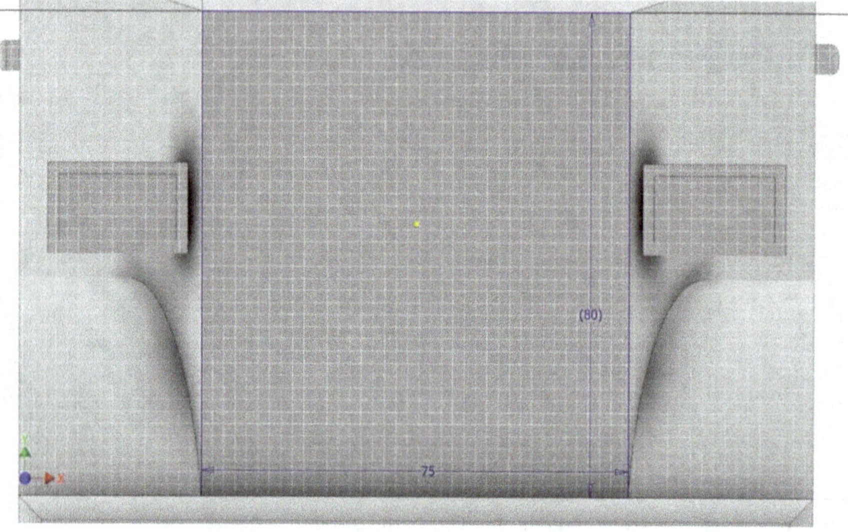

Figure 171: Sketching a rectangle (75 x 80 mm) on the front surface of the truck

In the next step, another rectangle, with 4 mm distance to the edge of the first rectangle, which borders our radiator cutouts.

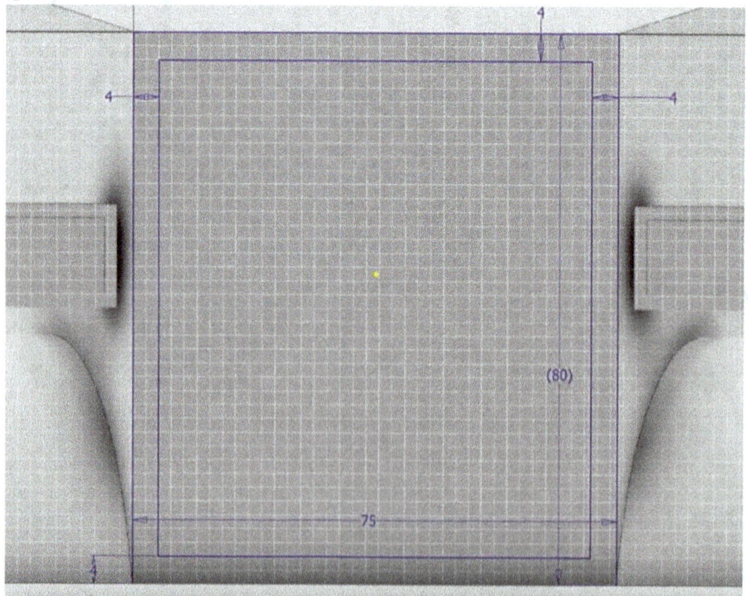

Figure 172: Sketching the second rectangle (each 4 mm from the first rectangle)

Then we draw a vertical line congruent to the center line.

Then we draw a line to the left and right of the center line at a distance of 1 mm from the center line. The start and end points should lie on the second rectangle drawn.

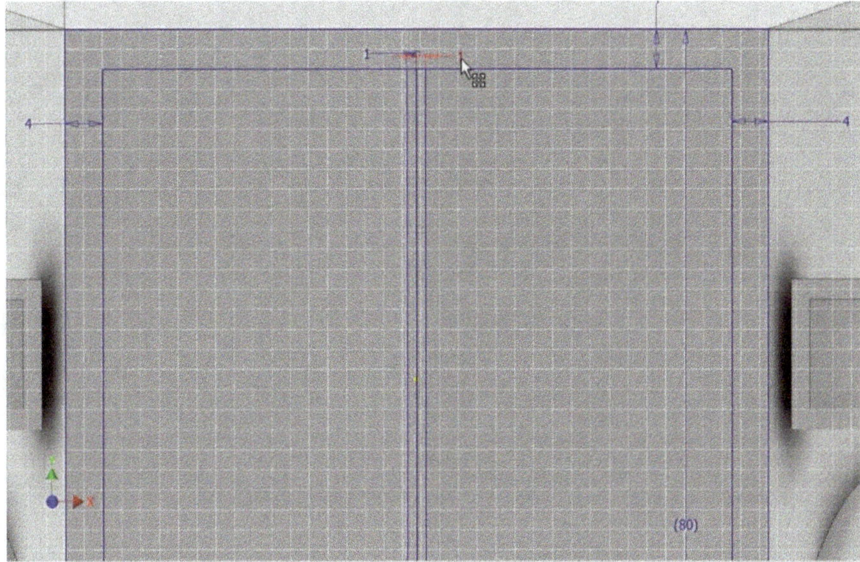

Figure 173: A vertical line congruent with the center line and one vertical line each to the left and right of it (the lines should start and end on the inner rectangle)

Now we would have to draw a lot of these lines, because we want to extrude every other space between them to get the shape of the grille. To make life easier, we will use a new command called "Pattern", or "Rectangular Pattern" in this case.

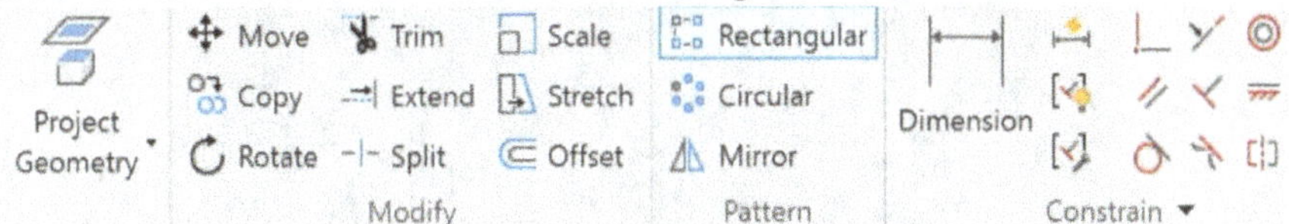

Figure 174: The Rectangular Pattern command in the Pattern section

To do this, we select each of the vertical line elements. First select the left line, start the command and then we have to specify a direction in which the pattern should be created. To do this, we simply select the upper or lower left line segment of the rectangle and, if necessary, turn the displayed green arrow with "Flip" (Options) in the desired direction, i.e. to the left. Then we have to enter a distance of 1 mm between the line elements and increase the number to 33. Tada, the program does the work for us.

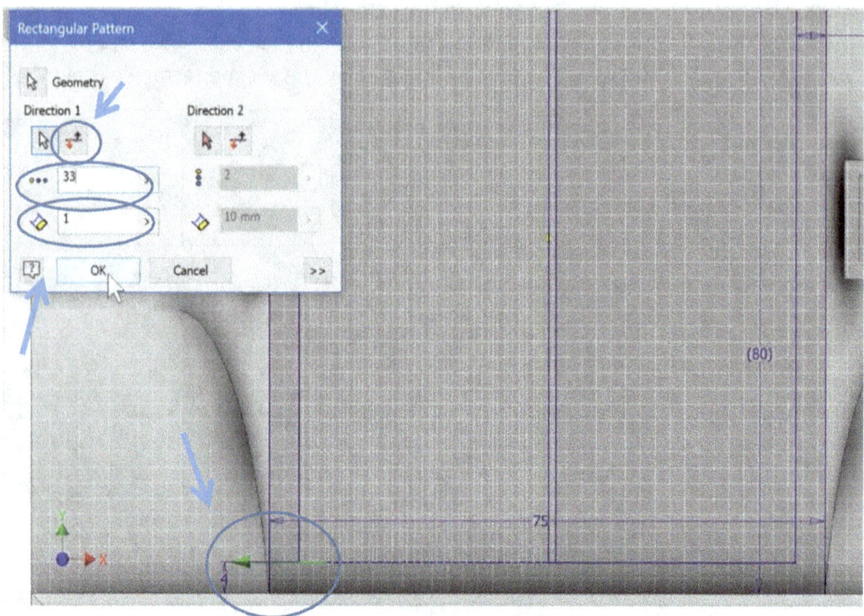

Figure 175: The command "Rectangular Pattern" in the application; the green arrow (circled) must point to the left, if necessary flip it with "Flip" in the "Direction" options

We then do the same for the other side, but to the right.

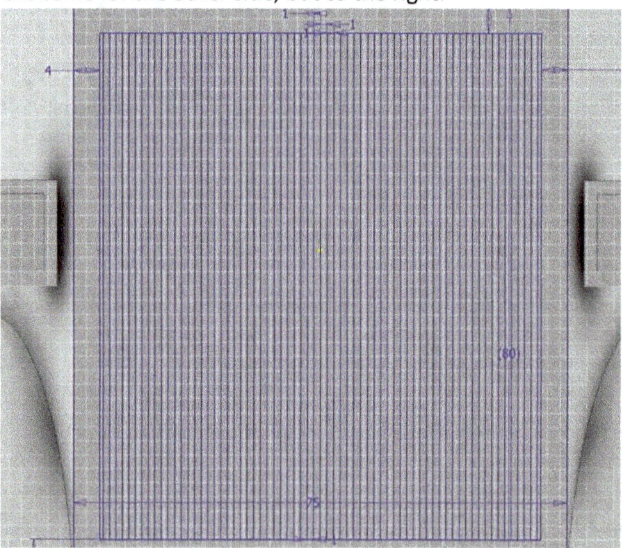

Figure 176: The result of the "Rectangular Pattern" command; applied in both directions

Now, to create the solid body of the radiator grille, we extrude the area between the two large rectangles and every second long, narrow rectangle 2 mm outward to create the following solid.

Figure 177: Extrude every second rectangle 2 mm outward to obtain the radiator grille

Very good! After we have rounded a few more edges, according to taste, with 2 mm each, we take a quick look at the individual bodies and then have this lesson done! Super if you stuck with it!

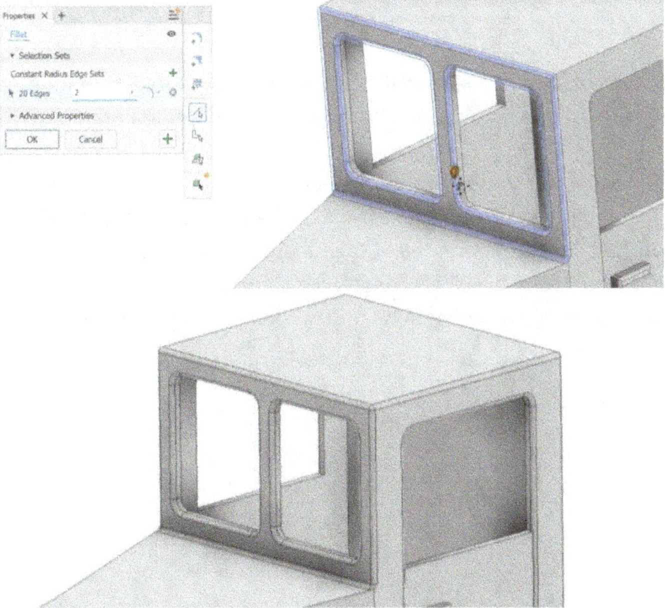

Figure 178: Filleting of edges (e.g. at the front of the windshield and at the top)

As we can see, we have now created several bodies in the "Bodies" folder in the part browser. More precisely: one each for the door handles, the body, the headlights, the struts, the bumper and the radiator grille. We can now hide / show these bodies as we wish or change the appearance per body separately.

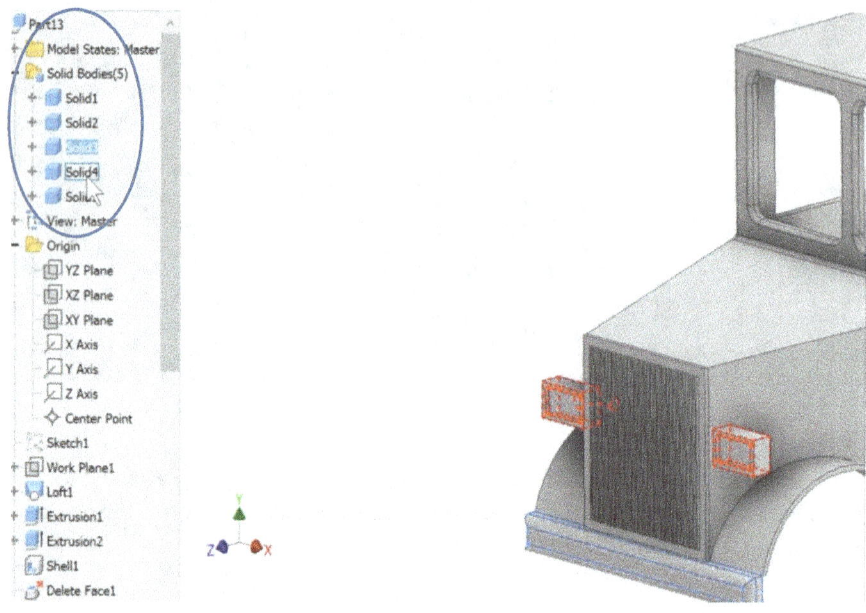

If we want we could print the model as it is with a 3D printer. If you are interested in 3D printing, feel free to take a look at my course "3D Printing | Step by Step".

However, if you prefer to design the bumper, the radiator grille and the headlights as independent components and then assemble them in an assembly, take a look at the next lesson first. In this lesson, we'll take a step-by-step look at how to work with components in an assembly. We'll construct a simplified model of a 4-cylinder internal combustion engine. This is going to be pretty cool! Let's get right to it!

4.4 Design project IV: 4-cylinder internal combustion engine

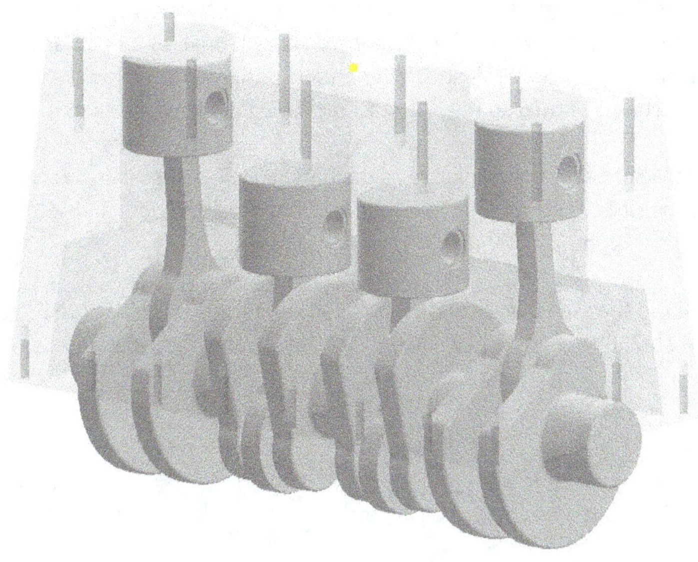

Figure 179: A 4-cylinder engine becomes our fourth design project

4.4.1 Part 1: Crankcase

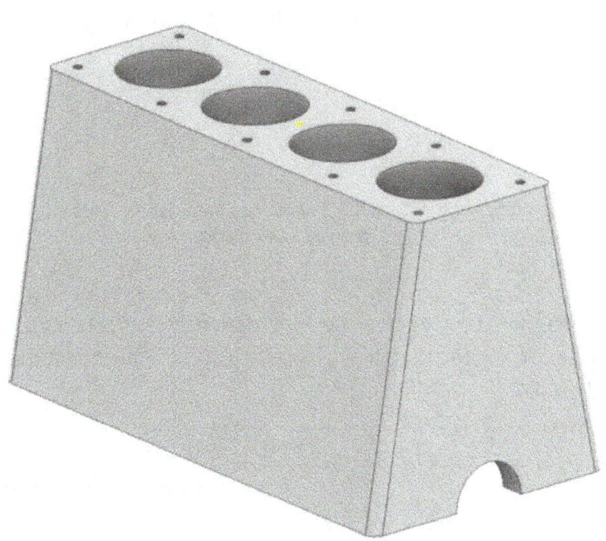

Figure 180: We start with the crankshaft housing or engine block first

In this chapter, as announced, we want to construct a simplified model of a 4-cylinder engine. We want to initially build this model from several main components, as in reality, but will then neglect some details so that the construction does not become too complex. To start with, we need a crankcase. We will omit an oil pan and a cylinder head with valve cover. So the first component we design is the crankcase, as it creates a central starting point. To do this, we start on the x-z plane with a sketch.

To create the shape for the crankcase as the basic body, we first span a rectangle from the center point and can immediately specify 500 mm as the width and 150 mm as the height as dimensions.

Then we finish the sketch and create a parallel plane to the x-z plane in 3D mode with a distance of -250 mm, as we have already learned in one of the previous lessons.

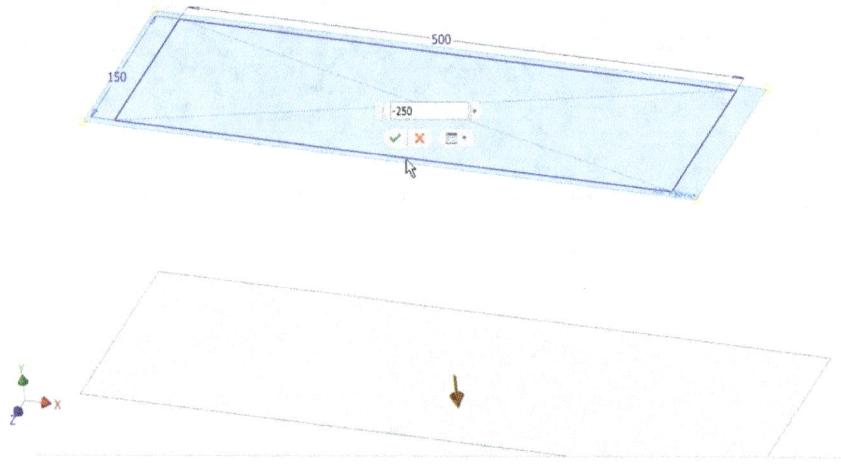

Figure 181: Draw a rectangular profile (500 x 150 mm) on the x-z plane; create offset plane (-250 mm) parallel to x-z plane

On this plane we then draw a rectangle with identical width, i.e. 500 mm and a height of 250 mm. After closing the sketch, we use the "Loft" / "Elevation" command to create a trapezoidal solid.

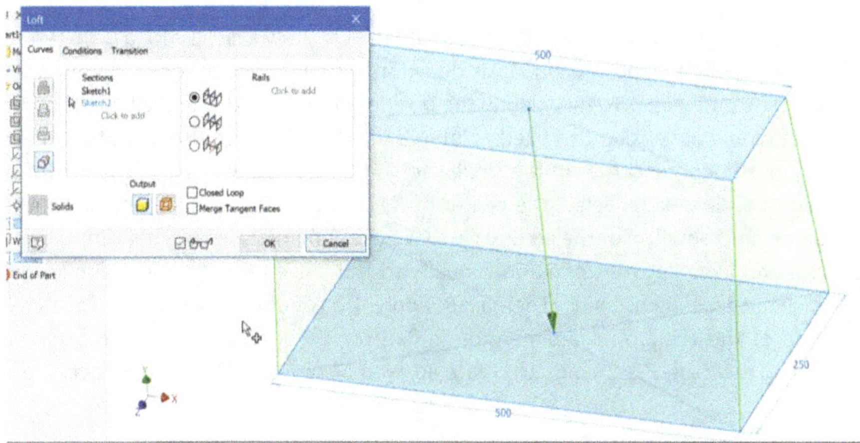

Figure 182: Creating a trapezoidal solid using the Loft command

Now we take care of the holes for the pistons, i.e. the cylinders. We can insert these in two ways, either with the "Hole" function or as a circular cutout with "Extrude". Since the holes have to go completely through the cuboid, we simply use the cutout in this case. For this we start a sketch on the upper surface. We want to create cylinders with 90 mm diameter and construct a 4-cylinder engine. Therefore we need the following dimensions and geometries:

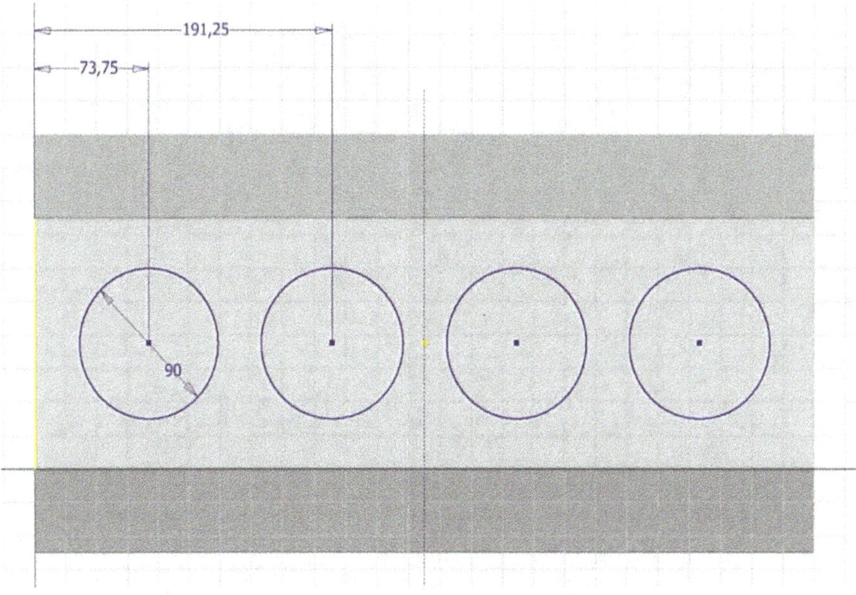

Figure 183: For the cylinders we need four circles as shown

What is the easiest way to draw these circles? First we draw a circle with a diameter of 90 mm and define its position in x-axis direction with a dimension of 73.75 mm from the center to the edge. To fully define the position of the circle, we need not only the diameter and a dimension to a fixed point in the x-direction, but also a position in the z-direction. Since the center of the circle should be on the x-axis, we use a condition instead of a dimension. Select the center of the circle and the origin, and select the condition horizontally. For the second circle we use conditions again. First simply draw a circle and then set the condition "Equal", so the circle gets the same dimension, without further dimensioning. Then again apply the condition "horizontal" for the z-position of the circle. And a dimension in "x", for the x-position in the coordinate system. In this case 191.25 mm, to create an even distance of 117.5 mm between the cylinders.

Since our geometry of the four circles is axisymmetric around the z-axis, we can now create the other two circles very quickly and easily with the "Mirror" command. For the command we first have to create an axis around which we want to mirror, because the z-axis is not selectable in this case. We do this by drawing a line, congruent to the z-axis and linking it coincident on the origin. We then convert this line into a construction or auxiliary line by right-clicking and selecting "Construction". You can recognize this by the dashed line type. We will not define construction lines completely, since they are not necessarily relevant. We only need a defined position in x-direction, which we already have.

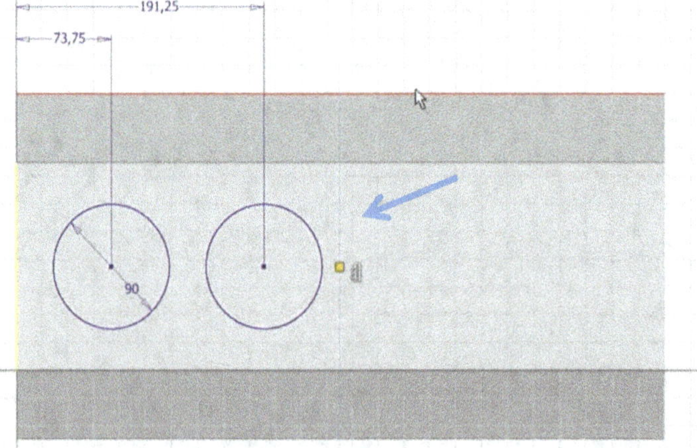

Figure 184: First draw the two left circles, then create a vertical line through the center point and convert it to a construction line by right-clicking on it and selecting "Construction Line"

Then select the "Mirror" command in the "Pattern" menu and select the two circles. In the options, switch the selection to "Mirror Line" and then select the construction line you just created. With "Apply" the other two circles are created and are already fully defined.

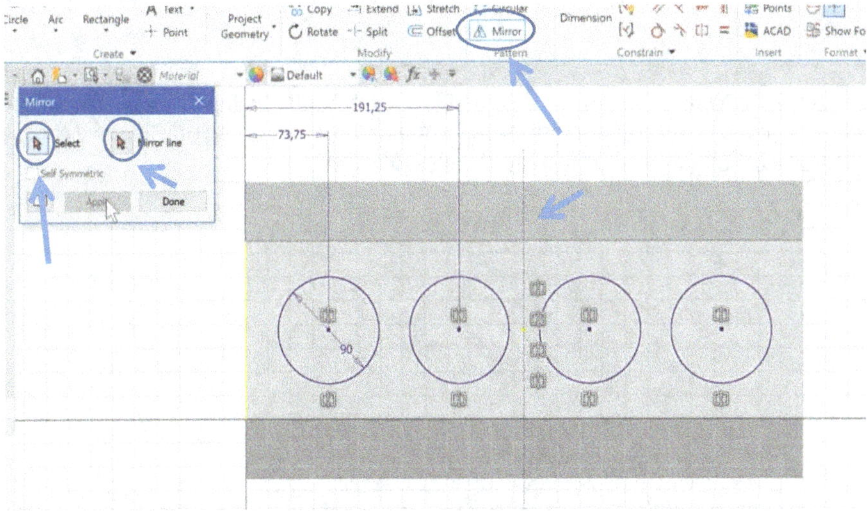

Figure 185: Creating the two circles on the right side of the mirror axis with "Mirror"

We close the 2D sketch and create the sections with "Extrude" by selecting the four circular areas. In the options, we can select "To" for "Distance" and then select the surface up to which the cutouts are to be made. In our case we select the ground surface. By the way, "Output" must be set to "Cut".

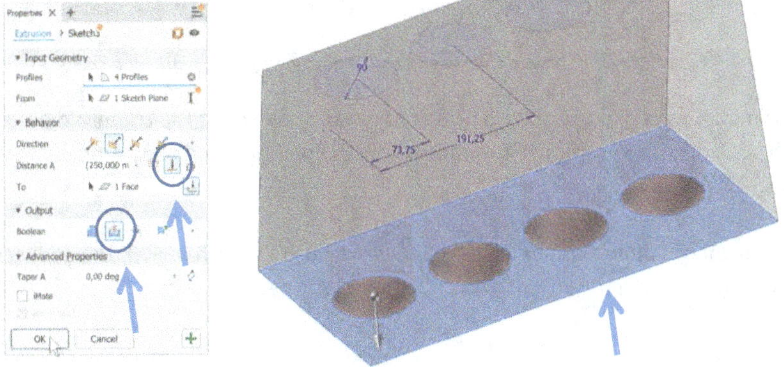

Figure 186: Create the cutouts with "Extrude"; at "Distance" : select "To" and select lower side of the case

By the way, we could have integrated these circular areas into the first sketch right away and thus saved ourselves a step.

Then we machine the lower part of the crankcase, which will later house the crankshaft. To do this, we create a trapezoidal cutout that spans symmetrically from the center of the housing. First, we draw a base line on the y-z plane and set it colinear with the crankcase bottom.

Then we draw the trapezoid as shown and dimension the height with 100 mm. Then dimension the lower corner points with 25 mm to the wall. For the side lines we choose a parallel condition to the side lines of the cabinet.

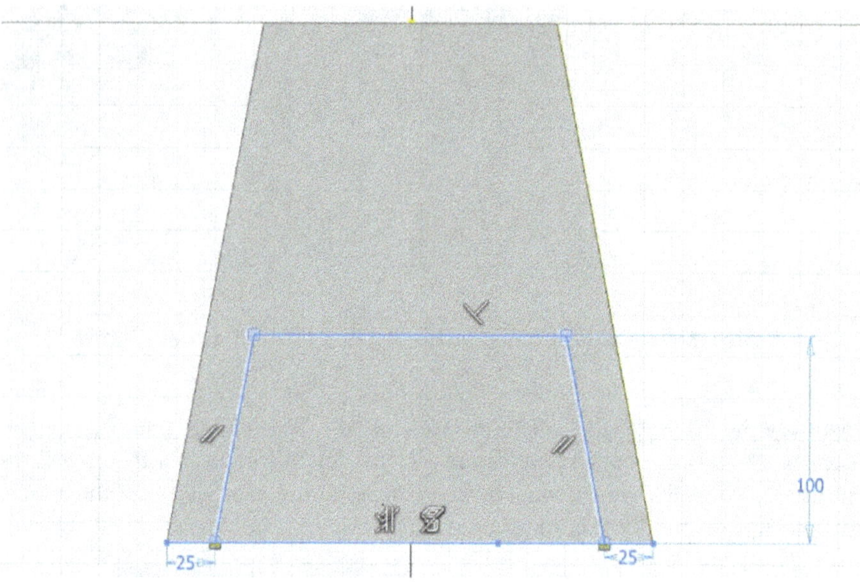

Figure 187: The trapezoid we need to draw on the y-z plane; mark for display

In 3D mode, we again use the "Extrude" command and select the trapezoidal surface. Then we select the option: "Symmetric" for "Direction" and the option: "Cut" for "Output".

We also enter a dimension of 450 mm, since we have a length of 500 mm and want to leave 25 mm of wall thickness for each. Confirm and ready.

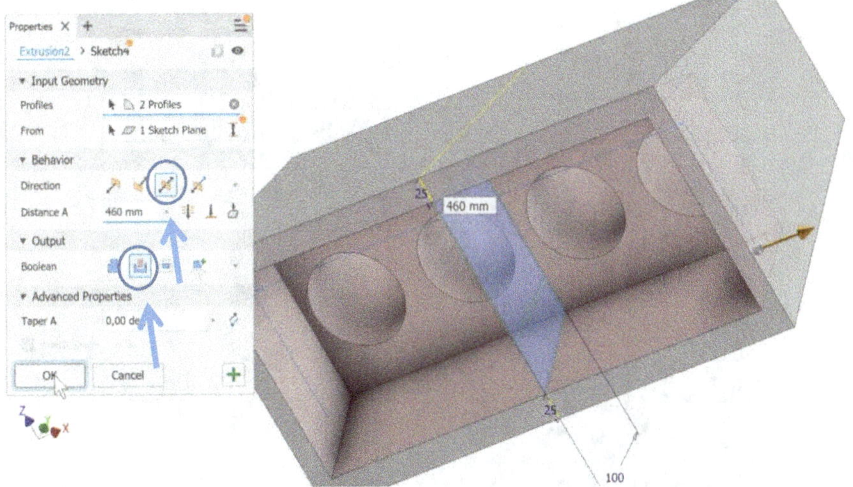

Figure 188: Convert sketch to a section with "Extrude"; use 450 mm instead of 460 mm

We now need to add material again for the crankshaft mounts. We draw the following three rectangular profiles on the lower surface of the housing.

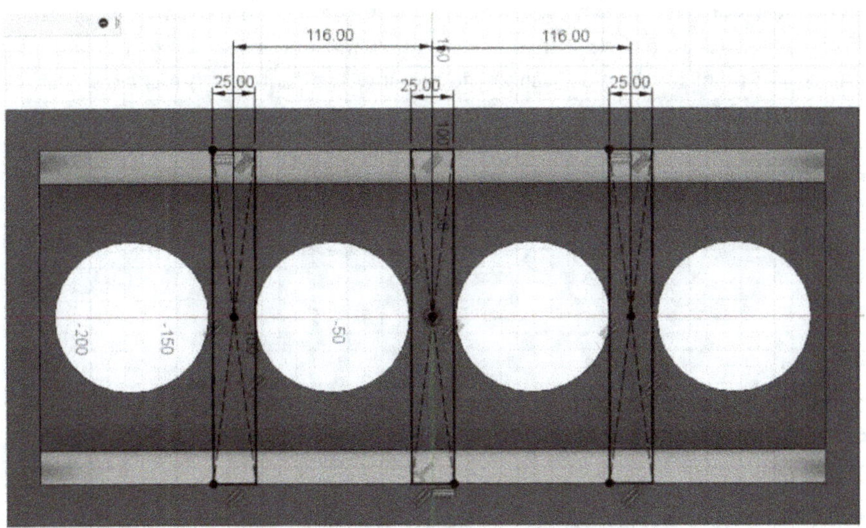

Figure 189: Draw the profile shown on the lower side of the housing

We then extrude these in 3D mode with the selection of "To" at "Distance", as well as "Join" at "Operation", at the extrusion options. This allows us to select the bottom face and extrude the three bars to it.

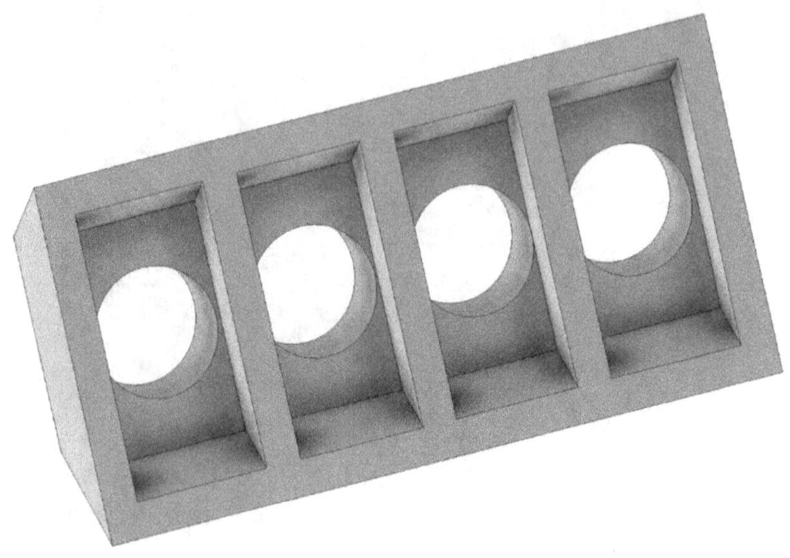

Figure 190: The three bars; already extruded

In the next step, we create a circular cutout for the bearing surfaces of the crankshaft. To do this, we draw a circle with a diameter of 70 mm and a distance of 125 mm from the corner point on the side wall of the housing. The center of the circle should be congruent with the bottom line.

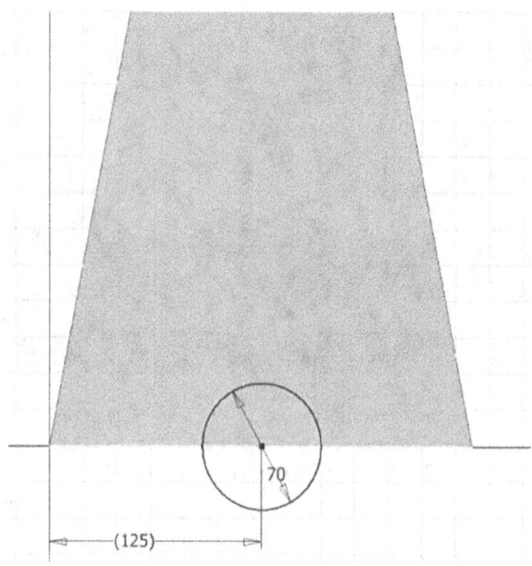

Figure 191: Sketching the circle shown on the side surface of the housing

We then extrude this completely through the entire housing using the "Cut" option. Of course, we could have drawn only a semicircle or used the "Trim" function.

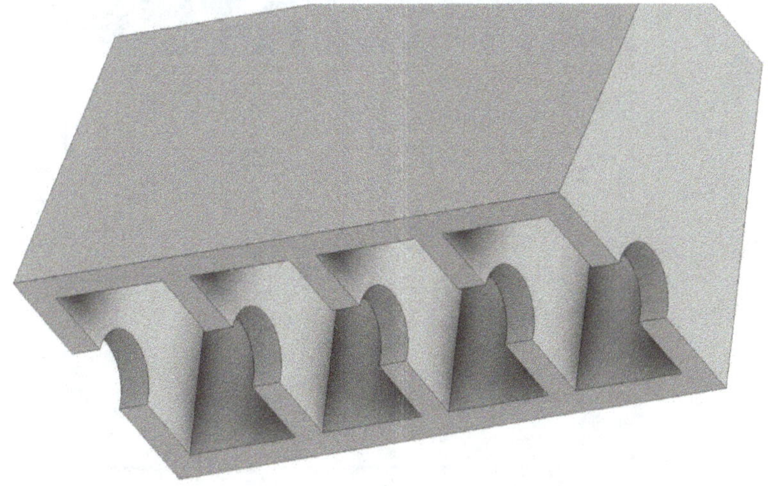

Figure 192: The housing after extrusion of the circular profile with the "Cut" option

In the penultimate step, we would like to create threaded holes for mounting the cylinder head and oil pan on our very primitive crankcase. First we create the holes for the cylinder head. We use the "Hole" function in 3D mode. However, in order to place the holes correctly, we first start a 2D sketch on the upper surface of the housing. We need ten holes for the cylinder head. To create them quickly and easily, we use the "Pattern" command from the "Create" section. In this case, we again need "Rectangular Pattern". We first create a point with 20 mm distance from each of the lateral lines of the cylinder head support surface. Then we select the point and the "Pattern" command.

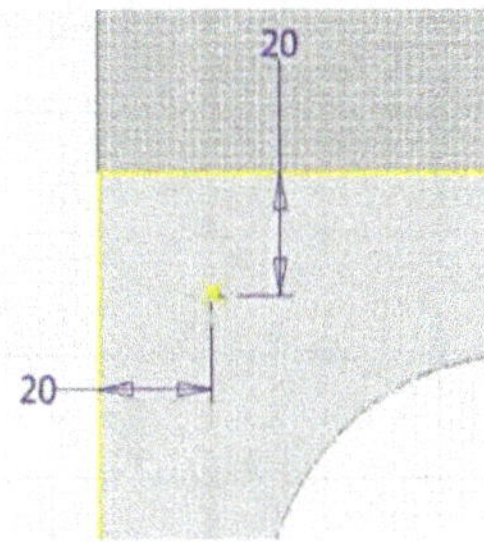

Figure 193: First draw a point on the upper surface in a sketch

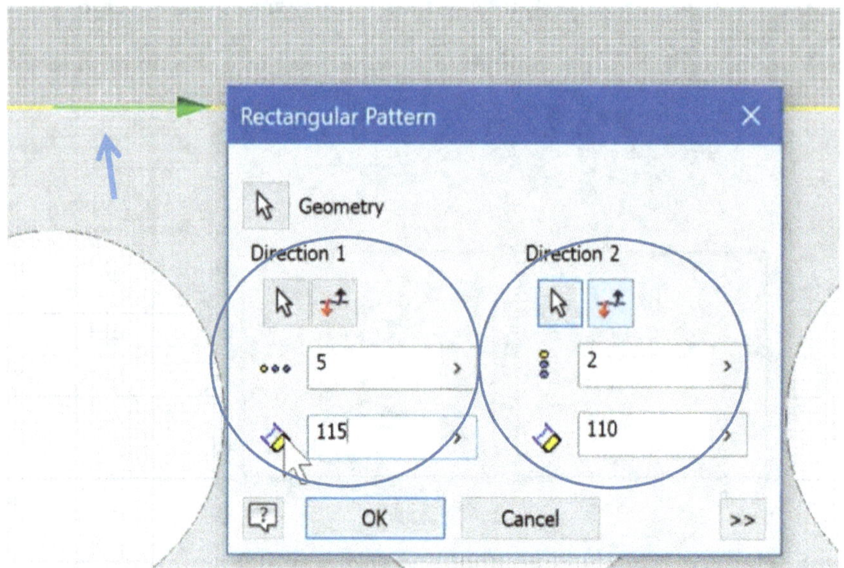

Figure 194: Select "Rectangular Pattern" command and enter values; the green arrow must point to the right

We are shown two selection fields for the directions, as well as input options for distance and number of the arrangement or pattern. If we select "Direction 1" and select the top line of the cylinder head, we will see a green arrow that should point to the right. If not, flip it with "Flip" in the options of the pattern. Then we select "Direction 2" and select the left vertical line of the cylinder head. The direction should point down in this case, if not flip with "Flip". Now we can set the values for number and distance in the options. Think of it like a table. In z-direction we need 2 lines if we like. In x-direction 5 rows. 2 x 5 equals 10 points for the holes.

The corner points should have a distance of 20 mm each to the edge, i.e. we need a distance of 115 mm for the pattern in x-direction and 110 mm in z-direction. We then confirm with Ok and get the desired pattern.

Then we select the "Hole" command in 3D mode and create the holes by entering the specifications and selecting the points.

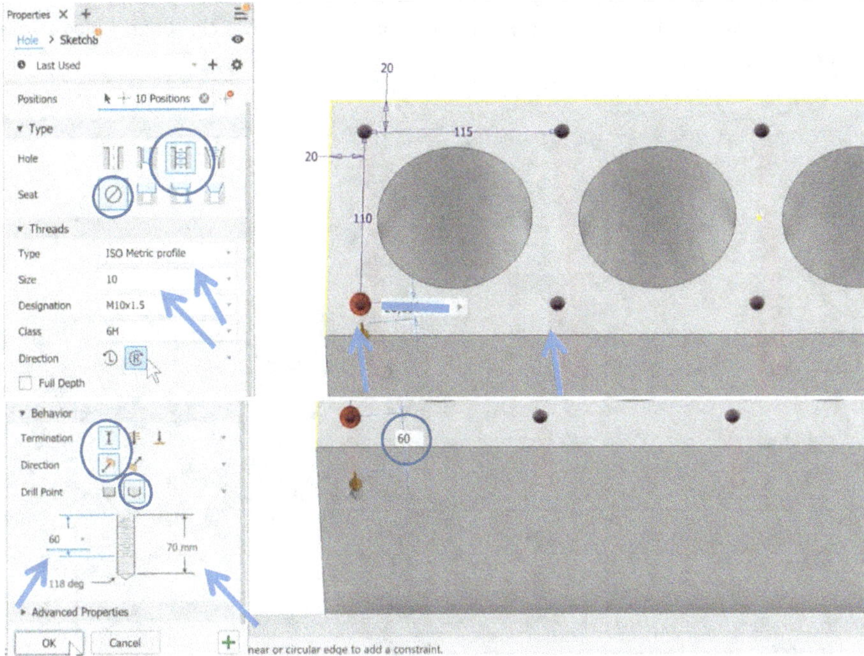

Figure 195: Select Hole command in 3D mode, select hole points and modify options

After selecting the points, we select the hole type "Tapped Hole", because we want to create a tapped hole. In the lower selection fields we can then choose which dimension the tapped hole should have. For example, we want our holes to be 70 mm long and 10 mm in diameter for a metric M10 thread. Also a thread pitch of 1.5. Confirm, and the tapped holes are created.

One more hint: As already mentioned many times, there are several construction methods, sometimes faster, sometimes slower, but basically all of them lead to the goal. So if possible, think along well, so that you also recognize other ways.

For the holes, for example, it is also possible to first create a hole in 3D mode and then use the "Pattern" function of 3D mode and place the holes in the same way as the sketch points.

Let's look at this for the oil pan mounting holes.
We select "Hole" / "Bore" and then first the bore surface, i.e. the underside of the housing. Then we determine the position of this hole in x and z direction. Simply click on the top edge first, enter a value, in this case 12.5 mm and then click on the side edge and enter 12.5 mm as well. It is important that you do <u>not </u>press "Enter" in between, but simply select the next edge immediately. Then select the hole type, as well as the

specifications as before. However, here we want e.g. only M8 threaded holes and a dimension of 40 mm.

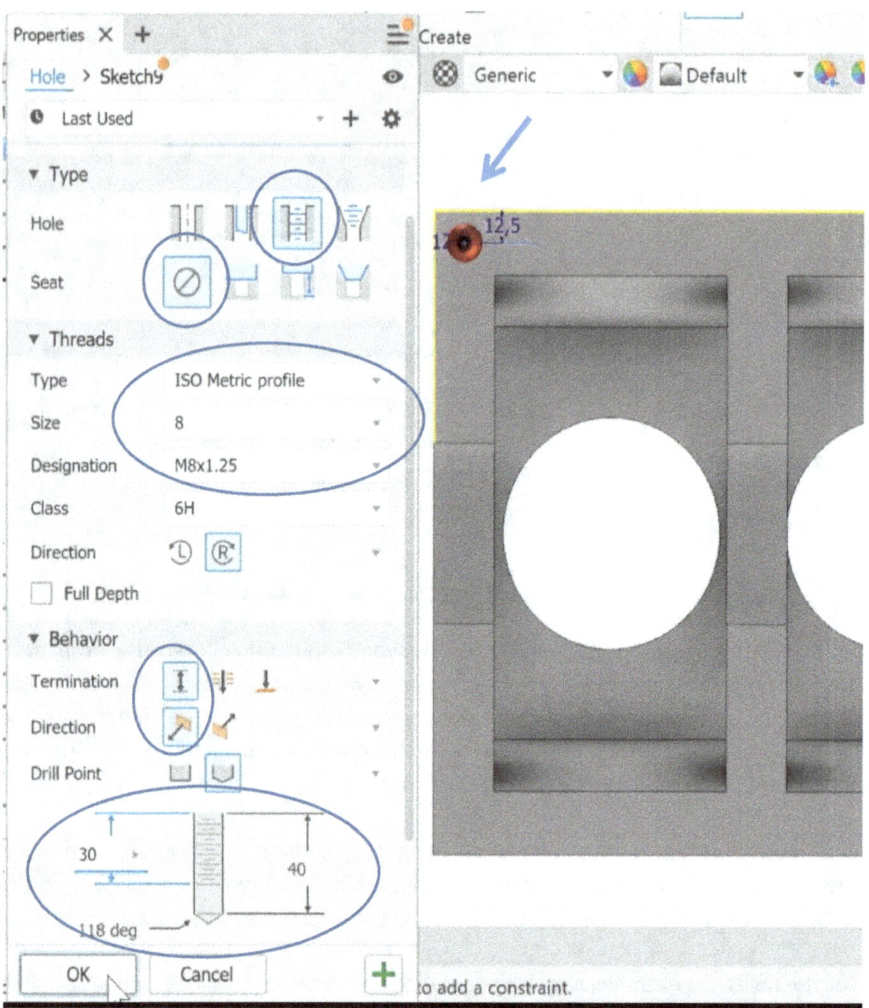

Figure 196: Use "Hole" to drill the first hole on the lower side; 12.5 mm distance from each edge; M8 x 1.25 30 mm thread for 40 mm hole

Now confirm with "OK" and the hole will be created. Then we select the hole and use the "Pattern" command. In the next step we change to "Directions" in the options and then click on the x-axis to indicate the first direction, possibly rotate the direction of the arrow with "Flip" and can proceed for the second direction analogously as with the 2D sketch before. In the x-direction we want 8 holes with a distance of 67.5 mm between the holes and in the z-direction 2 holes with a distance of 225 mm; in total 16 holes.

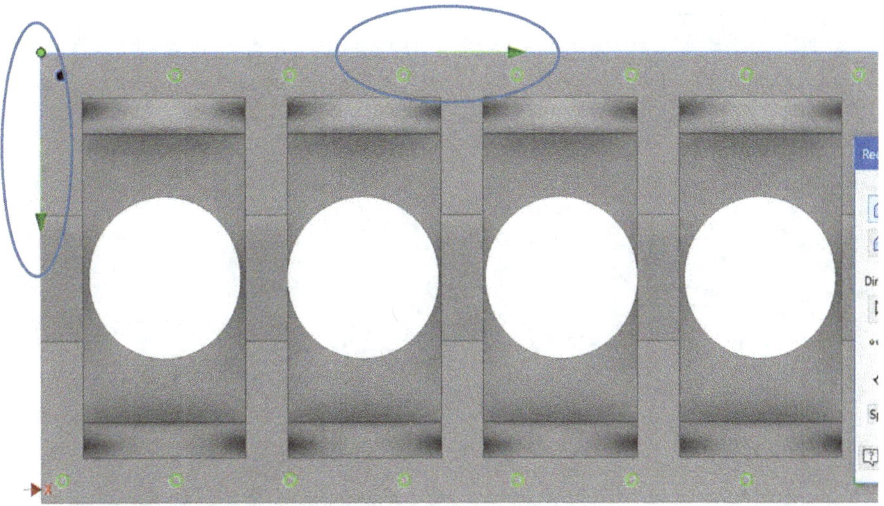

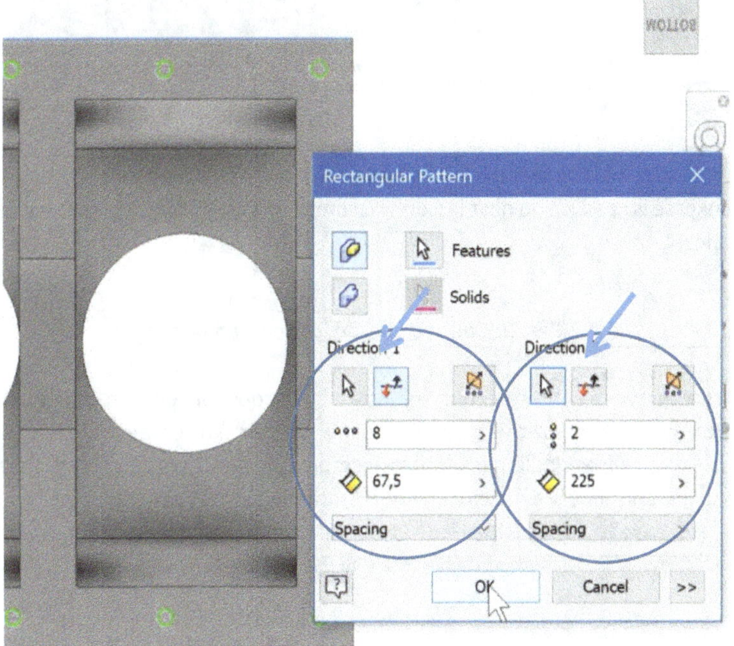

Figure 197: Select left and upper edge so that the green arrows appear (top image); reverse direction of arrows with "Flip" if necessary; enter values (bottom image)

In the last step for the crankcase and this lesson, we will use the Fillet command to round corners. Select the command, select the desired edges and enter a rounding radius of e.g. 10 mm.

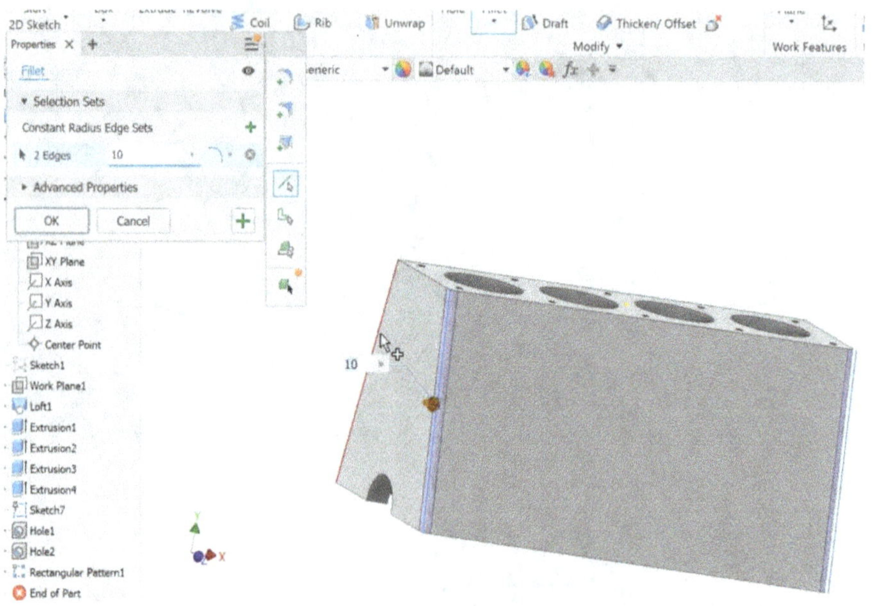

Figure 198: For example, rounding the corners by 10 mm

The crankcase is ready! The next lesson will continue with pistons, connecting rods and piston pins.

4.4.2 Part 2: Connecting rod, piston and piston pin

In this section we are interested in the connecting rods, pistons and piston pins. We start with the creation of the pistons. For this we start with a new file, because the piston is an individual single part of the assembly: "Engine". We then start a sketch on the x-z plane and first draw a circle with 85 mm diameter. Then we finish the sketch. Now we still have to extrude the circle area, we choose for example 70 mm. In the next step we hollow out the flask and give it a wall thickness of 5 mm.

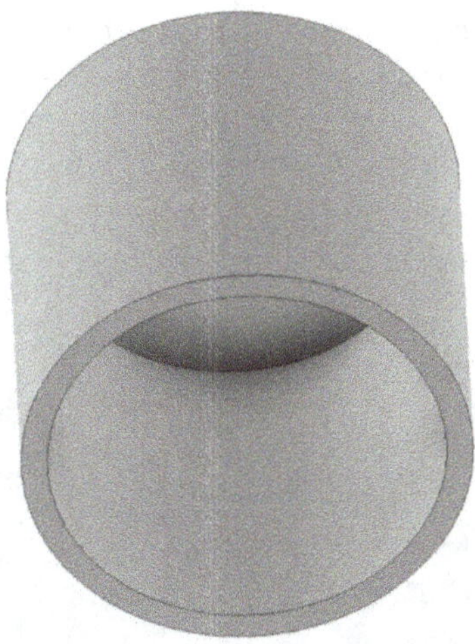

Figure 199: The basic body for the piston created with "Sketch", "Extrusion" and "Shell"

Then we start a sketch on the y-z plane of the piston to make a cutout for the piston pin, which later connects the piston and connecting rod. For example, we choose a diameter of 30 mm and dimension the circle with 35 mm to the lower edge so that it is centered. We also draw the circle so that it sits in extension with the y-axis.

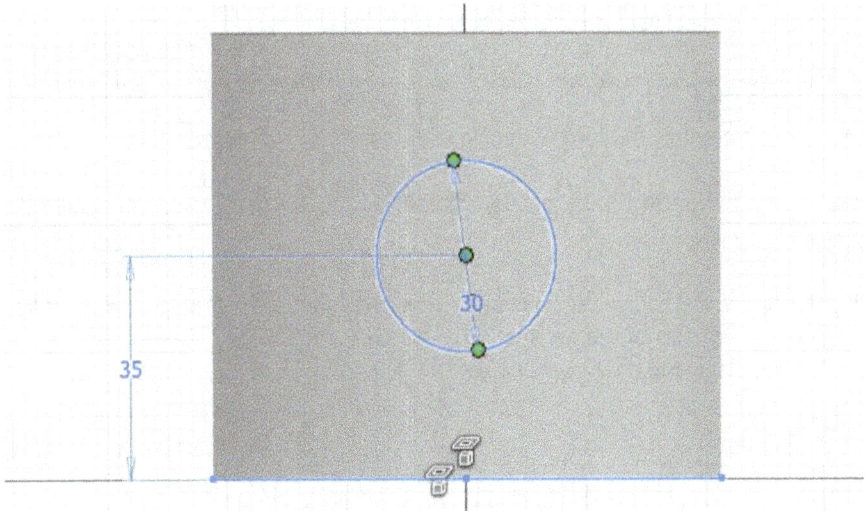

Figure 200: The sketch on the y-z plane for the section

Then we extrude the cutout in 3D mode, creating an opening. Finally, we round off the top and bottom edges of the flask with 2 mm each.

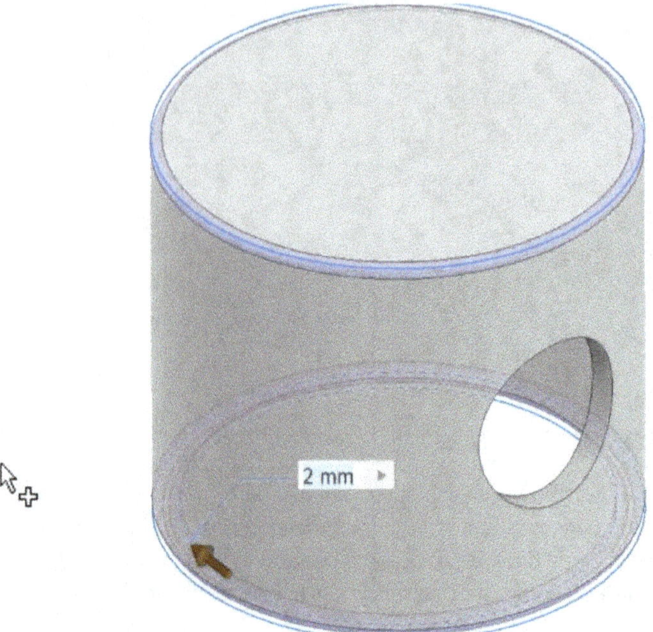

Figure 201: The cutout should go through the entire part; round off edges at the top and bottom

We save piston rings and further detailing for reasons of complexity and time.

We then move on to the connecting rod and piston pin first, before mounting the pistons in the crankcase.

For the connecting rod, we again create a new single part, since this component is also an independent part of the assembly. We sketch the following cross-sectional profile of the connecting rod on the y-z plane.

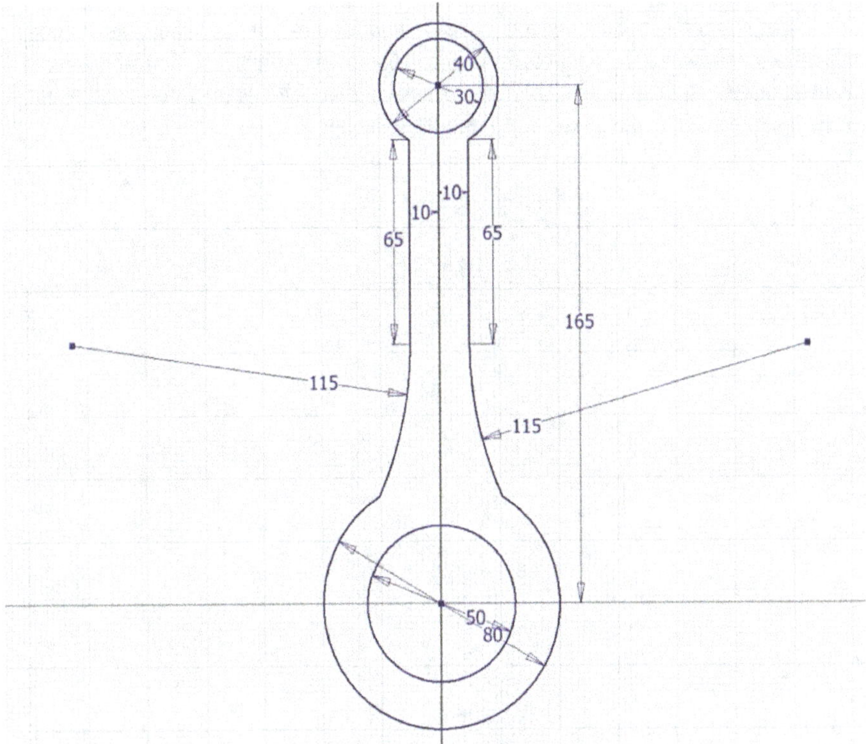

Figure 202: The cross-section of the connecting rod; you can also try to trace the profile on your own; alternatively, follow the individual steps

We will first start with the two "eyes". The upper connecting rod eye should have a diameter of 30 mm inside and 40 mm outside.

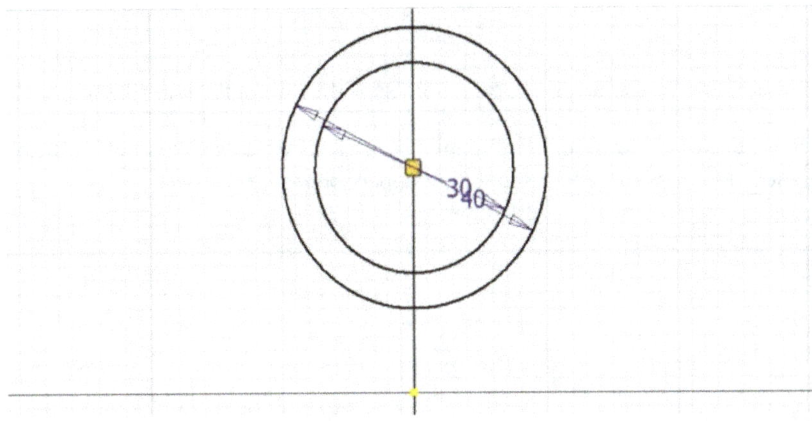

Figure 203: We start with two concentric circles (30 mm and 40 mm diameter)

The lower connecting rod eye 50 mm inside and 80 mm outside. Then we dimension the distance between the circle centers with 165 mm and set the two centers vertically to each other. We also set the center of the two lower circles congruent to the origin to completely define and position the previous sketch.

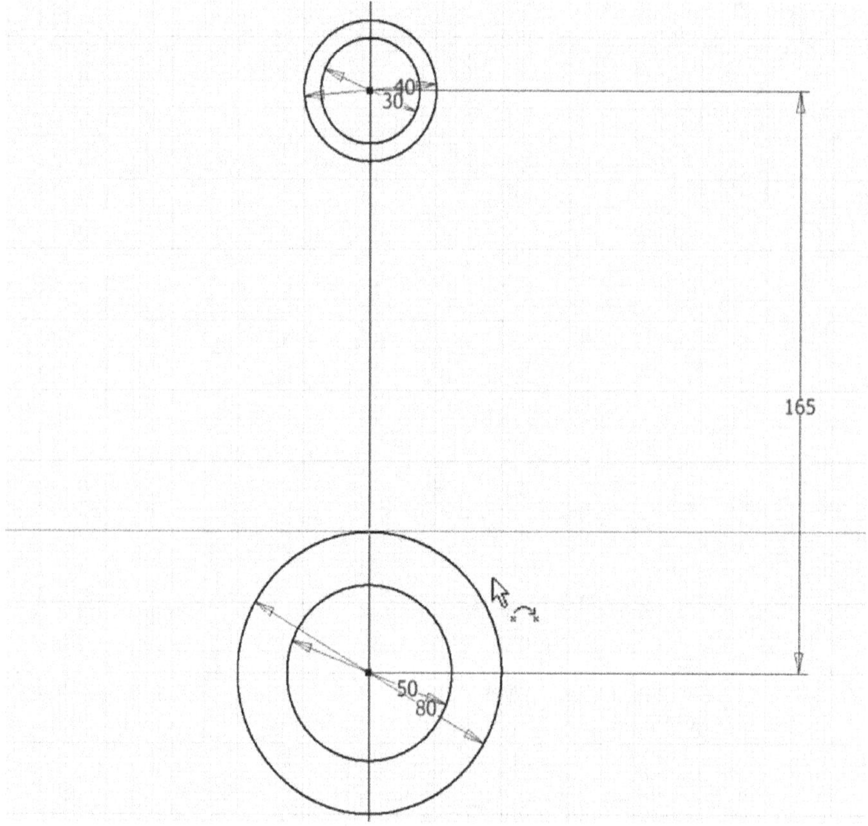

Figure 204: Add two more circles (50 mm and 80 mm) and dimension them 165 mm apart

Then we draw two vertical lines 65 mm long, each of which should have a horizontal distance of 10 mm from the center of the upper connecting rod eye.

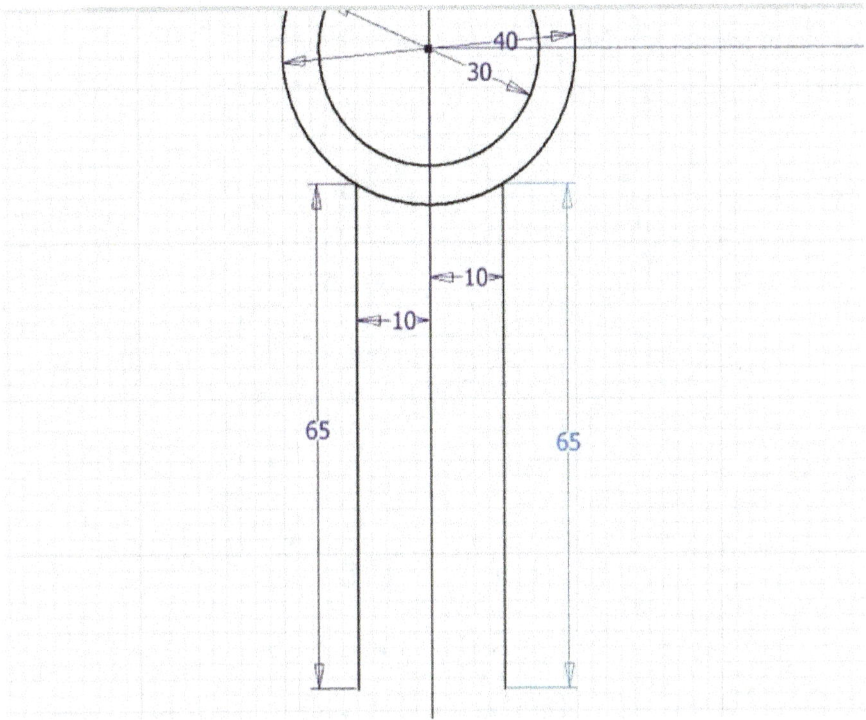

Figure 205: Draw two vertical 65 mm long lines at a distance of 10 mm from the center line

We complete the profile with two tangential arcs, each of which should have a radius of R=115 mm.

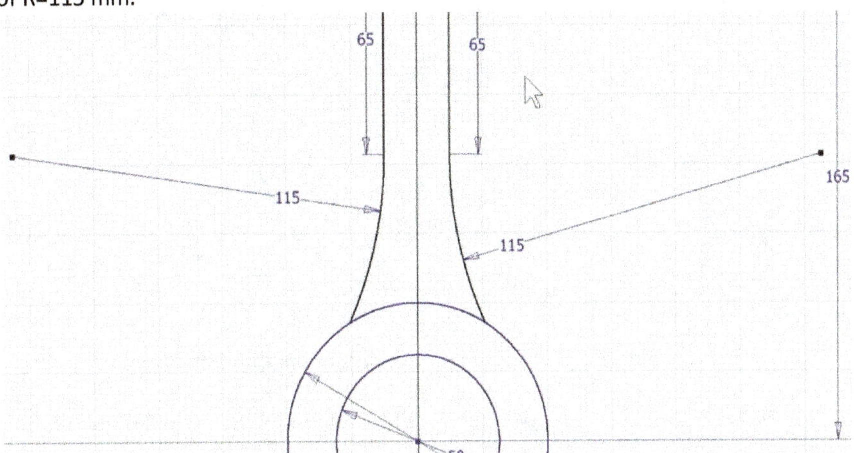

Figure 206: Connecting the upper and lower ends with two 115 mm bends

Finally, we use the "Trim" function and remove excess lines.

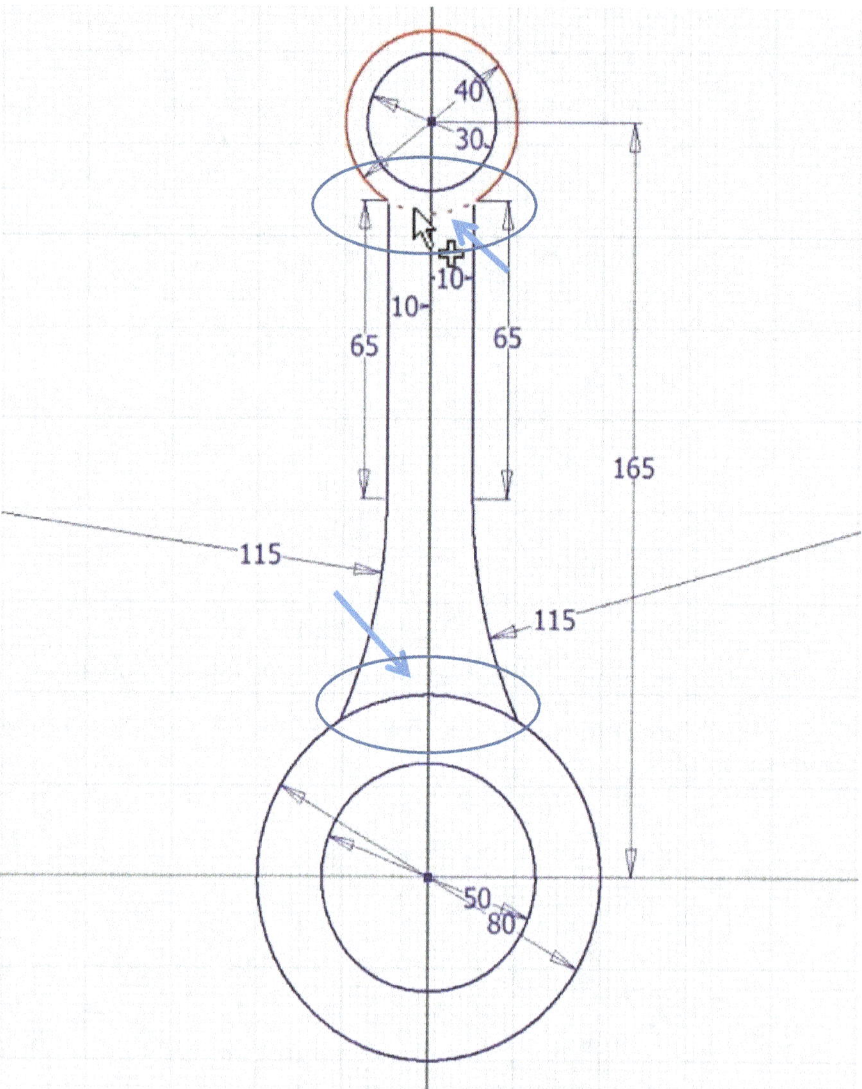

Figure 207: Remove the excess circle sections (see arrows) with "Trim"

When this is done, we can finish the sketch and extrude the connecting rod 20 mm.

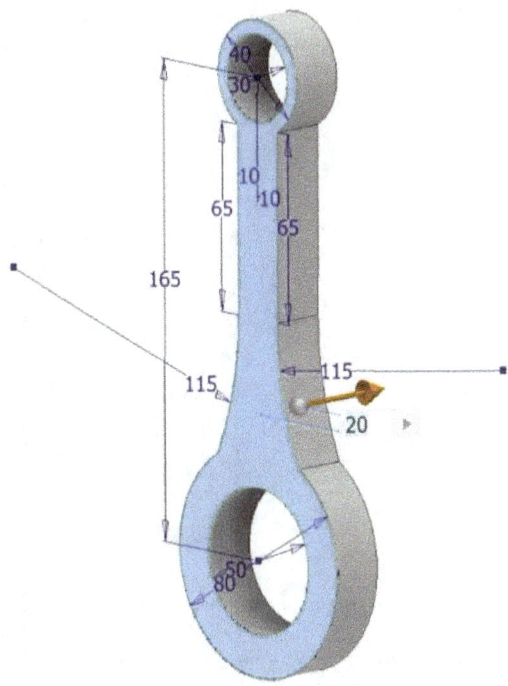

Figure 208: 20 mm extrusion of the connecting rod profile

So that the transitions are not too extreme, we can round off the transition at the bottom and top with 20 mm in the area of the connecting rod.

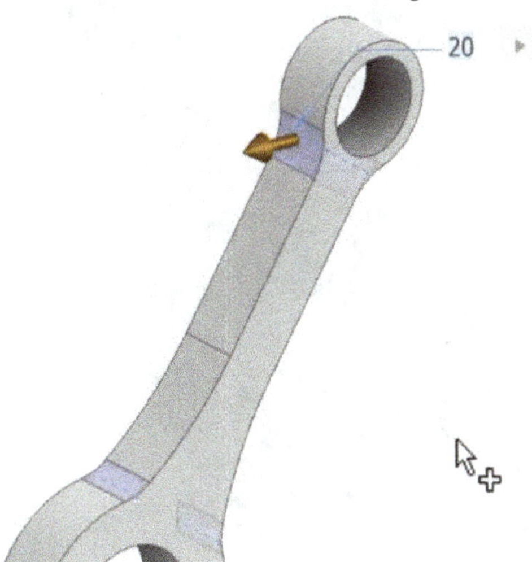

Figure 209: Rounding the top and bottom transitions on the sides with 20 mm each

Also round off the edges of the two surfaces with 1 mm each.

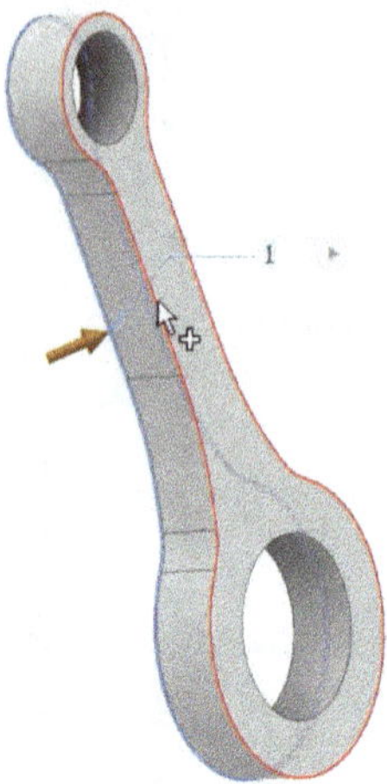

Figure 210: Rounding the outer edges of the connecting rod by 1 mm

The connecting rod in this case is also a highly simplified model. Normally, a connecting rod looks like the one in this picture.

Figure 211: A real connecting rod of an engine

In the lower area, it is divided into two parts, the geometry is more functional and, in addition, there are the so-called conrod bearing shells that would sit in the lower eye.

Let's then draw the piston pin first before we start assembling the components. To do this, we again create a new part and draw a circle with a diameter of 30 mm on the y-z plane, which we then extrude 76 mm symmetrically and hollow out to a wall thickness of 3 mm.

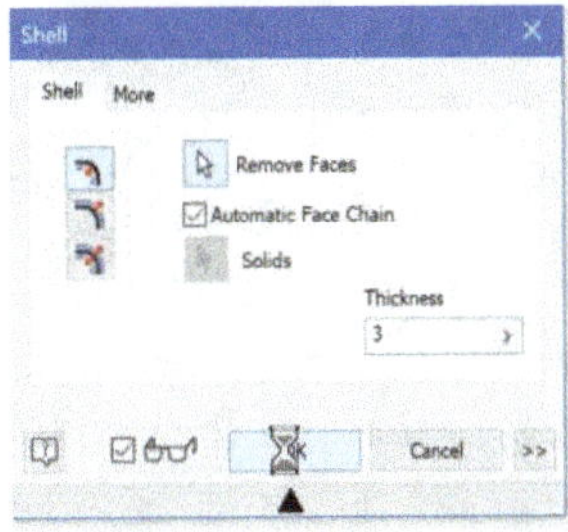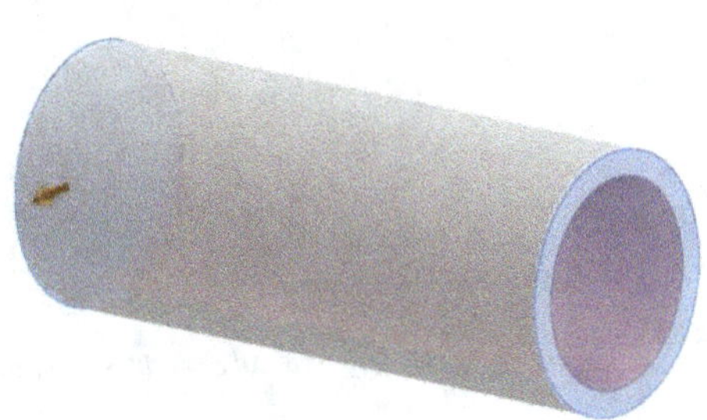

Figure 212: Extrude a 30 mm profile and extrude 76 mm; for "Direction": select "Symmetric"; hollow out to 3 mm wall thickness with "Shell", select both side faces for this purpose

For the assembly we create a new assembly file, i.e. an "Assembly" file. The crankcase is to be our base body, so we simply drag this into the assembly first. To do this, first open all the parts of the engine and then click on the small "window" icon at the top right to display all the open windows side by side.

Figure 213: Press the small window icon at the top right to display all open files side by side (if necessary, open all necessary files first)

Now you can click in each case in the desired window and then in the part browser drag the part with pressed mouse button into the correct window and drop it.

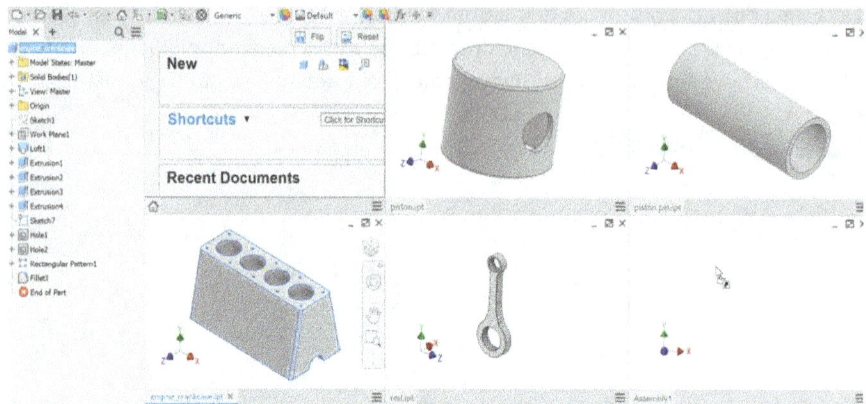

Figure 214: All open files are now displayed side by side

The crankcase is then automatically aligned and fixed based on the origin. We then drag all the other parts into the assembly as well. Once we've done that, the last thing we do is copy the pistons, connecting rods and piston pins four times each, since we have four cylinders.

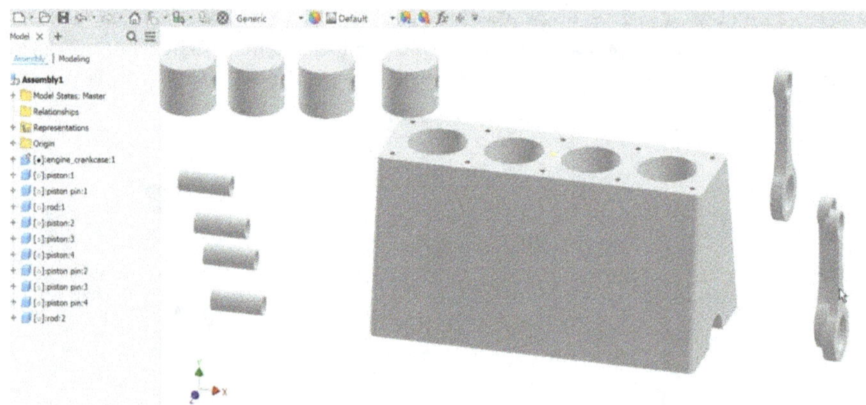

Figure 215: Dragging the piston, cobble pin and connecting rod into the assembly and then copying/pasting them

Then we first mount the connecting rod to the piston pin by selecting the following points as joint origins and selecting the joint type "Rotational".

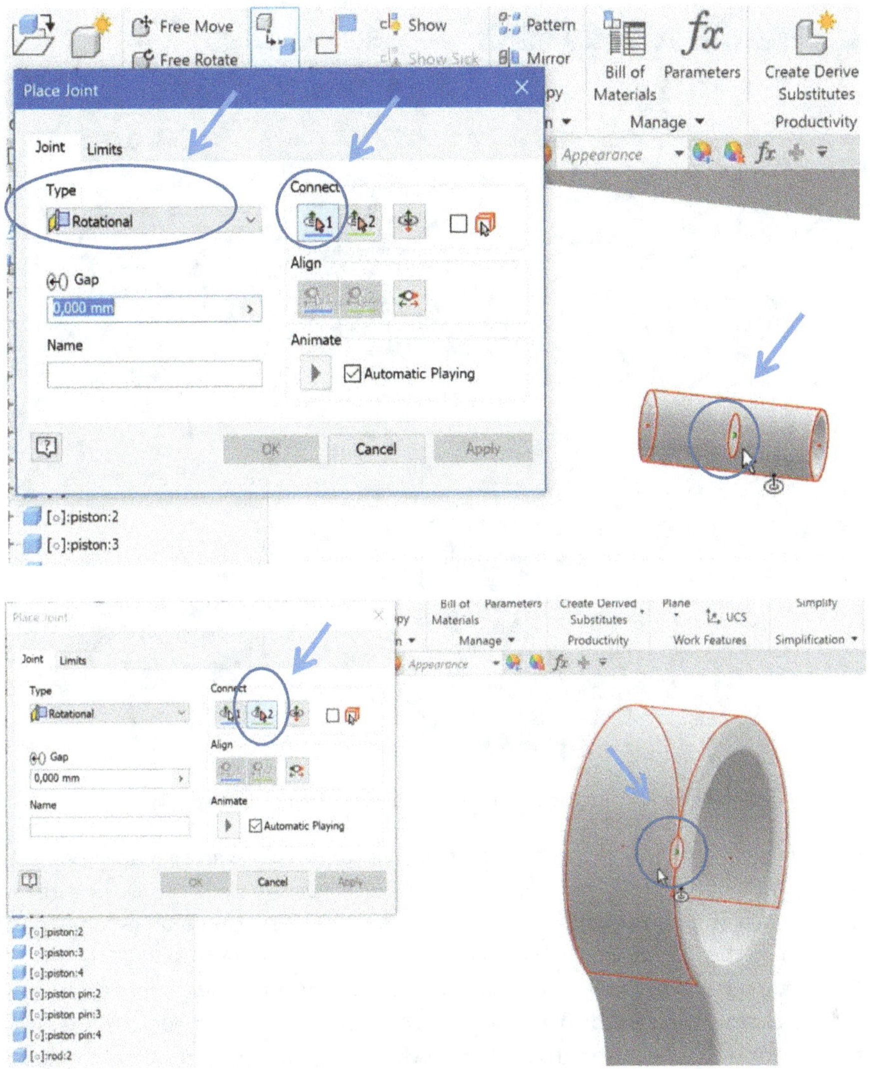

Figure 216: Select "Joint" command, "Type": Select "Rotational" and define joint origins as shown first on one of the piston pins and then on one of the connecting rods

Then we assemble the package of pin and connecting rod into the piston, with the help of a lateral joint origin on the pin and in the center of the pin opening on the piston. The type of joint is again "rotational". Some patience is required here until the two correct joint origins are selected or found. Pay particular attention to the correct alignment of the axes at the joint origins.

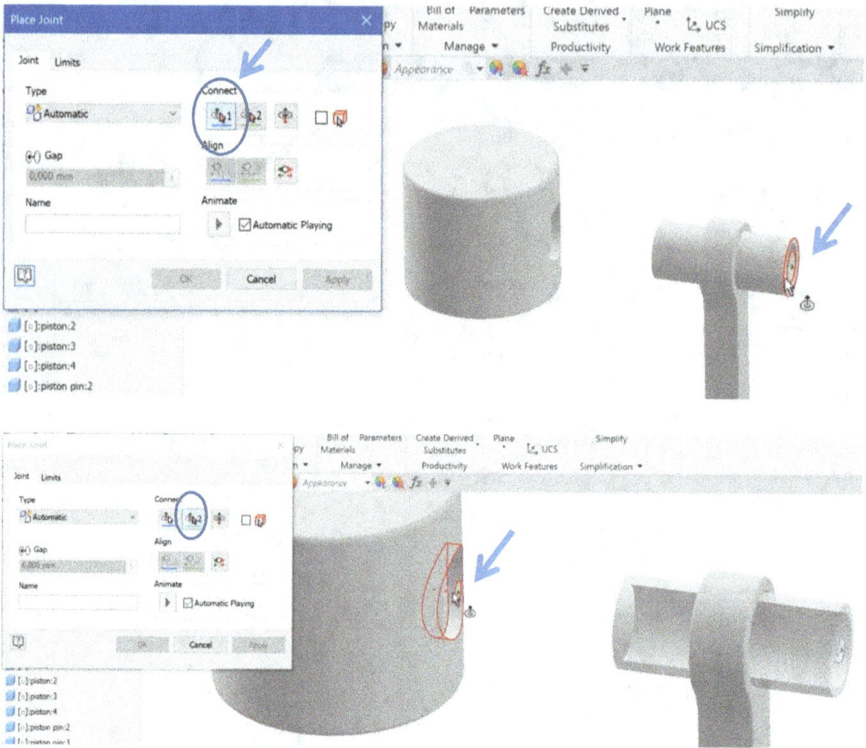

Figure 217: "Mounting" connecting rod with piston pin in the piston

Now we would have to link all the other pistons, piston pins and connecting rods in exactly the same way. To make life a little easier for us, we simply copy the already linked group of pistons, connecting rods and piston pins three more times in the next step. To do this, we select the three components and copy them using CTRL-C. With CTRL-V we paste them into the design environment. The great thing about this is that the links are also preserved! We notice this when we move the pasted parts. We have saved a lot of time and can delete the previously inserted parts that are no longer needed. We do this quickly and easily by selecting them and pressing the "Remove" key on the keyboard. So much for copying and deleting parts and linked parts within an assembly.

Now we have to link the pistons with the cylinders. For this we select the joint type "Cylindrical" and the shown joint origins.

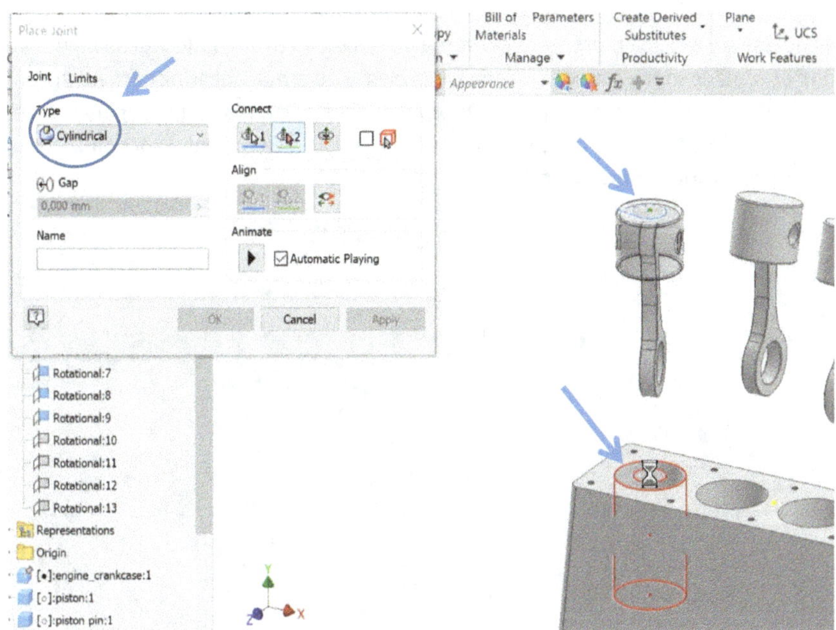

Figure 218: Connect piston, connecting rod and piston pin to crankshaft housing

Now we are almost done with our very simple 4-cylinder engine model. In the next lesson we will draw the crankshaft. Let's go!

4.4.3 Part 3: Crankshaft

For the crankshaft, the last part of our engine, we start again a new single part. Ultimately, the crankshaft should look something like this picture:

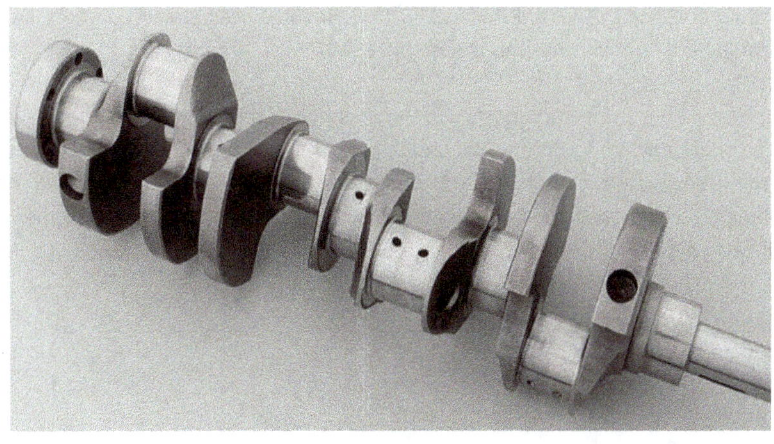

Figure 219: A real engine crankshaft

Of course, we will again proceed in a somewhat simplified way. We start a new sketch on the y-z plane in the side view. Then we draw the first main bearing of the crankshaft or its shaft journal with a simple circle of 65 mm diameter with the origin as starting point. In 3D mode we extrude this circular surface and select a distance of 20 mm in one direction and confirm with "Ok".

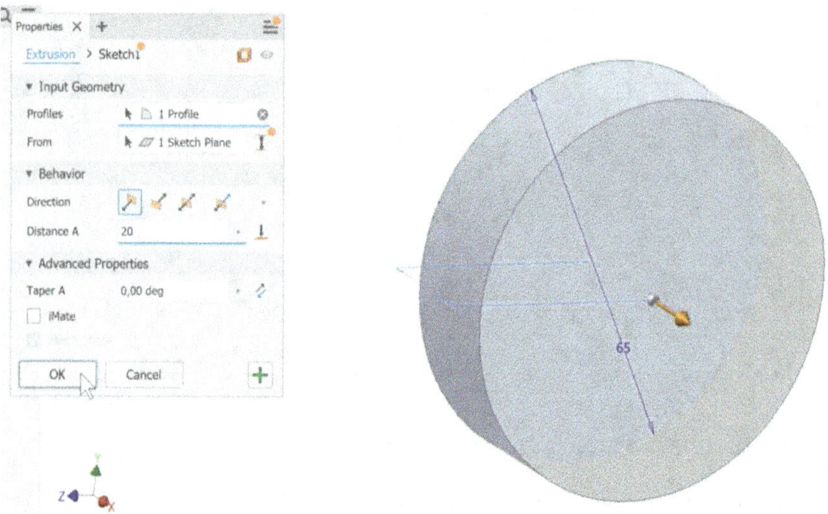

Figure 220: Sketch a circle on the y-z plane and extrude 65 mm

Since our crankshaft is to be symmetrical, we will draw only one half of it for the time being and will simply mirror it later on the y-z plane. We will now build up the crankshaft section by section using extrusion. You are also welcome to consider how you could construct the crankshaft using the "Revolve" / "Rotate" function, i.e. as a rotational part, and whether this is possible at all?

We start for the next section of the first crankshaft cheek, a sketch on the previously created shaft journal. To do this, we create two circles, one with a diameter of 70 mm and the other with a diameter of 160 mm at a distance of 45 mm from each other, including a vertical condition between their two centers. The center of the upper circle should also be 40 mm vertically from the center of the shaft journal and sit in line with it, i.e. be vertically connected.

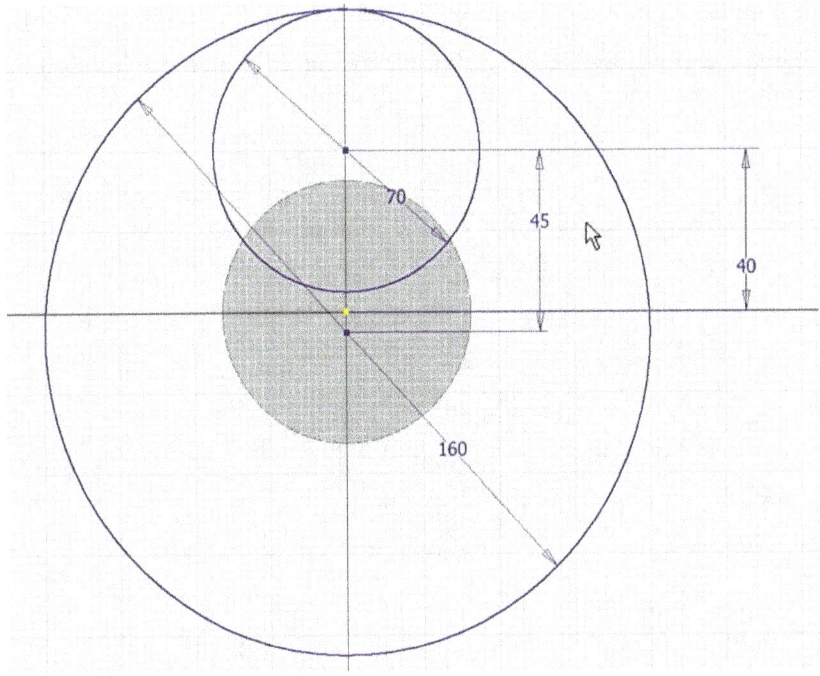

Figure 221: Sketch two circles as shown on one side of the body

Then we draw two connecting lines and dimension them vertically with 60 mm length and by means of parallel dimension with 30 mm to the upper circle center.

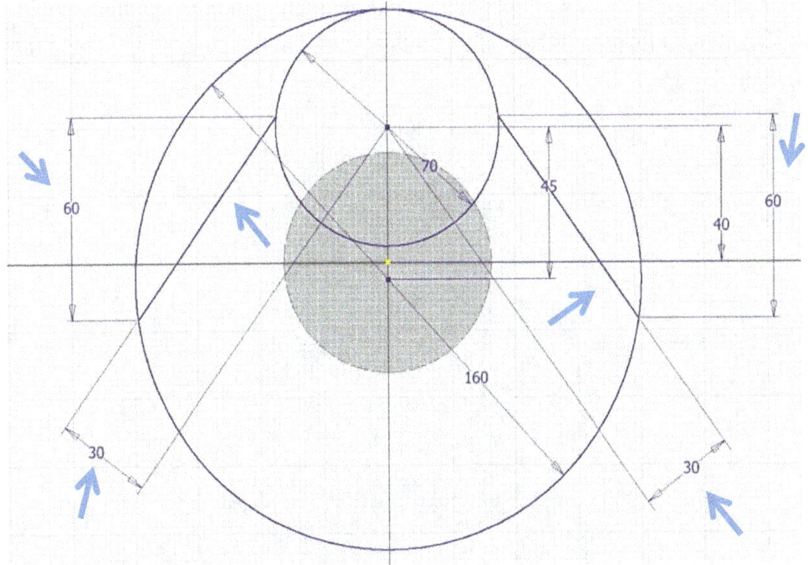

Figure 222: Creating and dimensioning two connecting lines between circles

In the last step we use the "Trim" function to cut away all superfluous lines and sections.

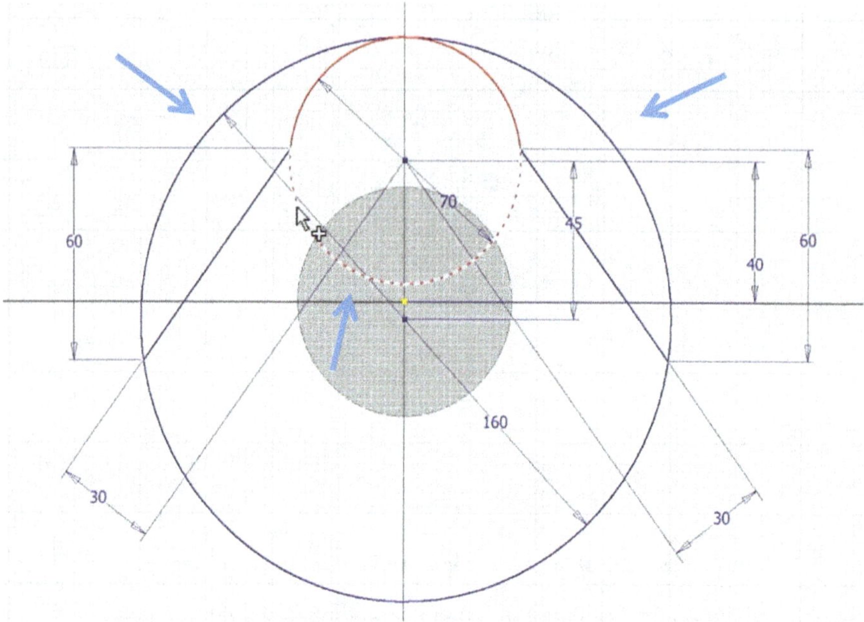

Figure 223: Removing superfluous circle sections (see arrows) with "Trim"

Then we extrude this cheek 22 mm.

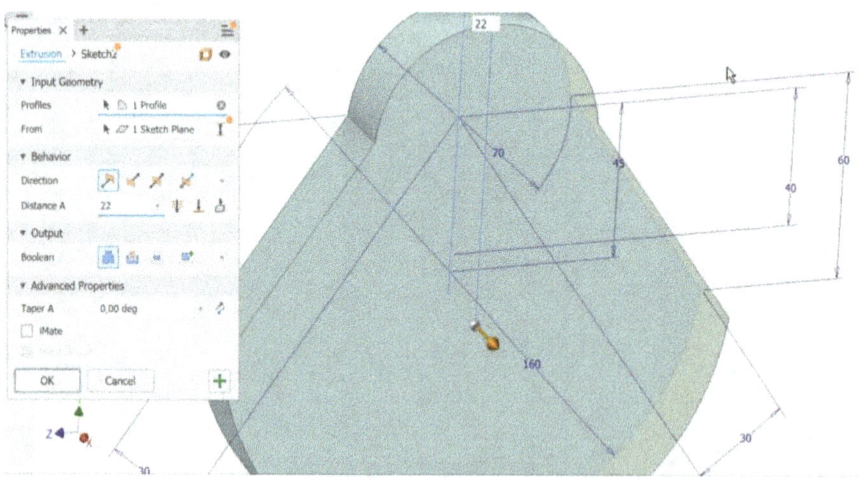

Figure 224: Extrude crankshaft cheek 22 mm

In the next step, we draw the shaft journal for the connecting rod on this cheek. To do this, we draw a 50 mm circle that should sit concentrically to the upper curve of the crankshaft cheek. We need a dimension of 16 mm for the extrusion.

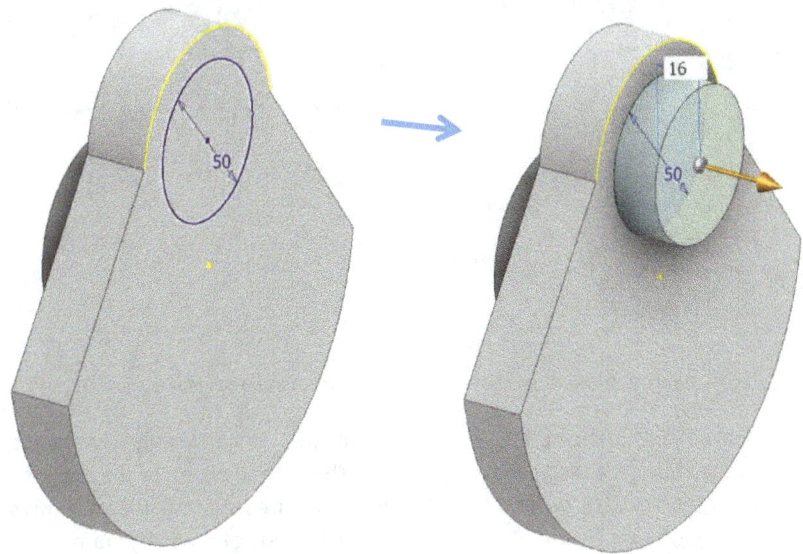

Figure 225: Draw a 50 mm circle in a 2D sketch and then extrude 16 mm

We could, if we were to take a more circuitous route, now draw cheek by cheek and shaft journal by shaft journal on top of each other as a 2D sketch and extrude them, just as we have done up to this point. However, it is much easier now to use only this half again for the first connecting rod. This body represents more or less 1/8 of the entire crankshaft.

In the following we will now skillfully use the "Mirror" function to save us some work. So for the second crankshaft cheek and the adjacent shaft journal sections we simply mirror the first body.

We do this by selecting the "Mirror" command and then switching to "Mirror solids" in the small options window that opens. Since we only have one body, this will then be selected automatically. In the next step, we switch to "Mirror Plane" in the options window and select the side surface of half the conrod's shaft as the mirror plane.

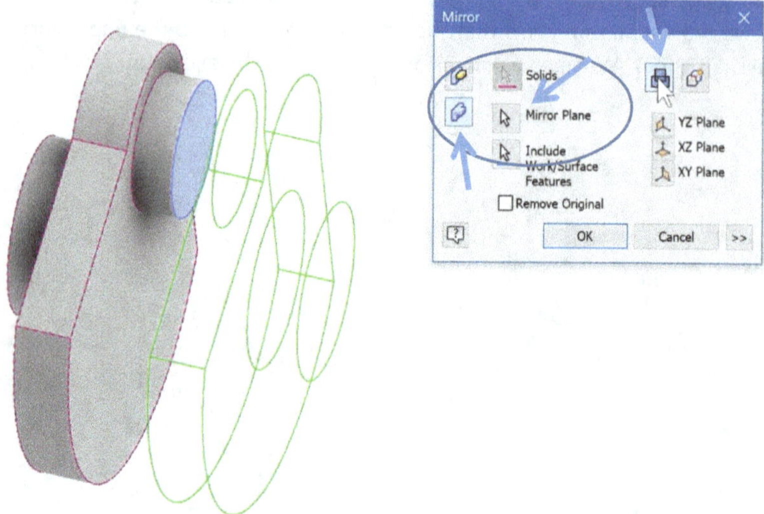

Figure 226: Mirror the first eighth of the crankshaft on the blue surface

We can leave "Join" in the options window for this step, since we only want to get one body and the cheek is already correctly aligned. The second eighth of the crankshaft is finished. For the next 2/8, we mirror the previously created crankshaft part in this step. Select the body, select "Mirror Plane". In this case, the side of the shaft journal that will rest in the crankcase. Now, however, we need to change our approach a bit, since we want to create a new body for the time being. So we need to select "New solid" in the options window of the Mirror command.

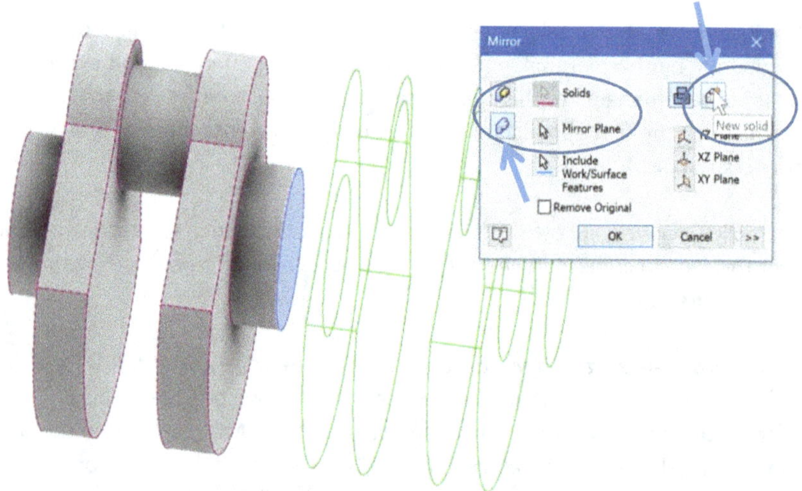

Figure 227: Mirror the second eighth of the crankshaft again on the blue surface

Why a new body? Because, as we can now see, this quarter of the crankshaft still has to be rotated 180 degrees around - in this case - the x-axis so that it is in opposition to the other quarter. Otherwise, all pistons would run in the same way, but only two of the four pistons may always be in the same position.

For this reason we have created the new body, because otherwise we would not be able to rotate this quarter of the shaft independently of the other quarter.

To rotate, we simply use the "Move Bodies" command from the "Modify" menu.

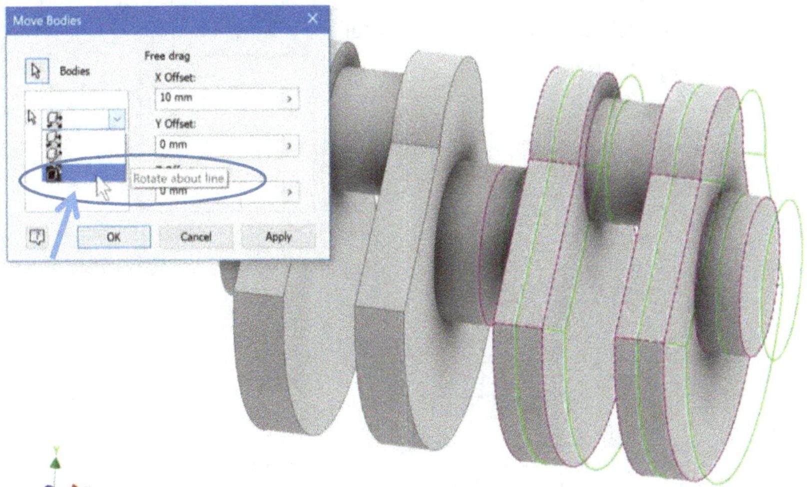

Figure 228: The Move Bodies command in the Modify drop-down menu

Then first select the body, in the options window in the left pane use the drop-down menu to switch to "Rotate about Line".

Figure 229: Select the second eighth of the crankshaft and then select Rotate about line

Then select the rotation axis, in our case the x-axis, and then enter an angle. We need a half rotation, that is 180°.

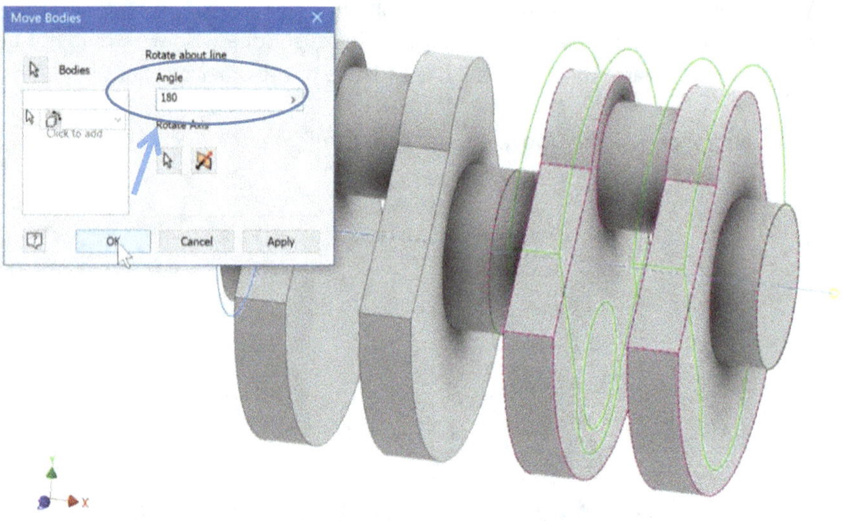

Figure 230: Enter an angle of 180°; select the x-axis in the part browser beforehand

Confirm with "OK". We see that the shaft journals for the connecting rods are now correctly positioned.

Before we continue, let's extend the shaft journal of the crankshaft, which is a bit too short due to the mirroring. Simply select "Extrude" and define a surface for the 2D sketch. Draw a concentric circle to the shaft journal and extrude 30 mm.

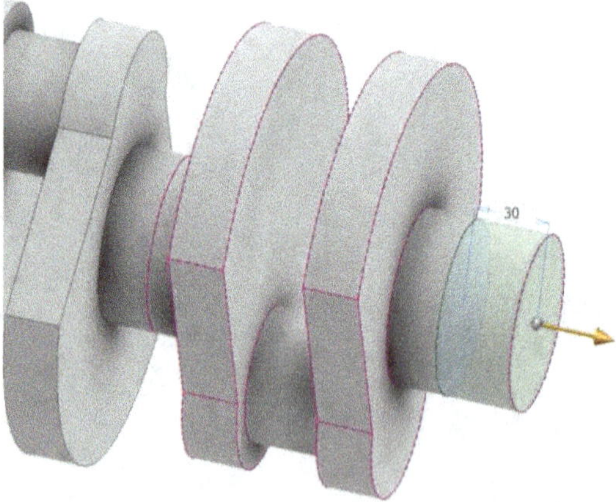

Figure 231: Extend the end piece of the previous crankshaft by 30 mm

Now we want to link the two existing parts of the now half crankshaft again to reunite the two bodies. To do this, we use the "Combine" function from the "Modify" menu. Select body and command, in the options at "Output": select "Join" and press "OK".

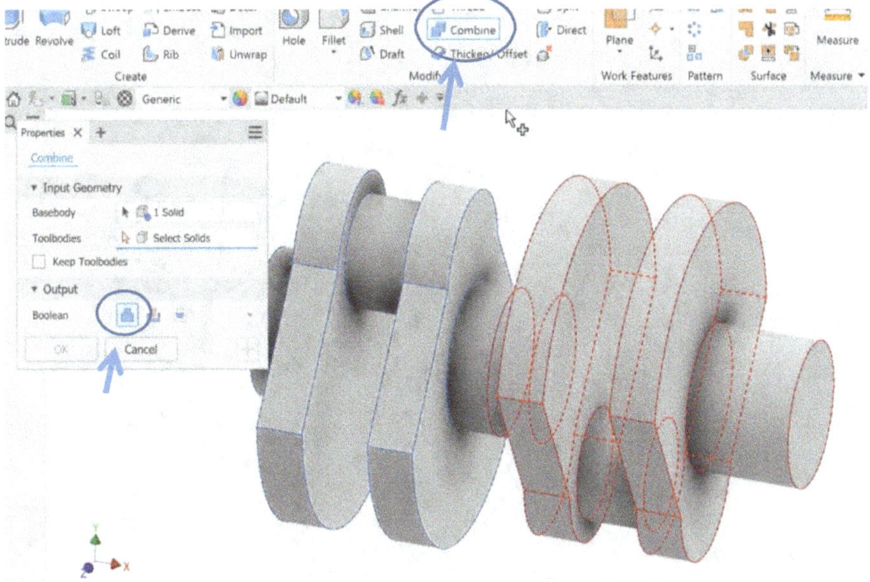

Figure 232: Reconnect the two still single bodies of the crankshaft with "Combine”

This approach has now already saved us quite a bit of work. To continue at exponential speed, we double our half-finished crankshaft one last time. This time we can again leave "Join" instead of "New Body" as the connection type, since the alignment is correct.

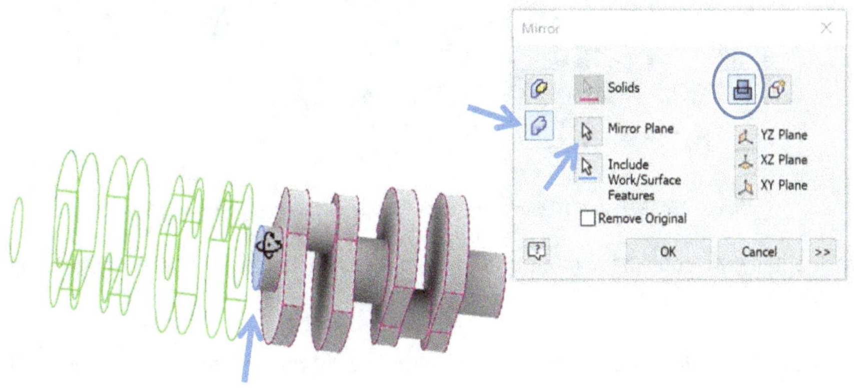

Figure 233: Create the last part of the crankshaft with "Mirror"; mirror on the blue surface

With one click, the crankshaft is finally almost finished. What is still missing? Firstly, a few fillets, which we would like to do as follows: 10 mm on the edges of the transitions in the lower areas of the stringers and 5 mm on the edges of the transitions in the upper areas.

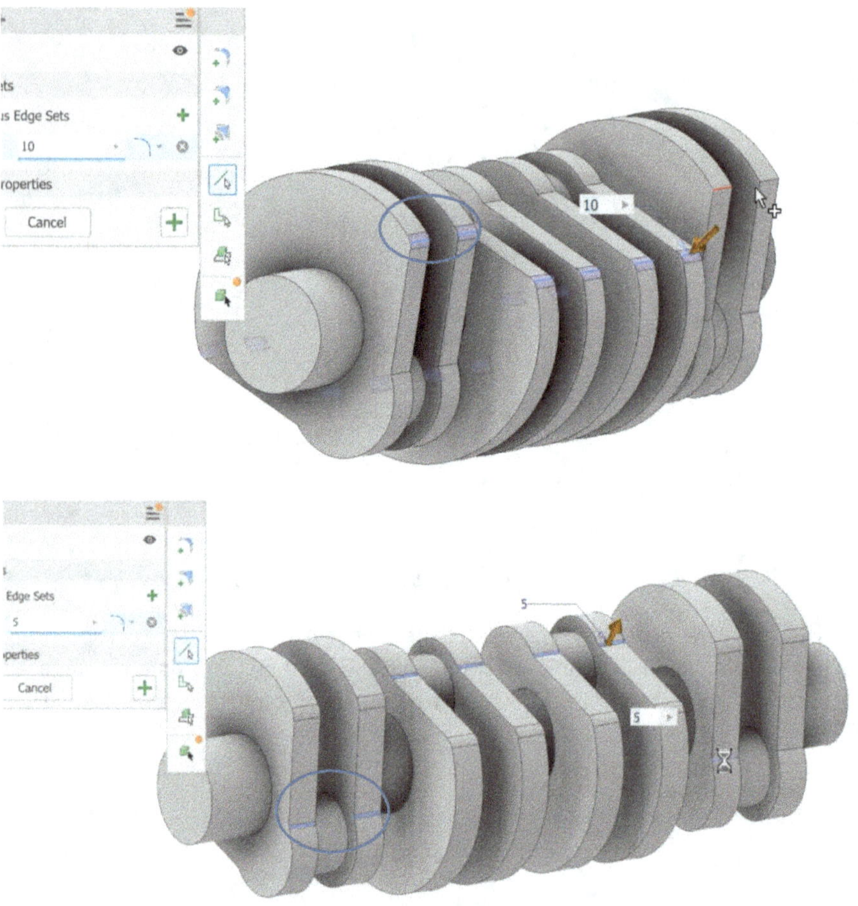

Figure 234: Filleting; 10 mm in the upper image and 5 mm in the lower image

Incidentally, we could have integrated these fillets into the sketch of the stringers right away.

And then 3 mm fillets for the edges on the side faces of the stringers and shaft journals.

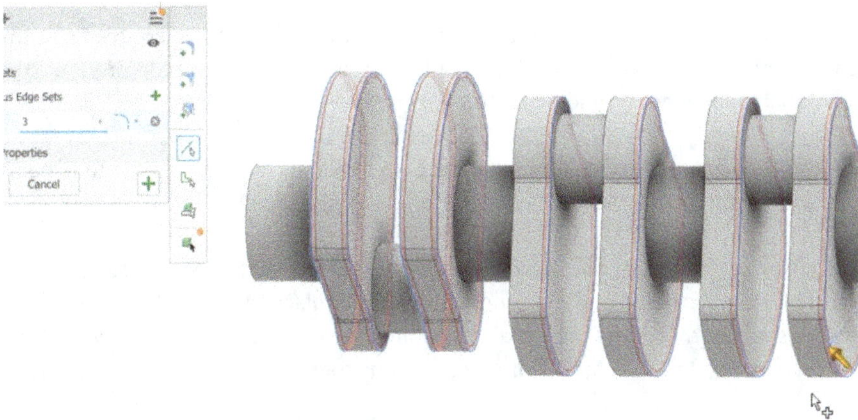

Figure 235: 3 mm fillets for the lateral edges of the crankshaft cheeks

In addition, we now have to insert our crankshaft into our engine assembly and then create the joint to the crankshaft housing. To do this, we simply select the joint origin, e.g. centered on the shaft journal we started with, and select the second joint origin centered on the main bearing of the crankshaft housing. We select "Rotational" as the joint type.

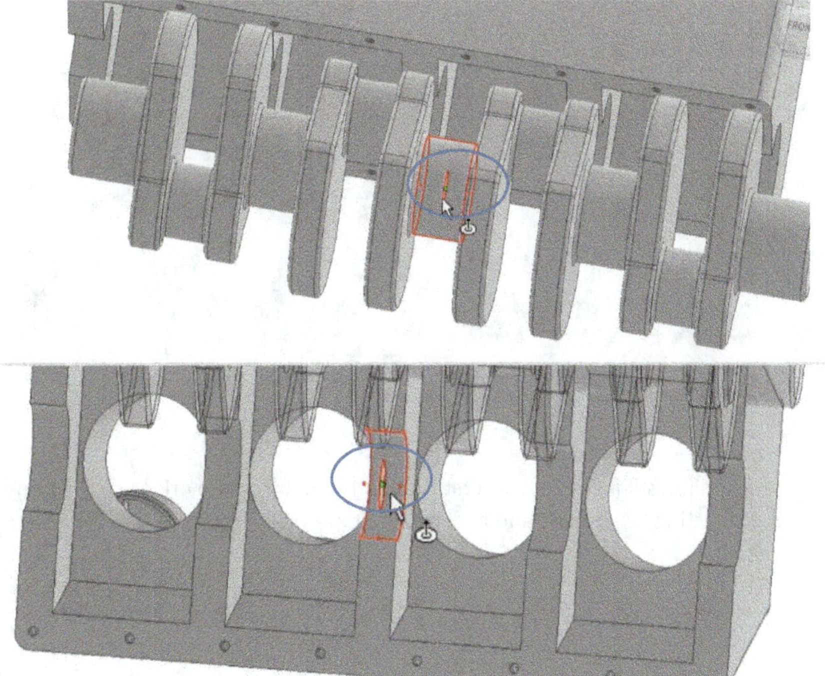

Figure 236: Apply Joint command and select these two joint origins

Perfect, finally all components for our highly simplified engine model are ready. At the end of the chapter, we would of course like to link all the connecting rods to the crankshaft and let our engine run virtually. Final spurt!

For the connecting rod and crankshaft links, we hide the crankcase for the time being for better clarity (right-click on the case and select "Visibility").

The linkage or joint creation is again relatively unspectacular. Place the first joint origin centrally in the lower eye of the connecting rod and place the second origin centrally on the shaft journal of the crankshaft. The joint type in this case is again "Cylindrical". Proceed in the same way for the other connecting rods.

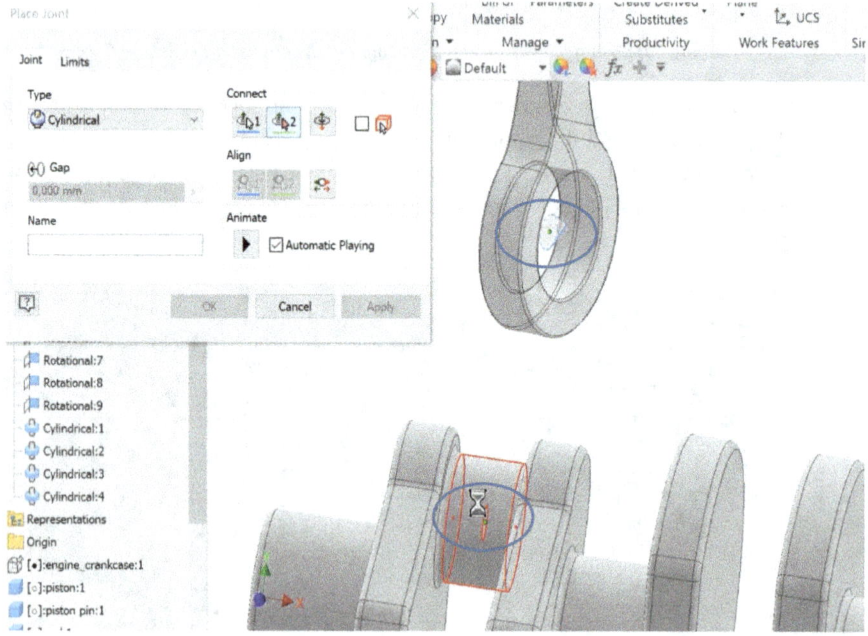

Figure 237: Linking connecting rod to crankshaft

When everything is linked, we can first unhide the crankcase by right-clicking on its body and selecting "Visibility", and at the same time make it transparent by selecting "Transparent".

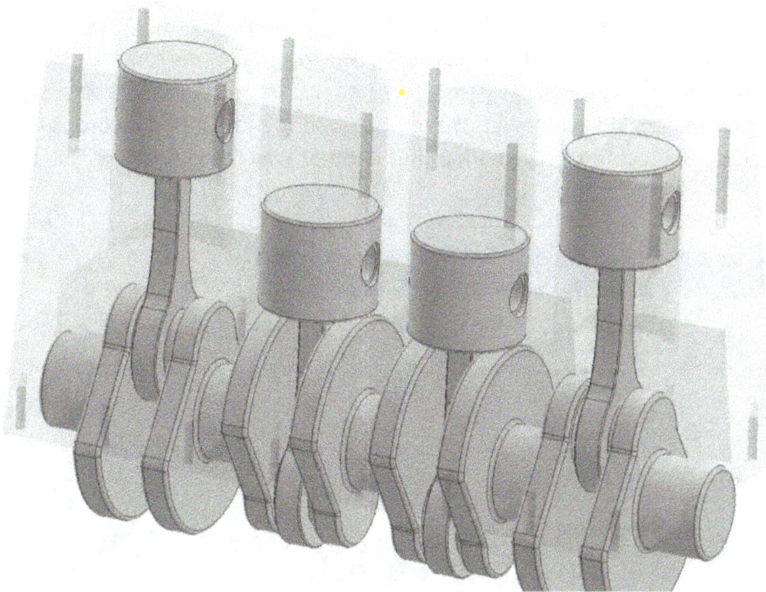

Figure 238: All joints are created and the crankshaft housing is now transparent

At the end of the chapter, we now want to run our motor virtually. If we have placed all the joints correctly, this should be no problem. To do this, we find the joint of the crankshaft with the crankshaft housing and right-click on it. We select "Drive" and then have to enter a start and end point, in this case two angles.

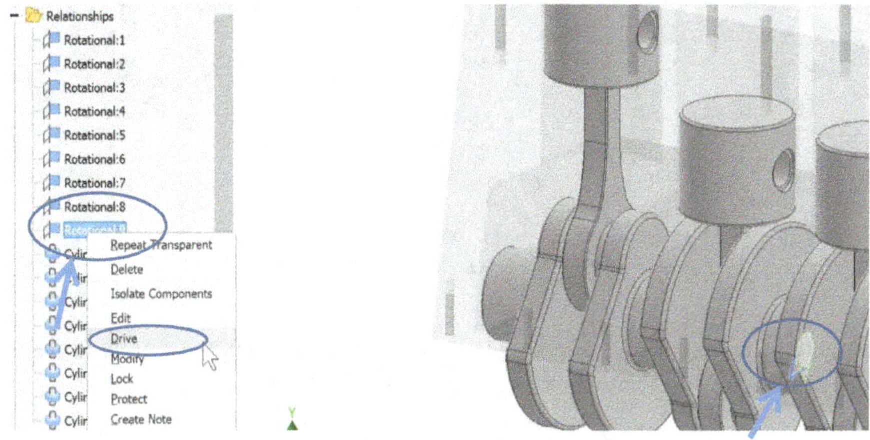

Figure 239: Select the correct joint and right-click on it; select "Drive"

For example, we can enter 0° as the start angle and a multiple of 360° as the end angle, since we want to see several revolutions. 360° is logically a whole rotation. So we enter e.g. 1080°, which corresponds to 3 x 360°! Then just press the "Play" icon and, buckle up please, the engine is running! By the way, with the integrated recording function you could now record this animation. But another way to do that later in "Inventor Studio".

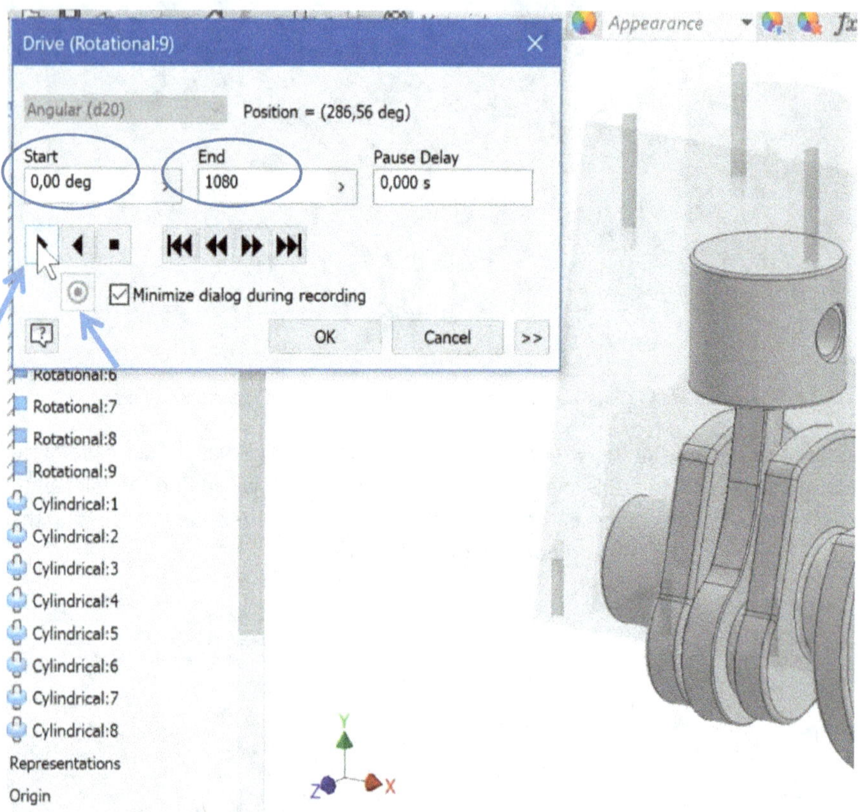

Figure 240: Controlling the animation of the joint with the options

Respect, if you got this far, you can really be proud of yourself! By the way, you can end the animation of the joint simply by pressing the "ESC" key.

5 Introduction to sheet metal design with "Inventor ".

Welcome back! Let us now turn to sheet metal design in this chapter. The dedicated "Sheet Metal" section is of great importance if you want to design sheet metal. The commands and functions in this tab are well designed for this.

If you want to design a sheet metal body, you especially need ease in dealing with bends, tabs, unwinds and other sheet metal specific elements and features.

If you want to design a curved sheet metal element, such as this element,

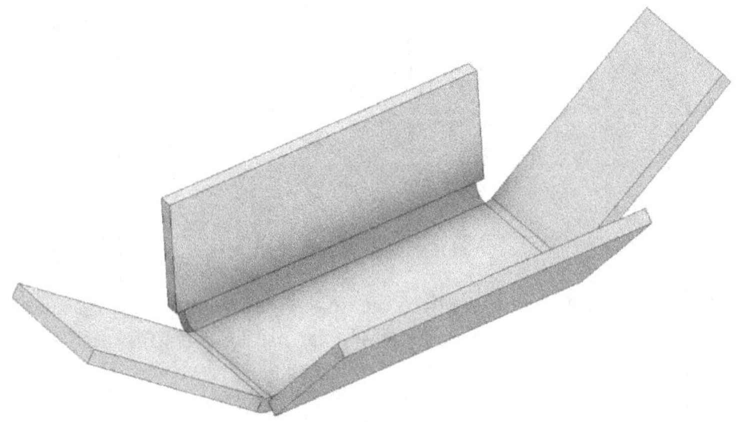

Figure 241: An example sheet that we will construct in this lesson

in practice, i.e. in the craft workshop, you need a cut piece of sheet metal in basic form, which you then bend or machine into shape.

This basic shape, also unwinding, can be easily created in "Inventor" in this section. To do this, you simply need to construct the finished and already bent sheet and apply a command.

This means that you design the desired, finished sheet metal body and then simply have the program generate the unwinding, i.e. the dimensions and geometries for the production documents.

Let's look at this with the example shown. The procedure for the construction is now very similar, but still a bit different, as if you were constructing a solid.

Let's go! We start a new part as usual in the "Part" environment. Before we start the design, we then select the "Convert to Sheet Metal" button in the upper right area.

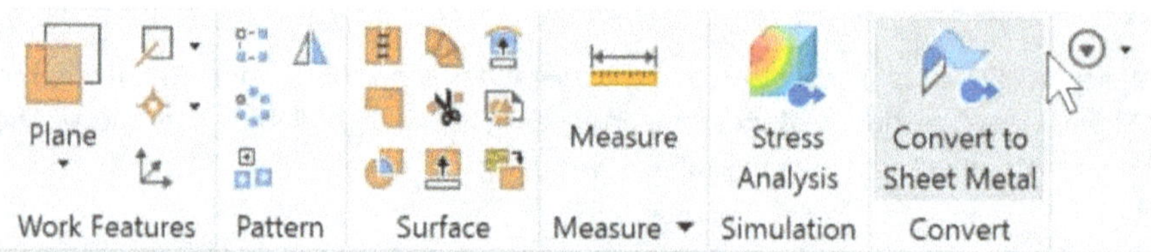

Figure 242: Converting a single part to sheet metal using Convert to Sheet Metal

The program now takes us into the field of sheet metal construction.

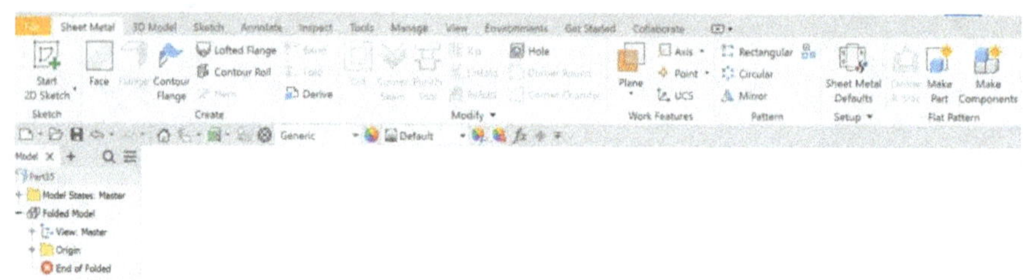

Figure 243: The "Sheet Metal" tab opens with sheet metal-specific features

For the floor or base element, we then create a sheet by starting a new sketch on a plane. We then draw, for example, a rectangular profile in a 2D sketch for our base element, just as usual.

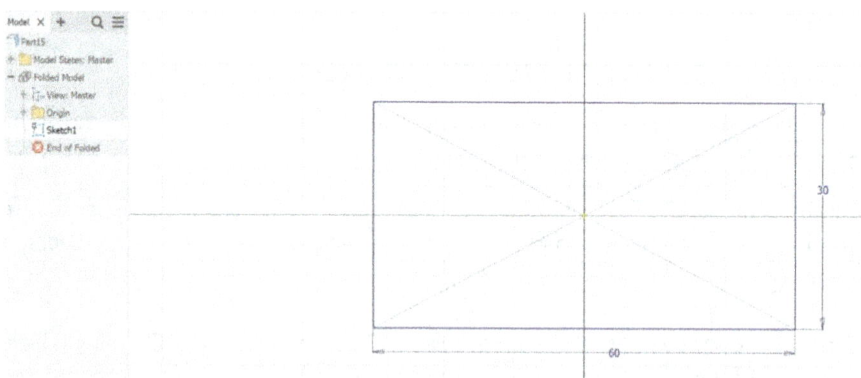

Figure 244: The rectangular base profile of our example sheet (60 x 30 mm) on the x-z plane

Now normally in 3D mode we would use the Extrude command, but we won't do that here. This is one of the biggest differences in the sheet metal construction. Because we are now building our sheet metal body with the two commands "Face" and "Flange". For the basic element, first select the "Face" command and the sketched profile. You only have to click on it, the thickness is already selected. We will see why this is so and how you can change the thickness in a moment.

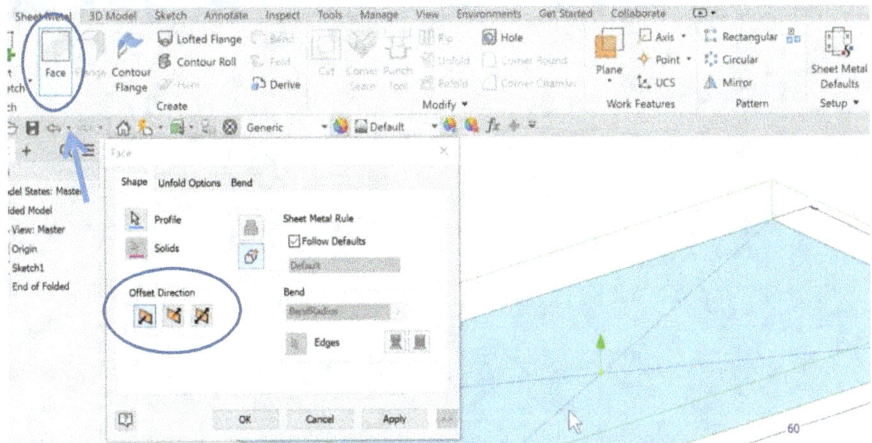

Figure 245: The Face command in the Create area of the Sheet Metal tab

With the button "Sheet Metal Defaults", which is located in the menu bar above at "Setup" in the tab "Sheet Metal", the so-called "Sheet Metal Rule" can be selected and edited with a click on the pencil symbol.

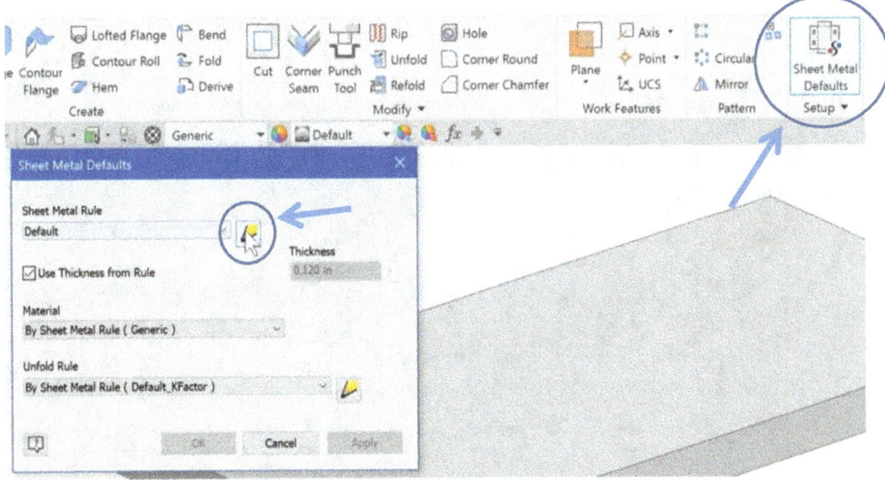

Figure 246: Editing the "Sheet Metal Defaults"; click on the pencil icon

Here we can also select the material. If we edit the "Sheet Metal Rule", we can set the thickness of our sheet metal and change all important sheet metal specific parameters for sheet metal constructions like the "K-Factor" or bending properties ("Bend conditions"). If necessary, you can change to another material here. However, it is recommended to adjust only the sheet thickness and to ask your sheet supplier for the parameters or to leave them with the default values.

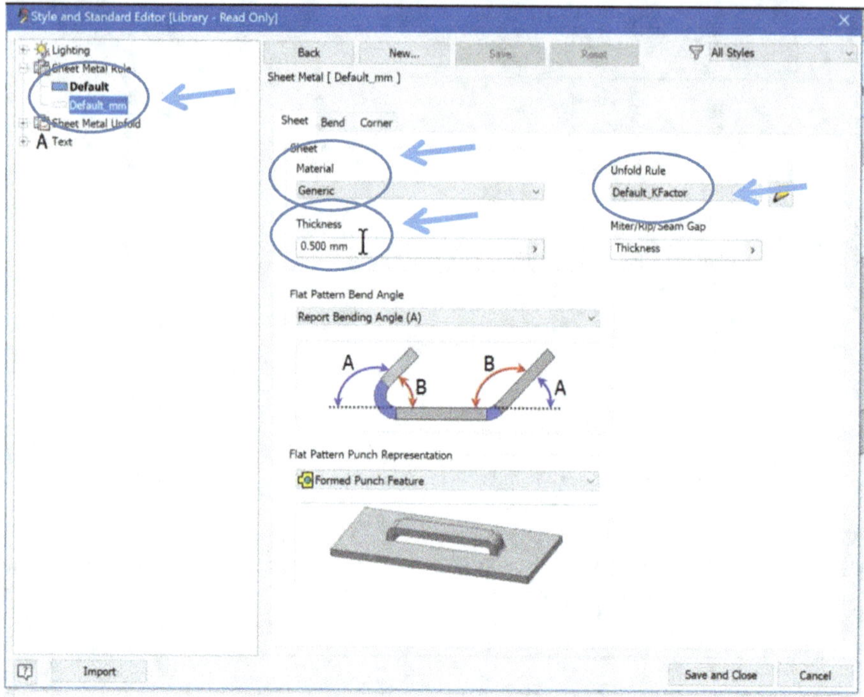

Figure 247: Sheet thickness, K-factor and other sheet-specific settings

How do we continue now? To continue building our sheet metal body, we now use the "Flange" command.

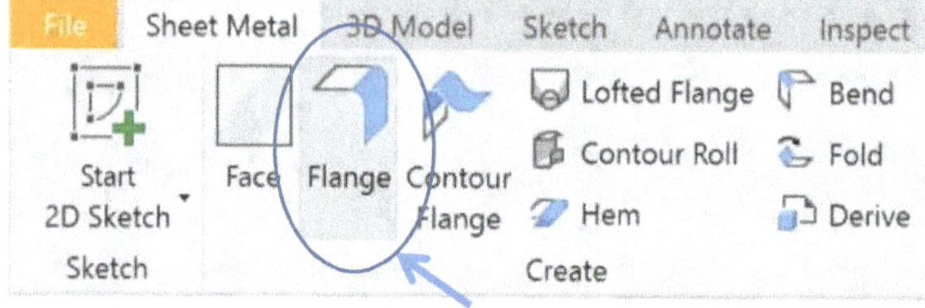

Figure 248: The Flange command in the Create section of the Sheet Metal tab

To do this, we always select edges or sketches in the following. Since our sheet is kept relatively simple, we simply select the lateral edge of the basic element. As you can see, the program now immediately creates the material with the correct bend.

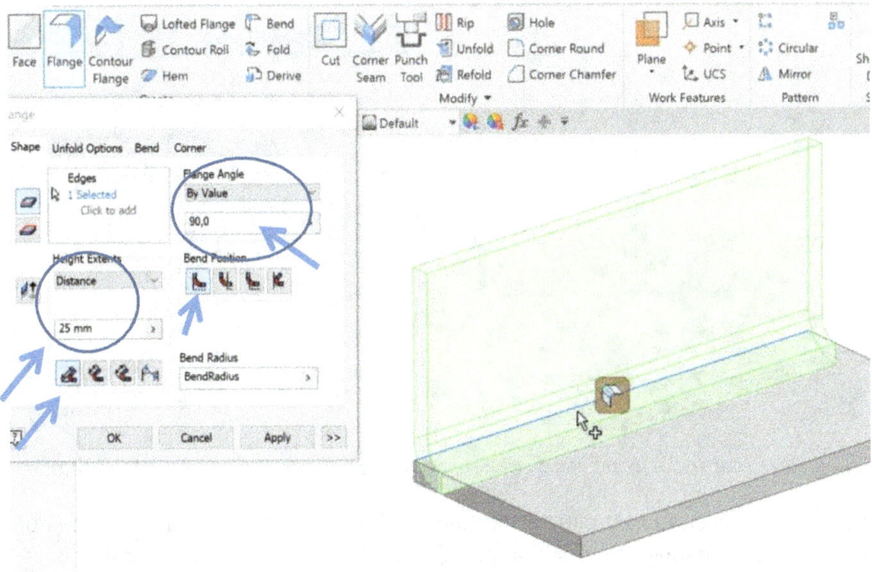

Figure 249: Select the "Flange" command, select an edge and set parameters; 90° bending angle and 25 mm height

In the options window you can change all important parameters, e.g. the bending angle or the bending position. Let's also construct the other missing elements of our example sheet.

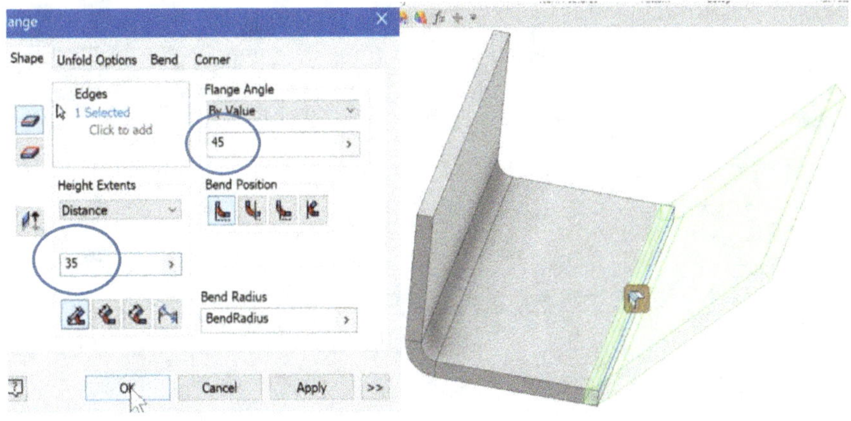

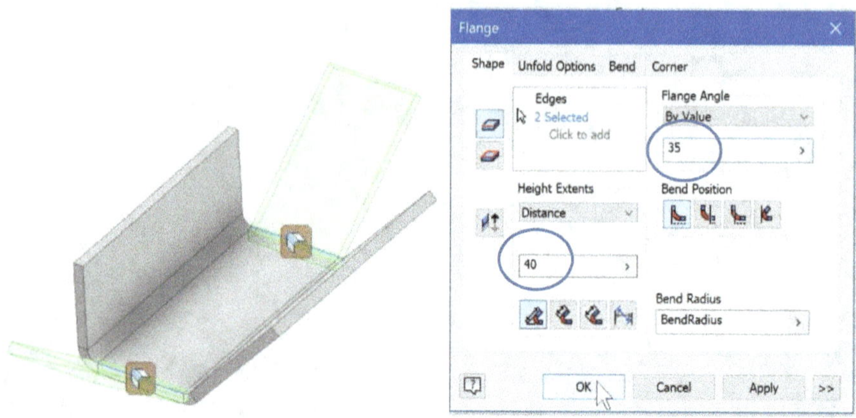

Figure 250: Further lugs for the plate; picture above: 45° and 35 mm; picture below 35° and 40 mm

By the way, you can also use matching commands from the other sections, such as the command for creating a hole or chamfers or edge fillets from the "3D Model" tab.

In the "Sheet Metal" area, there are two important functions for beginners that we would like to take a look at. One is the Unfold command and the other is Create Flat Pattern. To further process a sheet metal section in unbent form or to create supports for manufacturing, on the one hand we can use the "Unfold" command from the "Modify" section. To do this, first select the sheet section that should remain stationary, i.e. around which part of the sheet should be unfolded, e.g. this one:

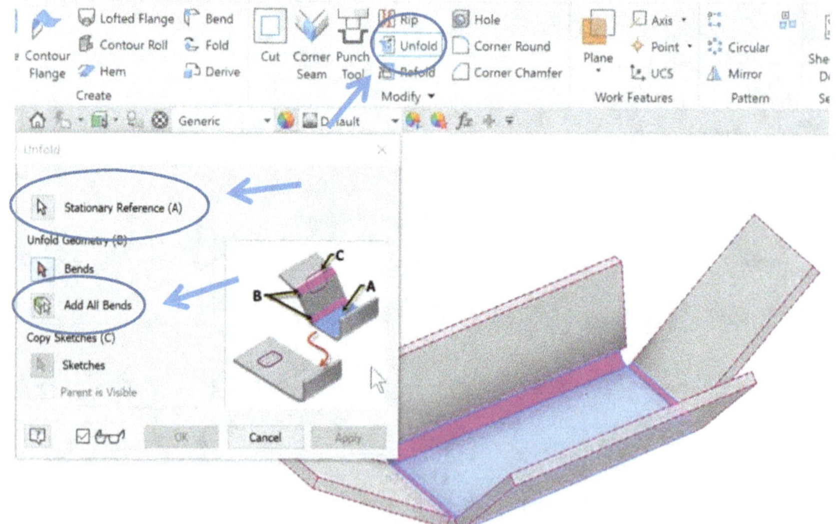

Figure 251: Use Unfold command; select blue area as stationary reference

In the options bar, select "Add all bends", for example, to select all bends, or select only individual bends.

For the actual production documents, however, it is better to use the "Create Flat Pattern" / "Abwicklung erstellen" command from the "Flat Pattern" section. To do this, simply select the command and you will then be transferred to the "Flat Pattern" workspace. The sheet will be unrolled automatically.

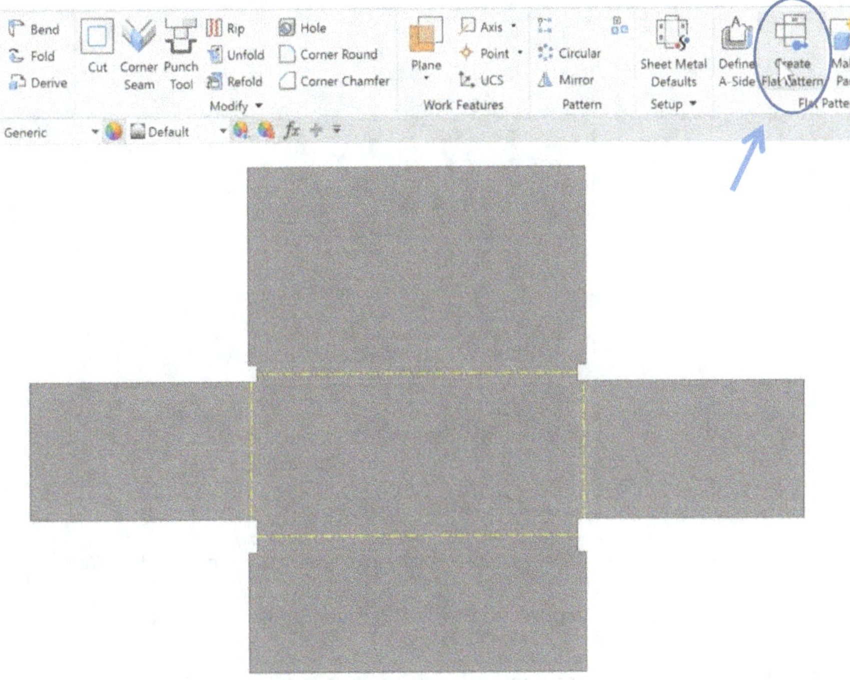

Figure 252: Create the unfold of the sheet using "Create Flat Pattern"
(undo "Unfold" before)

If everything fits, you can leave this workspace again with "Go to Folded Part" and then see the generated "Unwind" in the part browser on the left.

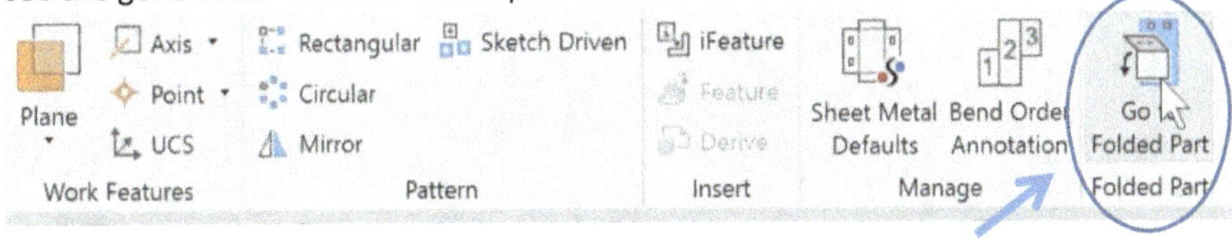

Figure 253: Exiting the "Flat Pattern" workspace again with "Go to Folded Part"

You can then export the generated development for manufacturing or create a technical drawing from it.

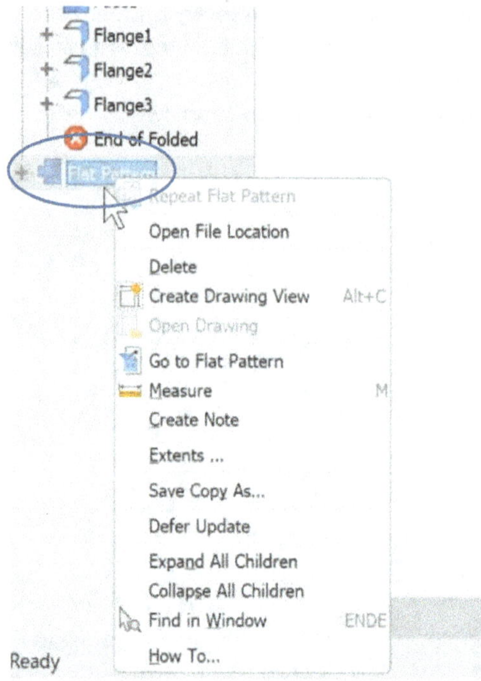

Figure 254: The created "Flat Pattern" appears in the part browser and can be edited

So much for the "Design" section and the CAD design! Super done so far!

Be sure to continue in order to get to know or use the full potential of "Inventor". In the next section, we will first briefly look at "Render" and "Animation" before moving on to "Simulation" and the technical drawings.

Section II: Rendering & Animation

In this part of the course we will deal with the two functions "Render" and "Animation". These two functions can be found in the so-called "Inventor Studio" under "Environments".

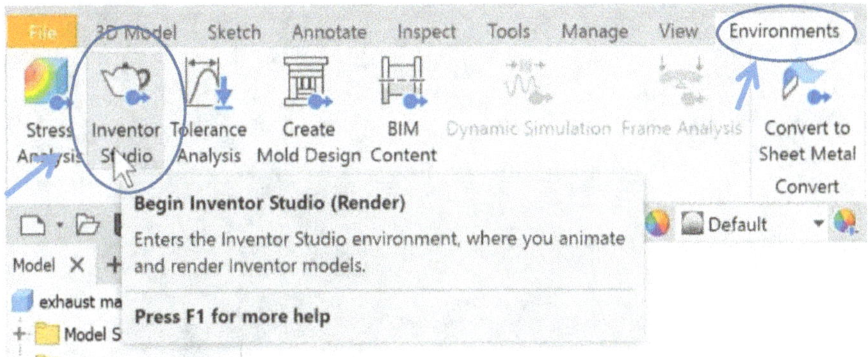

Figure 255: Switching to the "Inventor Studio" area; "Environment" tab

You need it whenever you want to present already designed individual parts or assemblies statically, i.e. in the form of photos, or dynamically, i.e. in the form of a video for a product presentation, for a website, for a meeting or simply for your circle of friends. It is, so to speak, an integrated photo and film studio for the constructed objects.

6 Rendering & Animation

In this lesson we will first start with the "Render" function. We will use as an object one of our construction projects, namely the exhaust manifold. As you can see, the program environment has hardly changed. On the left is the part browser and at the top is the "Render" tab with the individual functions or commands.

By the way, rendering here simply means that a graphic or image is generated from the geometric information of the CAD part. You could, of course, just take a screenshot if you're in a hurry. However, a rendered graphic will be significantly different in resolution and realism, but will also take more time to create.

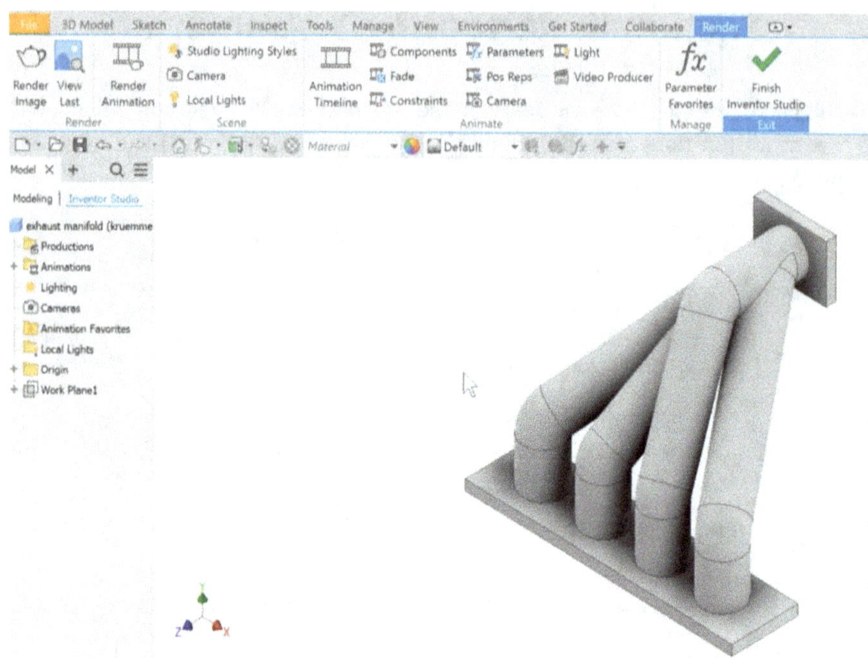

Figure 256: The Inventor Studio area

Let's just try it out step by step. First, of course, you can hide all the elements you don't want in the part browser by right-clicking on an object and selecting "Visibility", but this is not necessary in our case because we only have the exhaust manifold as a single part. In the second step we can change the appearance, the "Appearance" of our object. We can use this to apply the appearance and texture of certain materials to our entire design object or just to individual surfaces. A large number of materials are available for selection. However, this function is independent of the "Render" tab. We have to switch to the familiar "Tools" tab for this.

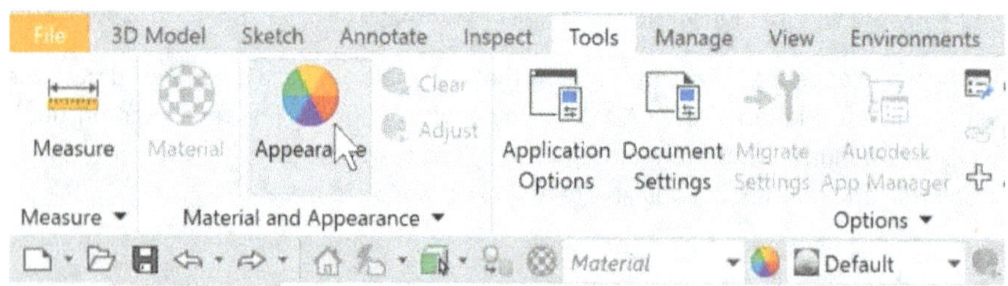

Figure 257: The Appearance command from the Tools tab

For example, we could simply have the exhaust manifold displayed in copper once. To do this, first select the individual part with the mouse, press the "Appearance" button, then search for the material in the material library and add it to the document by clicking on the small arrow in the right-hand area.

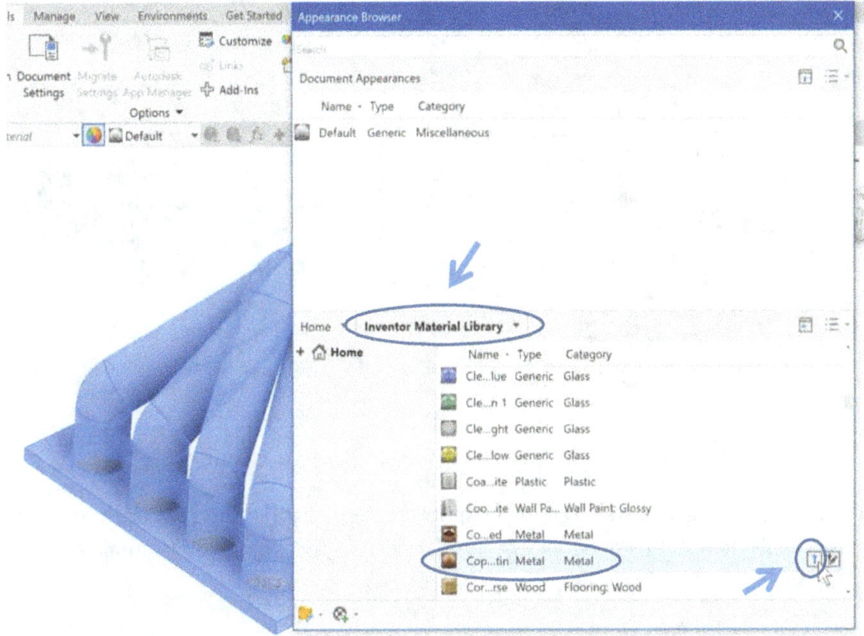

Figure 258: Displaying the exhaust manifold in copper or another material

Perfect, by the way, the final result is only shown when everything is rendered. In the "Scene" area we will then find a few commands with which we can edit our stage set, so to speak, i.e. the background and the environment.

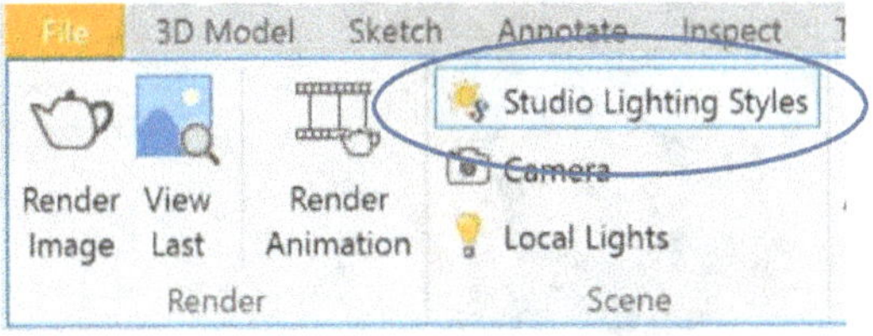

Figure 259: The Scene area in Inventor Studio

Here you can select a preset setting with "Studio Lighting Styles", e.g. "Warm Light" / "Warm Licht". With a right click and "Activate" it will be applied.

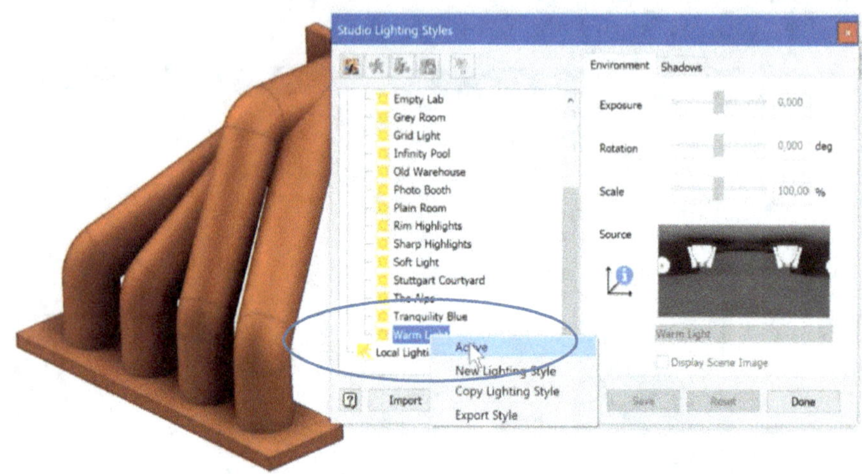

Figure 260: Changing the "Studio Lighting Styles"; e.g. to "Warm Light

Local Lights" can also be used to place "spots" for more light at specific locations. To do this, simply select "Position" and "Target" and a "Spot" that better illuminates the location will be placed.

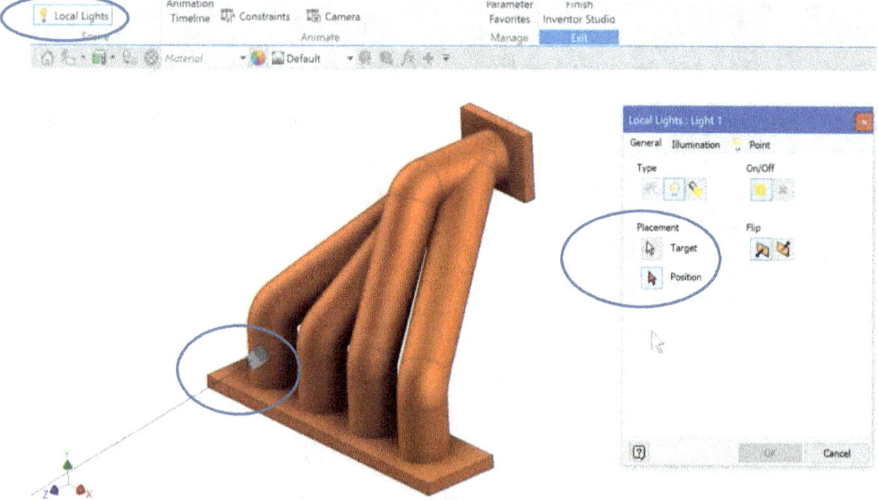

Figure 261: Placing a spot (gray rectangle) to increase the illumination of a location

The same procedure can be used to place a camera, which can then be selected during the rendering process. It is best to try out many different settings so that you find something that suits you best on an individual basis.

The actual rendering is now started with the "Render Image" command. Simply click on the "Teapot" icon and then make the desired settings.

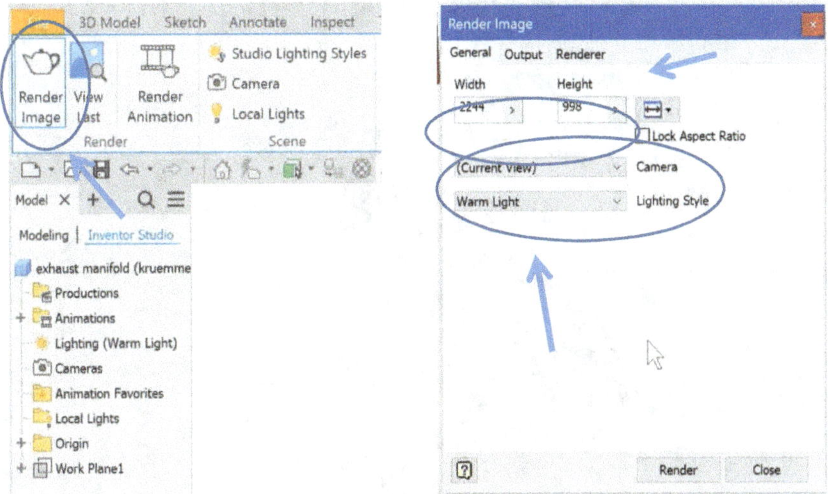

Figure 262: Starting the rendering process with "Render Image" (left); settings (right)

Here, you can set the desired size of the rendering and select either the currently displayed view or perspective under "Camera" or, as mentioned above, a created camera. The "Lighting Style" can also be changed again. In the menu item "Output" a directory can be set so that the image is saved immediately after rendering and in the menu tab "Renderer" settings can be made for the duration / quality of the rendering. But you can also leave the default values.

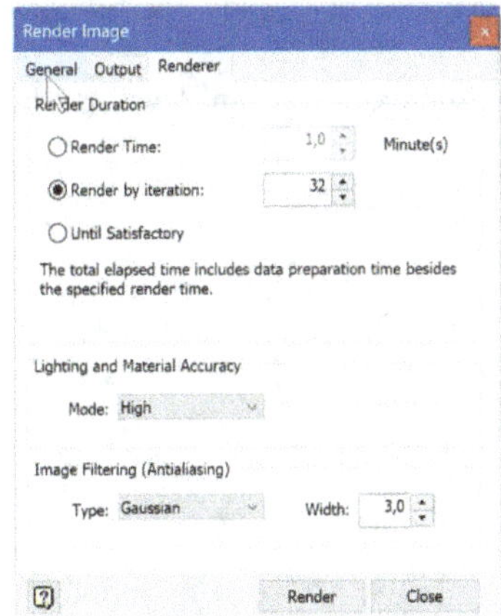

Figure 263: Render settings tab with default values

The higher the resolution and render quality, the longer it will take. Then just start the rendering and wait. The file and the progress will then be displayed. With a click on "Save rendered image" on the top right, you can then save the rendered graphic.

Figure 264: The rendering process that is not yet finished

That's it for rendering, there's not much more to talk about in this environment. We will continue with the "Animation" environment and then move on to more exciting topics.

For the "Animation" function, which can also be found in "Inventor Studio", we use the constructed model of our 4-cylinder engine.

With a click on the button "Animation Timeline" we first show the timeline that opens in the lower area.

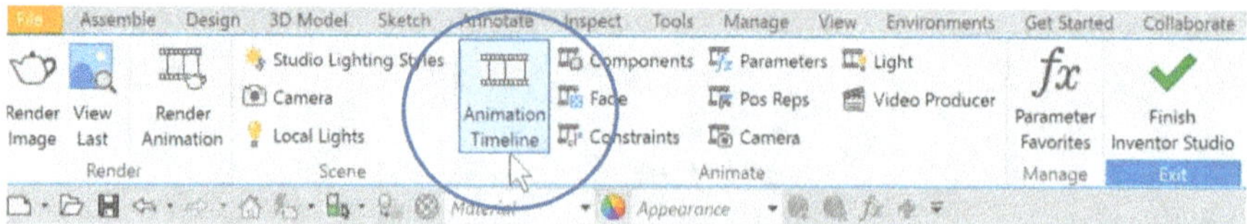

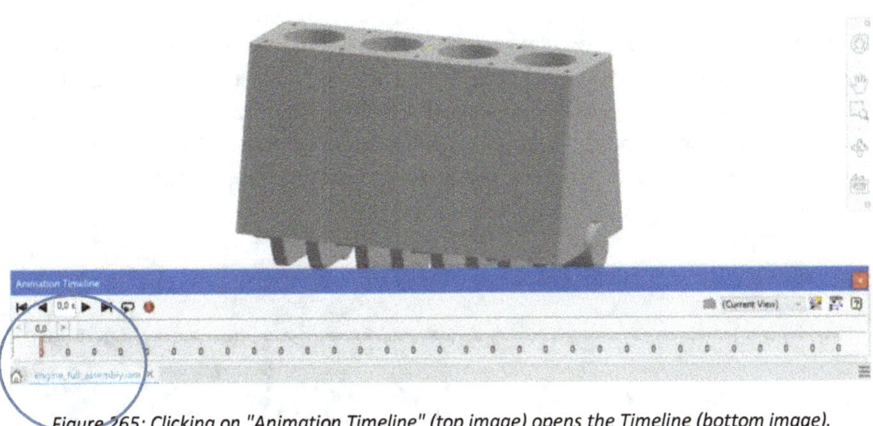

Figure 265: Clicking on "Animation Timeline" (top image) opens the Timeline (bottom image).

We would now like to create a kind of video in which the pistons move up and down in the cylinders. Unfortunately, the existing joint of the crankshaft cannot be animated in this environment, because joints are not displayed in "Animation". "Constraints" on the other hand are displayed to us and can also be animated. I had already mentioned this at the beginning. Therefore, if you are planning to animate, it makes sense to use "Constraints" in the design, or at least apply them specifically for animation. This is what we will do in the following. The animation is then very simple. To do this, we need to replace the joint of the crankshaft with two "constraints". We close "Inventor Studio" for the time being and find the joint of the crankshaft in the assembly environment. Since we want to replace this joint, we suppress it by right-clicking and selecting "Suppress".

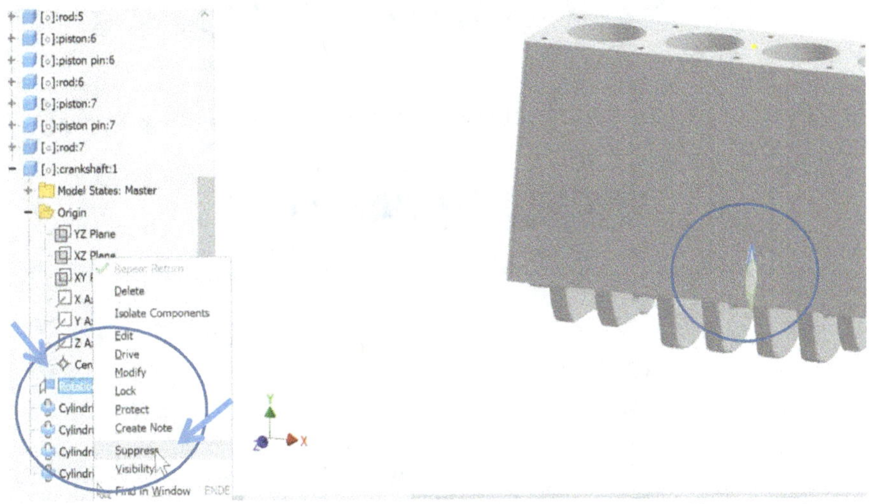

Figure 266: Searching for and suppressing the joint of the crankshaft ("Rotational") in the part browser

Alternatively, you could also delete it, but then it is permanently gone. Then we can move the crankshaft freely again. Now we have to reconnect the crankshaft to the crankcase with "Constraints". For this we first use the "Constrain": "Insert" to link the axes of the crankshaft and the receptacles in the housing. Then click on the left edge of the middle face of the crankshaft mount and select the counterpart in the housing.

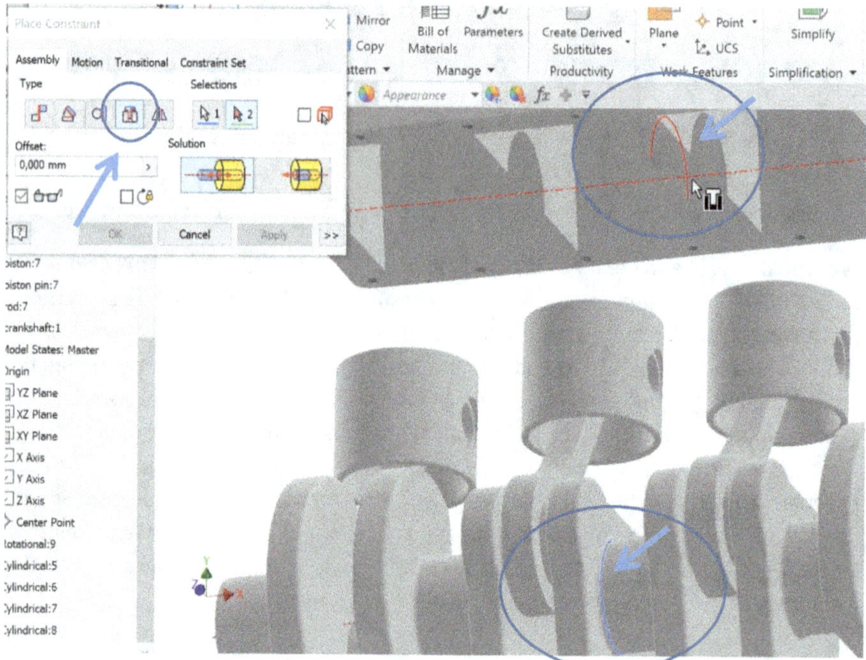

Figure 267: The "Constrain": Use "Insert" and link crankshaft with housing

In the options we have to correct the alignment. To do this, we select "Aligned" for "Solution" and an offset of -5 mm.

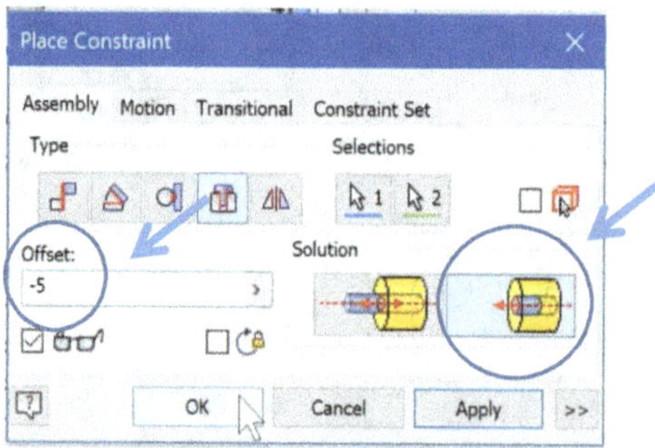

Figure 268: Change "Solution" to "Aligned" and enter a -5 mm offset

The crankshaft is then correctly centered. The crankshaft is now rotatably mounted in the crankshaft housing. To get a complete definition, we still create an angle dependency with the "Constrain": "Angle". We also need this for the animation. For this we link the x-z plane of the crankshaft with the x-y plane of the crankshaft housing.

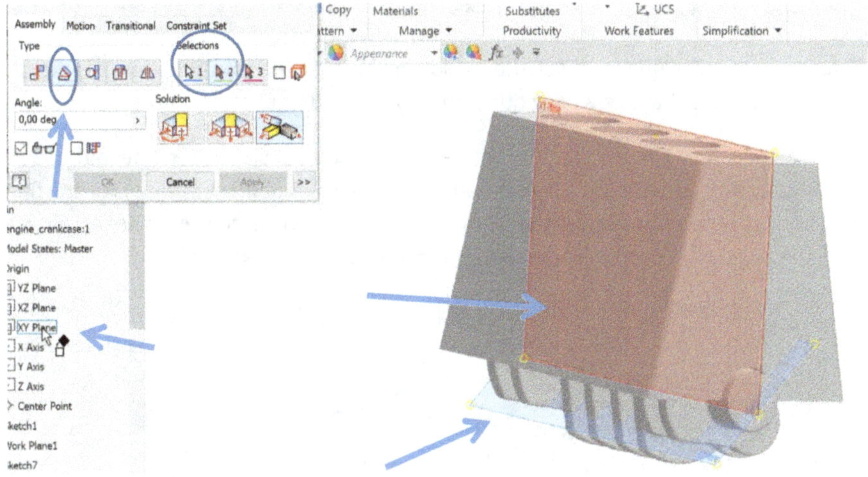

Figure 269: Select "Constrain" and choose "Angle" as "Type"; then select x-z plane of the crankshaft and x-y plane of the crankshaft housing in the part browser one after the other

For "Solution" we select "Directed Angle" and enter an angle of 90 degrees so that the pistons align as shown.

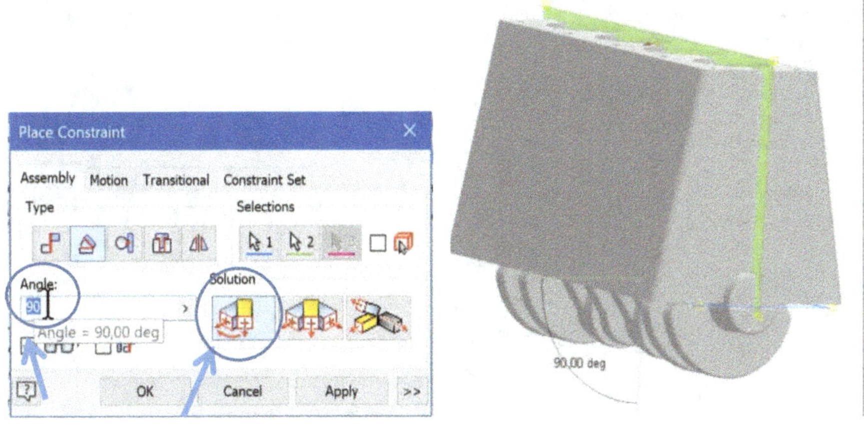

Figure 270: For "Solution": Select "Directed Angle" and enter 90° as the angle

Perfect! Now we have defined the crankshaft with "Constraints" instead of a joint and can switch back to the "Inventor Studio" area.

Another tip: For very simple and quick animations, you can also simply do without the animation in "Inventor Studio" and instead animate the crankshaft joint in the "Design" environment, as we had already done and create a screencasting video, i.e. a screen recording, of it with the integrated recording function - perhaps you remember - or else with external software.

Before we start, we have to set the cursor in the timeline to a duration, e.g. to 10 seconds, because that's how long our animation should last.

In the following, we would like to animate a few revolutions of the engine in these 10 seconds, as well as make the crankshaft housing transparent in the course. For the first part, the movement, we select the "Constraints" command in the "Animate" area and then the angle relationship from the part browser at the crankshaft.

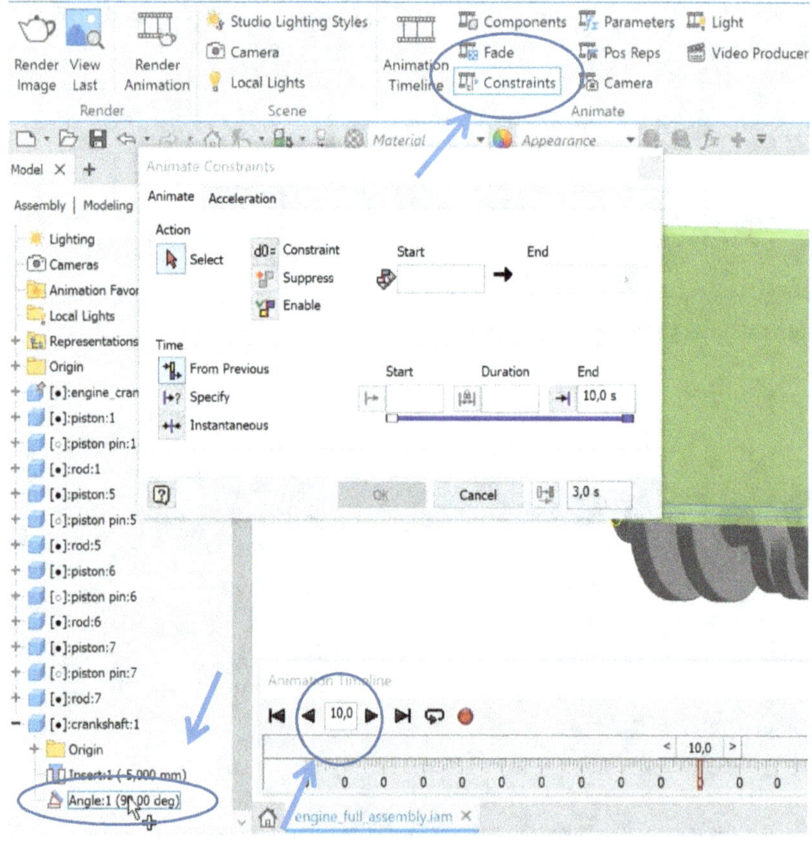

Figure 271: Using "Animate Constrain" in the "Animate" area

We must now determine the positions for "Start" and "End". The start position is 90°, we leave it like this. As end position we select e.g. 1170°. Why this number? Because we want e.g. 3 whole revolutions. One complete revolution has 360°. 3 x 360° for three revolutions gives 1080°. Then we have to add our starting point, which is 90°, and we get 1170°. The start and end time is already entered, because we have set the timeline to 10 seconds. We could change that here - if desired. Then simply click on "OK".

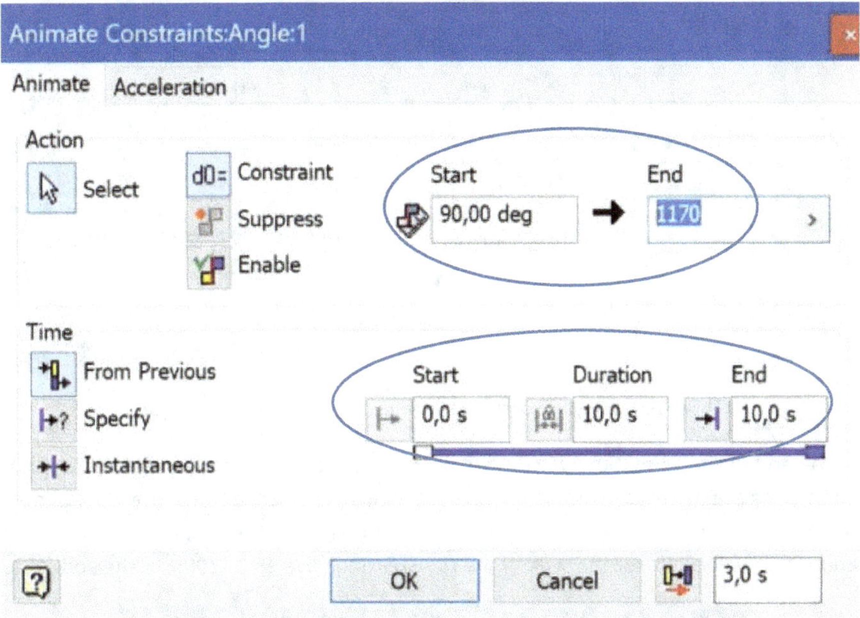

Figure 272: Enter start and end point and, if necessary, start and end time

For the second part of the animation, i.e. to make the crankshaft housing transparent, we select the "Fade" command.

As a component we choose the crankshaft housing and we let the transparency start with 100%, i.e. no transparency, and increase to e.g. 50% until the end of the process.

For example, we want this process to start at the first second and to finish at three seconds, i.e. to last two seconds. To do this, we select "Specify" for "Time" and enter the values for start and end. Finally confirm with "Ok".

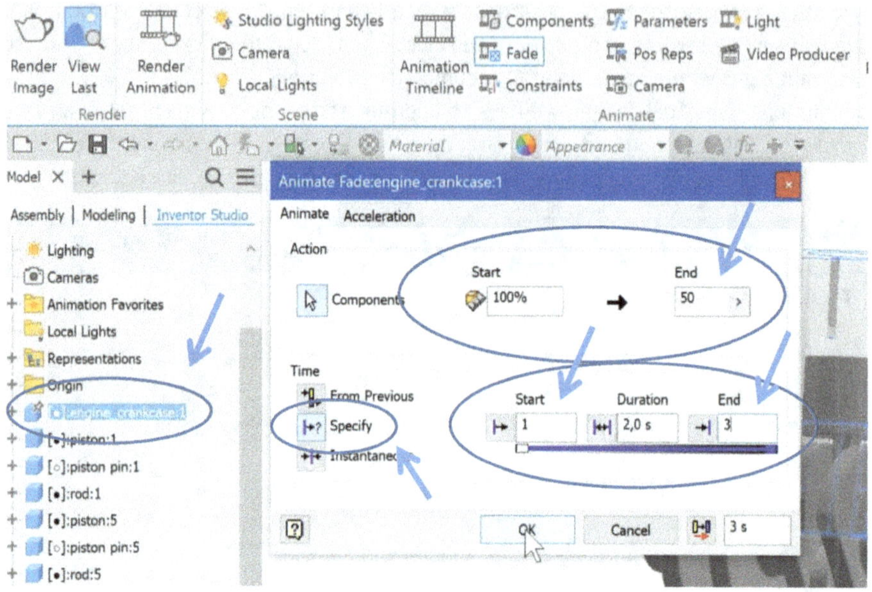

Figure 273: Applying the "Fade" command with the displayed settings

at the end of the animation we could make the crankcase opaque again. We do this in exactly the opposite way with the same command. First set the start time, for example, to seven seconds and the end time to nine seconds, then the program automatically adopts the value 50% for the start of the transparency. We enter 100% as the end value.

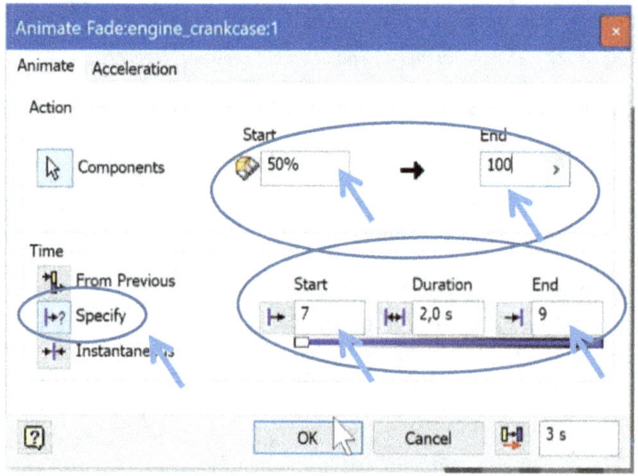

Figure 274: Using the "Fade" command again with new settings as shown

Very good. With a click on Play in the timeline we can let the animation play, the cursor must be at the beginning. By the way, with the button "Expand Action Editor" on the upper right side of the timeline we can view all created animation commands and edit them again.

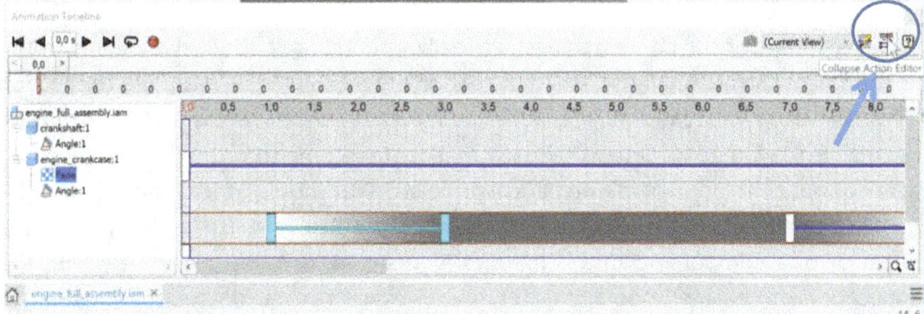

Figure 275: Maximize / minimize the "Animation Timeline" with the button in the upper right corner

With a click on "Render Animation" or on the small red button in the animation timeline, we have to render our animation with the desired settings to a video and can then save it.

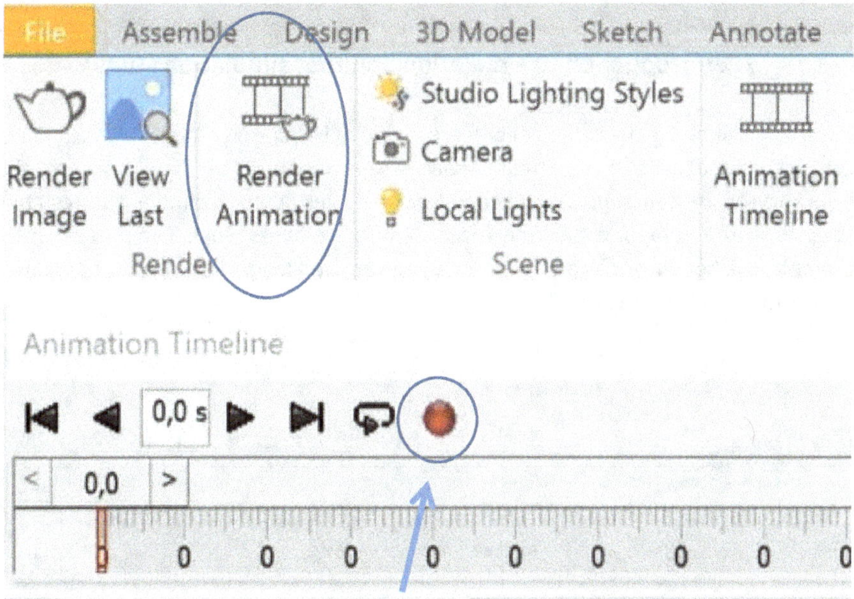

Figure 276: Starting the animation rendering or recording in two ways

Superbly done! That's it for the Animation / Rendering section and the "Inventor Studio". We will continue with a very exciting area of "Inventor". In the following we will deal with FEM simulations in the area of "Stress Analysis". Be sure to continue!

Section III: FEM Simulations & Technical Drawings

In this last part of the course, things get really interesting, because we deal with the environment "Stress Analysis", and the creation of technical drawings. With the section "Stress Analysis" you can simulate loads and material behavior. Possibly the term FEM, i.e. the "Finite Element Method" already means something to you. Without going into detail about this complex mathematical principle, you should at least have heard the name once and know that FEM software can be used to simulate loads and material behavior of a component. In this practical course, we will deal exclusively with the application of the methodology. After that, we will take a look at the creation of technical drawings. You need these for the transmission of information to the machine production and for documentation purposes.

7 FEM simulations with "Inventor"

7.1 Introduction to simulation and first simulation study

We would like to use the carabiner created in one of the design projects as a sample to get acquainted with the "Stress Analysis" environment of "Inventor". In this environment we can simulate loads and get as a result, for example, the resulting stresses in the component or the resulting displacements, so in simple terms, for example, the bending of a component under an applied load. First we have to create a load study with "Create Study".

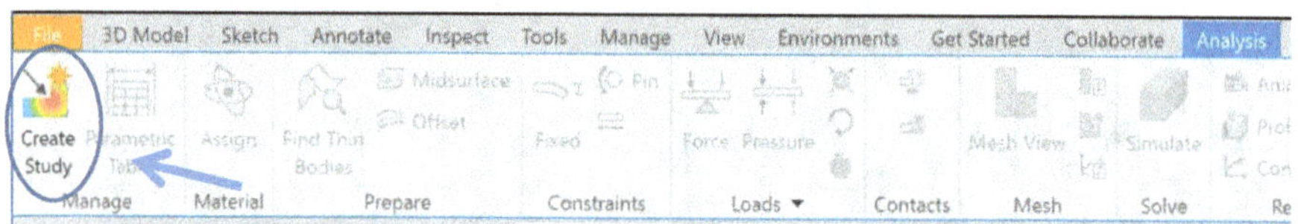

Figure 277: Create a stress study with "Create Study"; first open the carabiner and select "Stress Analysis" at "Environments

A window opens in which we can select which simulation we want to run. In this beginner's course, we will deal exclusively with probably the most common application: static loading. Therefore we select this one. We can leave the set values as they are.

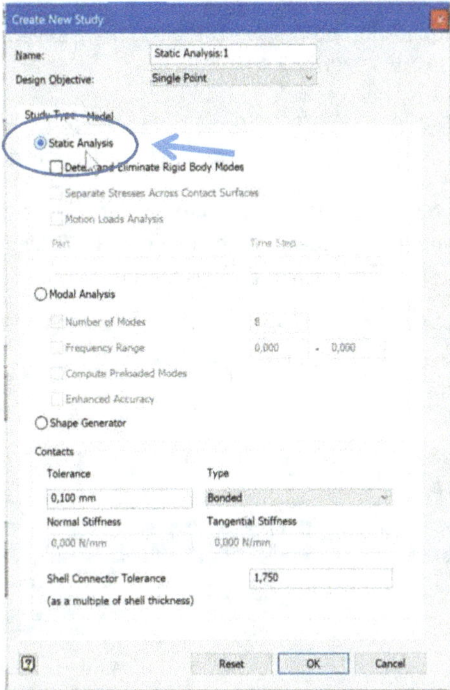

Figure 278: A window opens; select "Static Analysis" and leave settings as they are

This load study is then displayed to us with all relevant options and settings on the left in the part browser.

Figure 279: The created study is displayed in the part browser

In the "Analysis" section, in the upper menu bar, there are all the settings we need for the simulation. If we want to have different load situations calculated, e.g. simulate two different force application points, we can also create several such studies. To do this, we would simply click on "Create Study" again.

For the simulation of a load on a component, we now proceed successively in four steps. This procedure is relatively identical for each study, only the content differs.

The first step is to check if the correct material is assigned for our part. To do this, we use the "Materials" menu with the "Assign" command. Clicking on "Assign" opens a window that shows us the respective materials for all components.

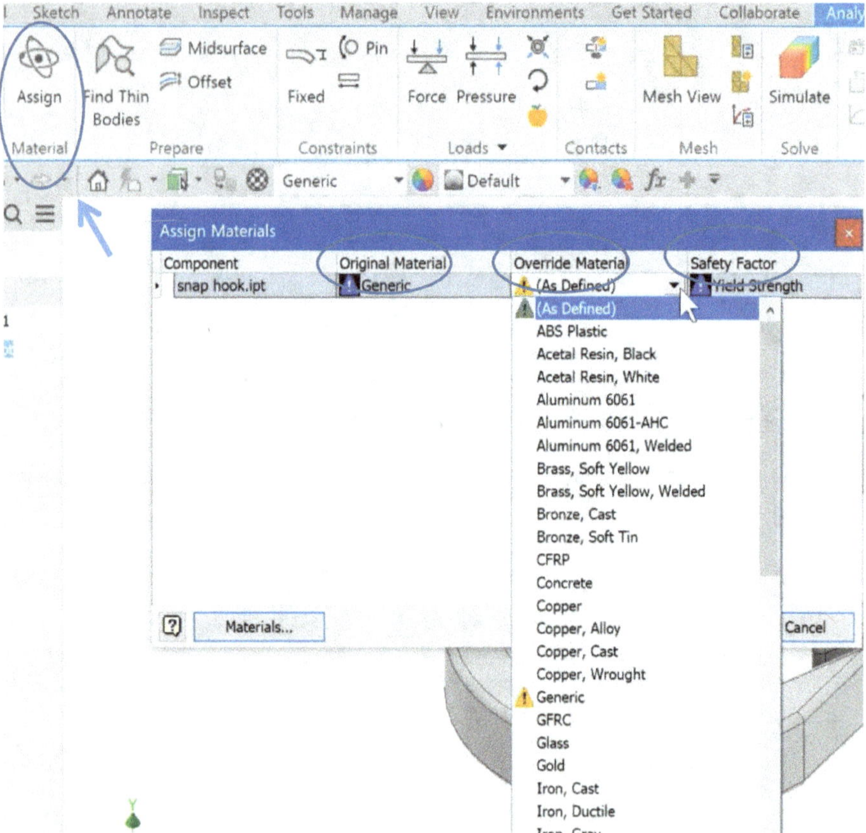

Figure 280: Setting the material of the component for the load study with "Assign"

In this case we have only one, because it is a single part. Depending on what we selected as the material during the design, the material is displayed to us under "Original Material". In the "Override Material" field, we can now select the material of the part for this study. Currently, it is set to "As defined", so the actual material of the object will be used for our load study. If we want to select a different material for, say, a different loading study, we simply select it from the drop-down menu. Alternatively, we can change the material in the design environment, but this will be more laborious for multiple studies. For this simple karabiner, for example, we now select "aluminum" as the material for the calculation once, since steel would have a much too high Young's modulus for opening the karabiner here, i.e. it would provide too high a resistance to deformation. For the calculation of the safety factor, the yield strength of the material should be used, i.e. the point in time from which plastic deformation occurs in the material due to the load. However, if necessary, we could also select the tensile strength, the "Ultimate Tensile Strength", i.e. the maximum stress that the material can withstand.

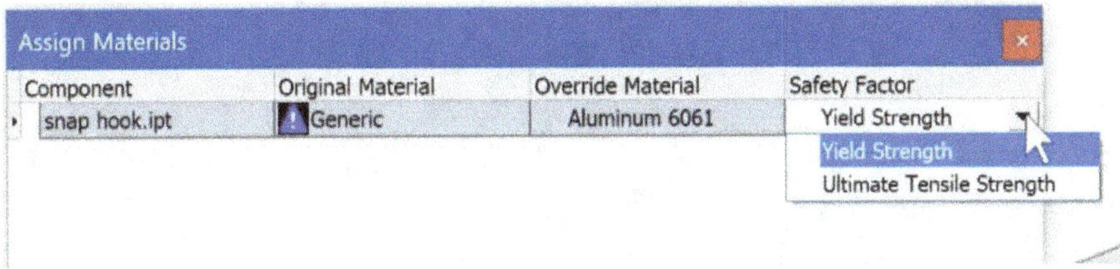

Figure 281: Select e.g. "Aluminum 6061" as material; "Yield Strength" as safety factor

The second step before we can start a calculation of the simulation is to select "Constraints" / "Dependencies" and "Contacts" or "Contacts" for the calculation. We only need "Contacts" for an assembly with several components, because with "Contacts" we define the load transfer between the individual components, i.e. the connection points between the components. However, we will take a closer look at this in the second example.

So here we only have to define "constraints". "Constraints" simply represent constraints in the "Simulation" area. That is, at which points or surfaces our component is fixed in space, or how or where it is supported. Imagine it in a very practical way: You would take the carabiner in one hand and hold it with the palm of your hand against the back or press the back against the palm of your hand, so we select the back surface of the carabiner as the bearing. For this we create a constraint with the command "Fixed" from the menu section "Constraints".

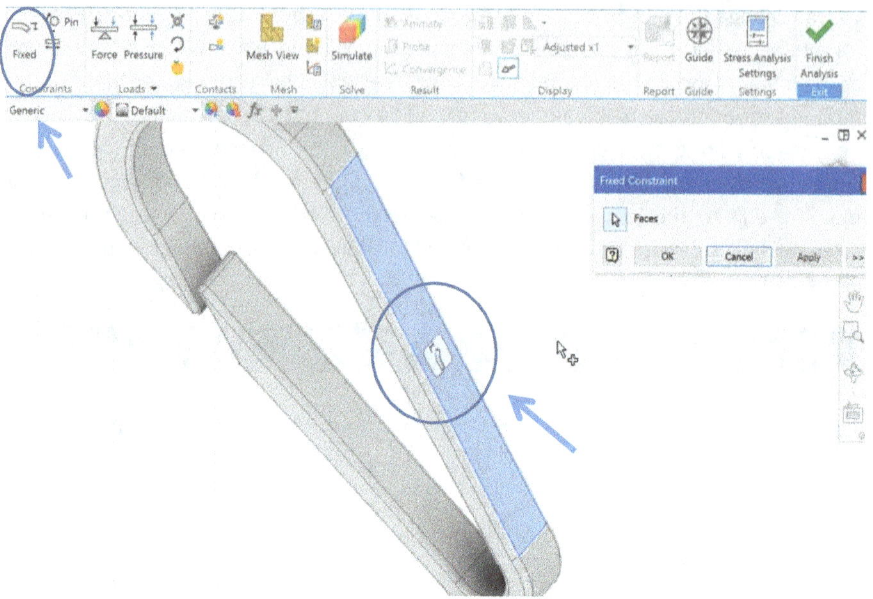

Figure 282: For the creation simply select the command "Fixed" and the desired surface

Here we can choose between "Fixed", "Pin", "Frictionless". For the carabiner, we select "Fixed" as the simplest constraint and assume as a simplification that this applies in all directions, i.e. that the carabiner does not move a bit in the palm of the hand.

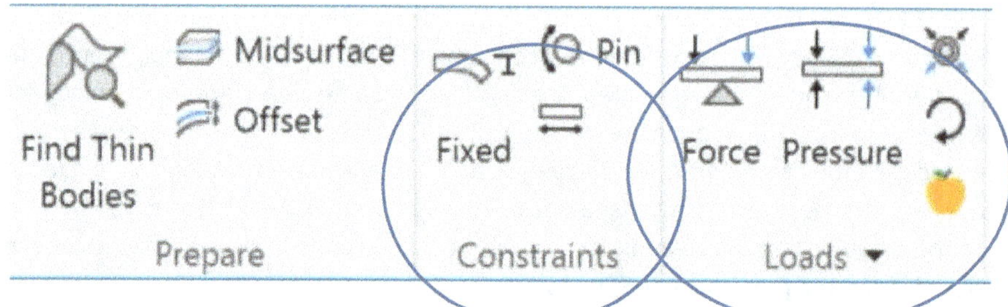

Figure 283: The available constraints (center) and load types (right)

Then, in the third step, we still need a load, of course. We consider how the carabiner is actually loaded. In the present geometry, the front element of the carabiner is loaded by pressing it, so as to widen the opening of the carabiner in order to thread a rope, for example. For example, one will press with the index and or middle finger against the upper edge of the carabiner, i.e. just before the opening. For the simulation of this load we select the command "Loads" and as type a force, i.e. "Force". We could also apply a "pressure load", a "moment" or other load here, depending on the situation.

Then we select the front upper rounding of the carabiner, just before the opening, and enter a value for the force of 100 N, for example. This corresponds to a load of approx. 10 kg.

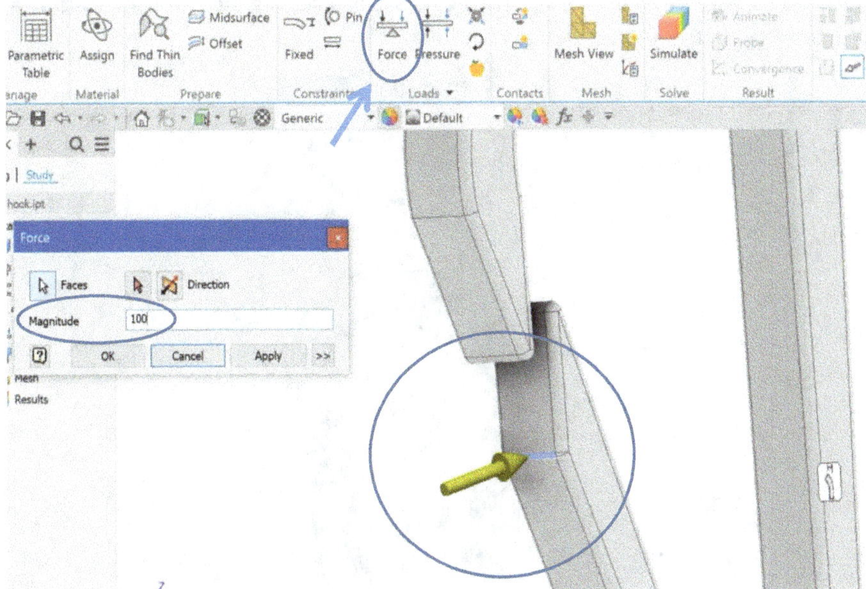

Figure 284: Select "Force", select the edge of the opening and enter 100 N as the size

Incidentally, a man can apply up to 500 N of gripping force as standard, i.e. approx. 50 kg, if he exerts himself more strongly. We assume a perpendicular direction of force on the surface here. However, we could also change the direction of the force vector here.

Then we have almost everything we need. In the fourth and last step, before we can start the calculation of the simulation and the results are displayed, we have to generate a mesh. In the FEM method, the calculation is performed using a mesh with nodes, which is placed over the solid body. We do this by simply clicking on "Mesh View" in the upper menu bar under "Mesh". The generated mesh will then be displayed.

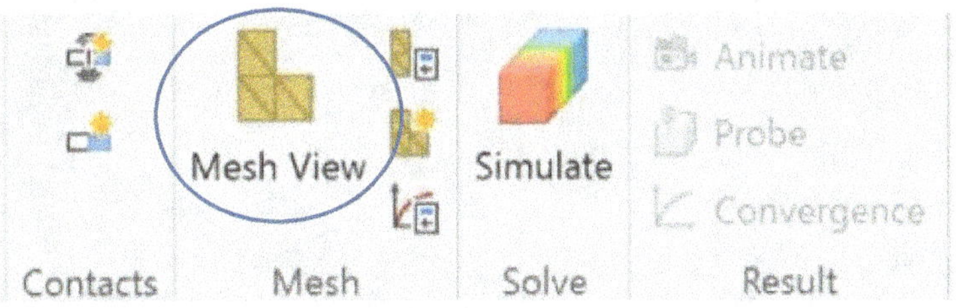

Figure 285: Select "Mesh View" to create or display the mesh.

In fact, you could also skip this step because the software automatically creates the mesh during a calculation anyway.

Afterwards, we let ourselves calculate the results by pressing the "Simulate" button at the top and starting the simulation with "Run".

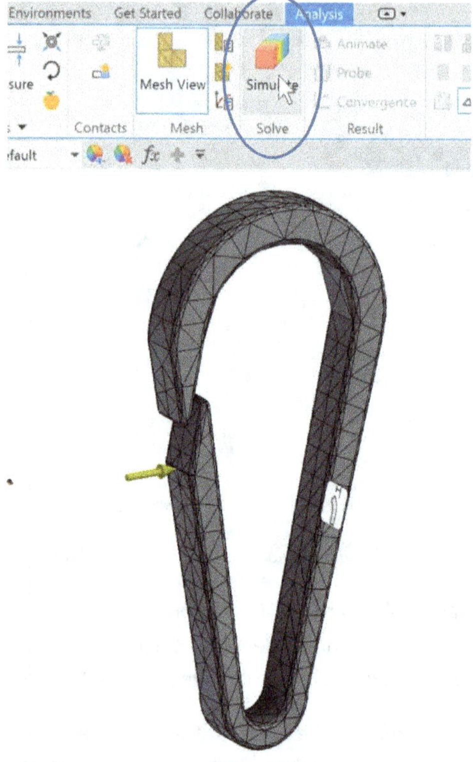

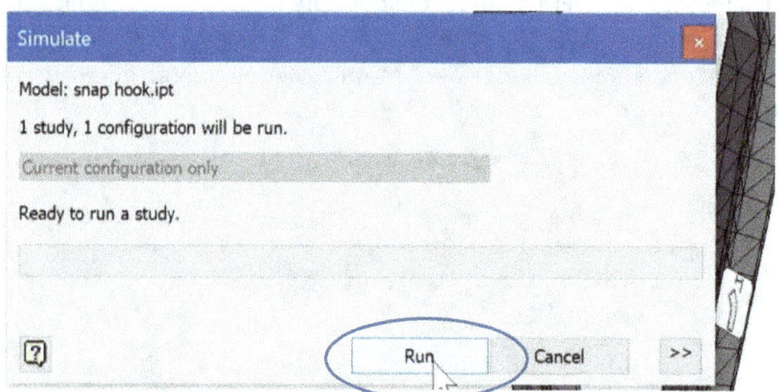

Figure 286: The mesh has been created and the simulation can be started

After the calculation, the results are then displayed graphically using a color gradient. The color gradient in the component indicates which value is present in which area.

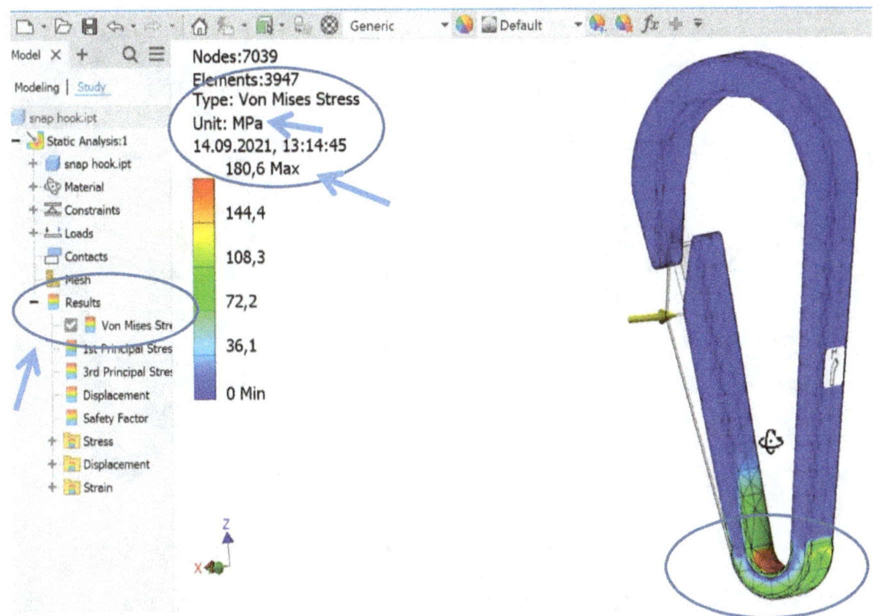

Figure 287: The result of the simulation (Von Mises voltage; largest at the bottom)

At the moment, the "von Mises stress" is selected in the part browser, i.e. the equivalent stress according to the shape change hypothesis. In the area of the lower curvature of the component, it can be seen that a stress of probably about 180 MPa prevails. This was to be expected for this bending load, and this is also where the stress will be highest in the real component. If the carabiner breaks when it is opened, it will first break somewhere in this area.

To display the displacements or the safety factor, we switch to the respective result in the area of the part browser.

When displaying the displacement, we see that we could open the carabiner by approx. 1.8 mm in the negative x-direction with the applied force. On the one hand, this is graphically exaggerated here, but on the other hand it is of course too little to open the carabiner. We would therefore have to apply more force and, if necessary, reinforce our carabiner in the lower area if the safety factor were no longer sufficient.

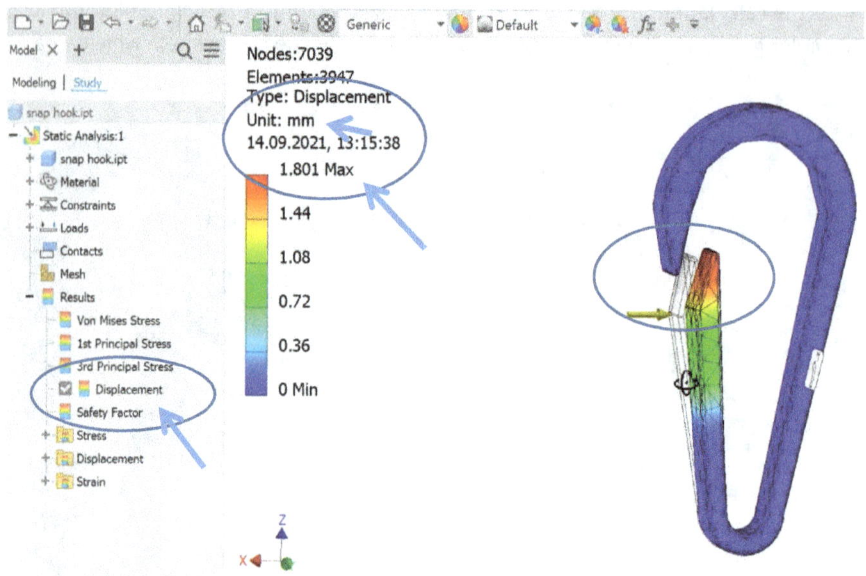

Figure 288: Displaying the displacements ("Displacement") in the component

Perfect! That was the first part of the "Simulation" section. With this knowledge we can already simulate a simple component to a load situation. In the second part, we'll take another look at our engine model. Stay tuned, it continues in an exciting way!

7.2 Performing a simulation study with an assembly

In this chapter we want to deepen our knowledge and skills in simulation by means of an assembly. Here there are a few small differences to individual parts to consider. We will choose our exemplary 4-cylinder engine as a model. For this, we start a new study in the model of the engine.

Before we begin, we will first simplify the model for our purposes. We want to simulate the forces acting on a piston, and for this we will only consider a piston, with piston pin, connecting rod and the crankshaft. Therefore we remove all other components. You can do this easily by right-clicking on the unneeded components in the part browser and selecting "Exclude from Study". For a better view we additionally suppress the visibility of these components.

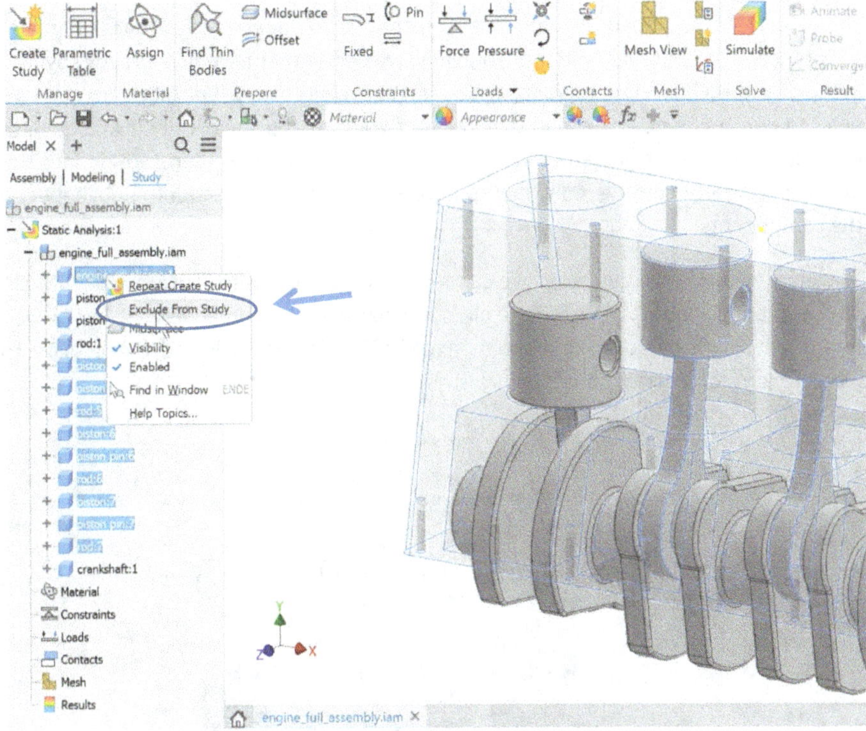

Figure 289: Exclude components from the load study with "Exclude from Study"

The simulation in an assembly runs relatively identically to the simulation in an individual part, i.e. we must first select the correct material. In our case we choose for all components: steel.

Component	Original Material	Override Material	Safety Factor
engine_full_assembly.ian			
engine_crankcase:1	Generic	(As Defined)	Yield Strength
piston:1	Generic	Steel	Yield Strength
piston pin:1	Generic	Steel	Yield Strength
rod:1	Generic	Steel	Yield Strength
piston:5	Generic	Steel	Yield Strength
piston pin:5	Generic	Steel	Yield Strength
rod:5	Generic	Steel	Yield Strength
piston:6	Generic	Steel	Yield Strength
piston pin:6	Generic	Steel	Yield Strength
rod:6	Generic	Steel	Yield Strength
piston:7	Generic	Steel	Yield Strength
piston pin:7	Generic	Steel	Yield Strength

Figure 290: Select "Steel" for all or only the three remaining components

In the next step we need to define the "Constraints" / "Dependencies" and "Contacts" / "Contacts". What "Constraints" are and how we define them, we had already covered in the previous chapter. In this chapter, however, we also need "Contacts" because we need to determine how the load that we later want to apply vertically from above to the piston surface is transferred via the components. Contacts" therefore defines the load transfer between the individual components, i.e. the connection points between the components.

There are two possibilities here. We can let the software create "automatic contacts" or use "manual contacts", i.e. create all "contacts" ourselves. In general, it has proven to use "automatic contacts" first and then to check them manually and, if necessary, to modify them according to one's own wishes.

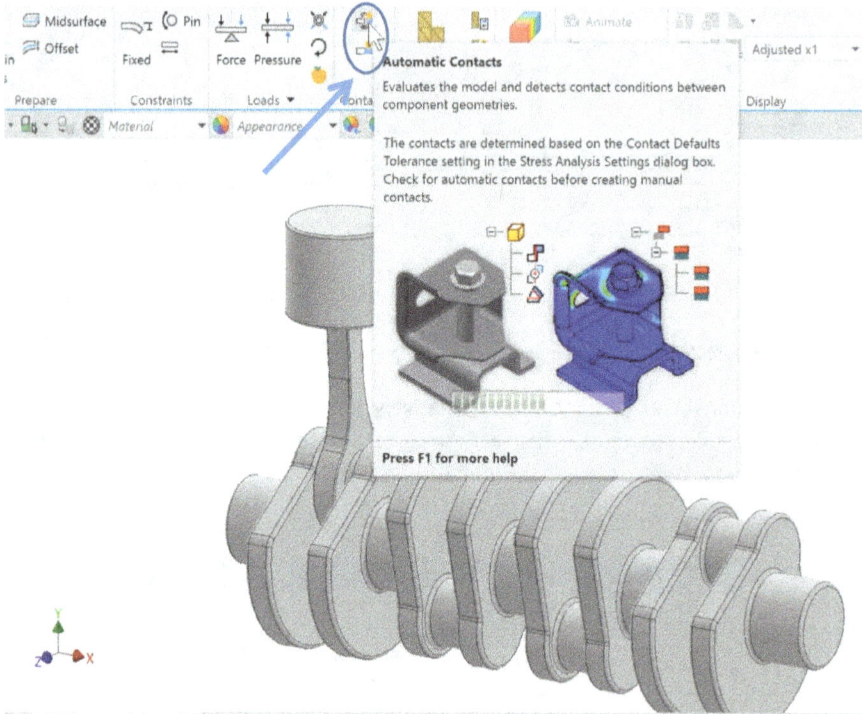

Figure 291: Create "Automatic Contacts" with a click on the command

If we have activated the command "Automatic" at "Contacts", we see the created contacts in the part browser in the folder "Contacts". In our case we need: Contacts between piston and piston pin, between piston pin and connecting rod, and between connecting rod and crankshaft. With a right click on a contact and "Edit" we can edit it.

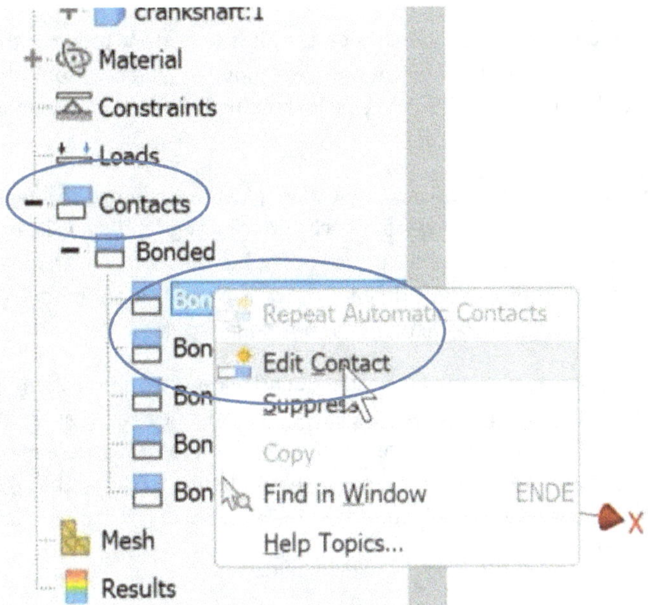

Figure 292: The automatically created contacts in the part browser; edit with right click

We can then select the "Contact Type". As type we have six basic "Contact Types" available.

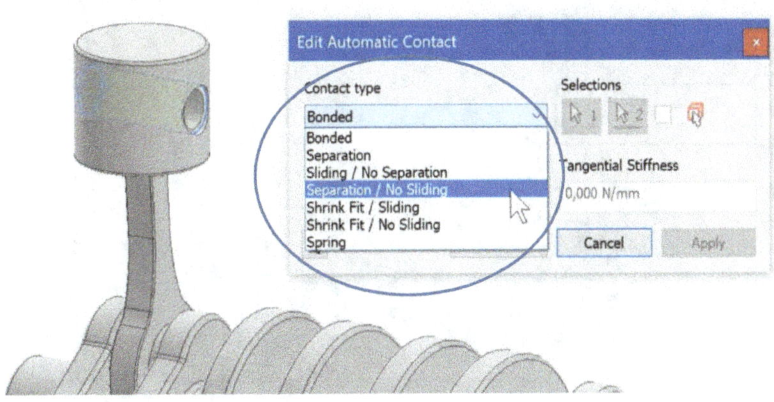

Figure 293: The different "Contact Types" available for selection

"Automatic contacts" has the type "Bonded" selected by default, which corresponds to a fixed or bonded connection state. In our case, we will leave all "Contact Types" set to "Bonded" to perform a simplified calculation on our anyway simplified model. However, we will briefly look a bit more closely at how we would select the correct

"Contact Type" in a manual contact creation. To do this, it is important to know the individual "Contact Types". The most important ones are "Bonded", "Separation" and "Sliding". There are also "Shrink Fit" and "Spring" and combinations with and without "Sliding / Separation".

"Bonded", as mentioned earlier, gives a fixed connection, glued together so to speak. "Separation" allows bodies to move away from each other during loading. "Sliding" does not allow components to move away from each other, but the surfaces can move tangentially to or from each other, i.e. slide on each other. However, in our model, as mentioned, we only use "Automatic Contacts" in this beginner's course.

What are we still missing for a calculation? Exactly! "Constraints", i.e. the fixation in space, as well as a load that is applied. As "Constraints" we select all crankshaft surfaces, with which the crankshaft is mounted in the crankcase. We fix them in all directions and select as "Type": "Fixed", that means we simulate in this case that the crankshaft does not move, normally it would rotate. However, we only want to simulate a static and not a dynamic case.

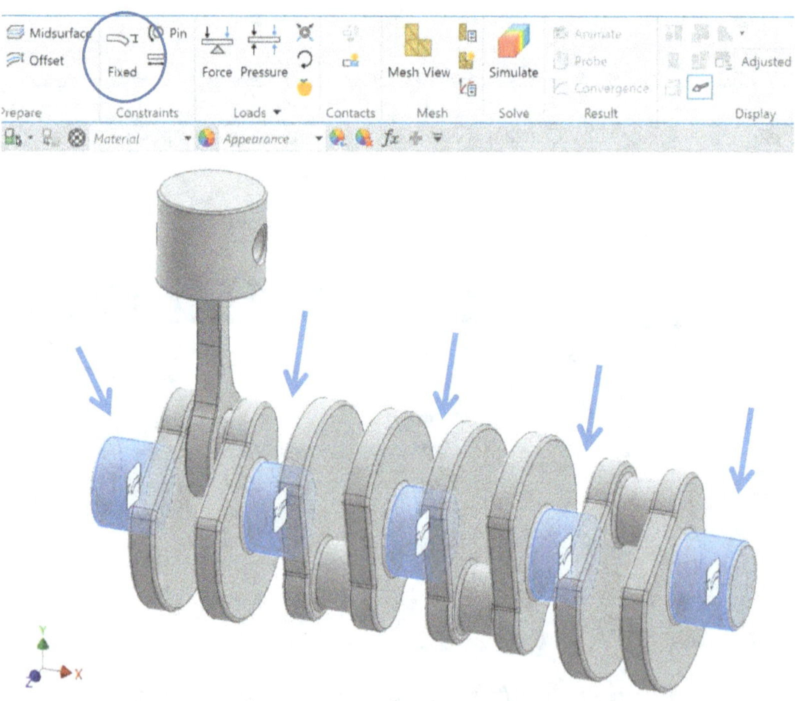

Figure 294: Fixing the crankshaft to the journals of the main bearings

Finally, we define a load, perpendicular to the piston surface, e.g. 1000 N.

190

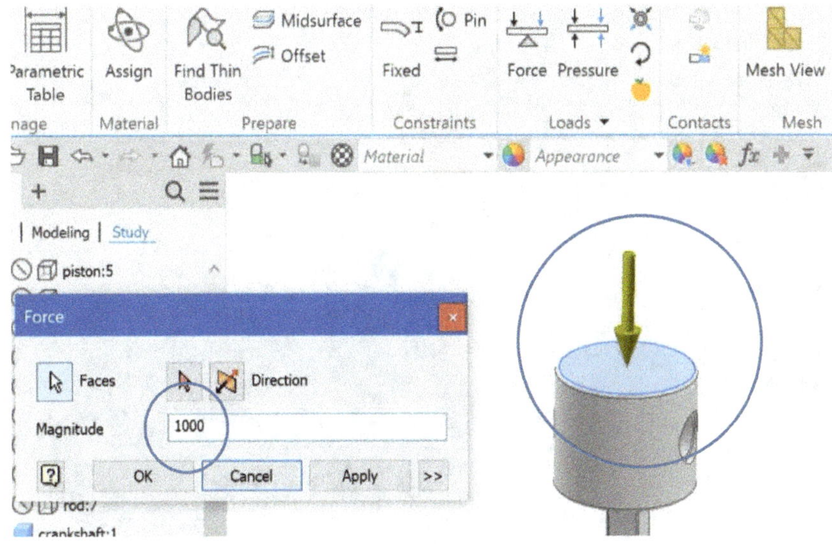

Figure 295: The last step is to apply a force of 1000 N with "Force".

Now we could generate the mesh, but with a click on "Simulate" the software will do it for us automatically. After the model has been successfully calculated, we can again display the desired results such as stress, strain or the safety factor. In our case, we can see how the connecting rod would deform under the load. Of course, this is again very exaggerated here.

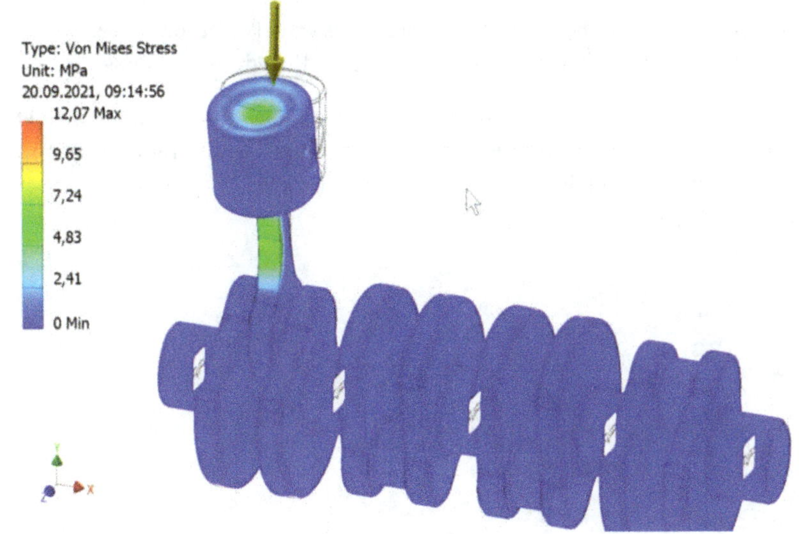

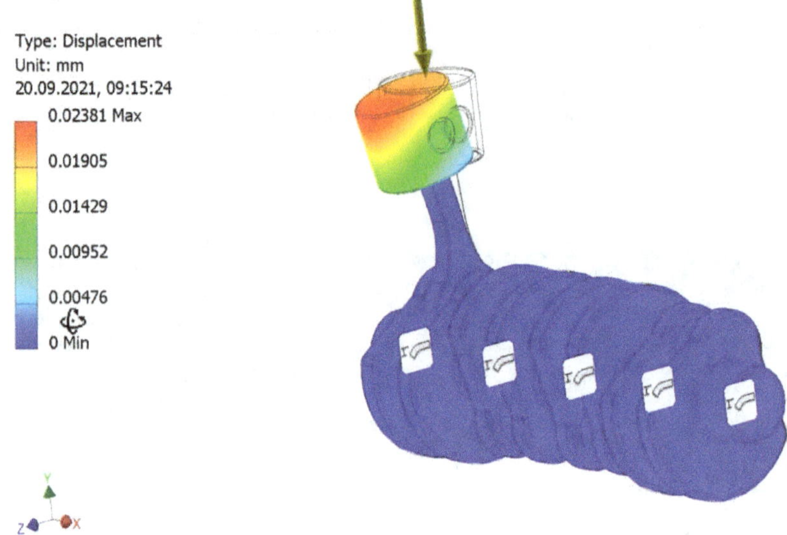

Figure 296: The results of the stress study;
The von Mises stresses (top image) and the displacements (bottom image).

Very good! That should be enough for us as an introduction to the world of FEM simulation with "Inventor". You have learned how to perform a load study on a single part and on an assembly.

More advanced case studies and other applications would go beyond the scope of this beginner's course. Look forward to a continuation in the advanced course!

"Inventor", like any other professional CAD program, now offers us the possibility of creating technical drawings that we can then pass on to a manufacturing company. We will see how this works in the next and last chapter. Now we're almost there, let's move on to the last chapter!

8 Technical drawings with "Inventor" - An introduction

Welcome back to the last chapter of this course! As already mentioned in the previous chapter, we can of course use "Inventor" to create a technical drawing for a manufacturing company. For this we will create a very simple single part, which would be manufactured e.g. by CNC machining. Please design the very simple example part on your own using the following dimensions and as shown below.

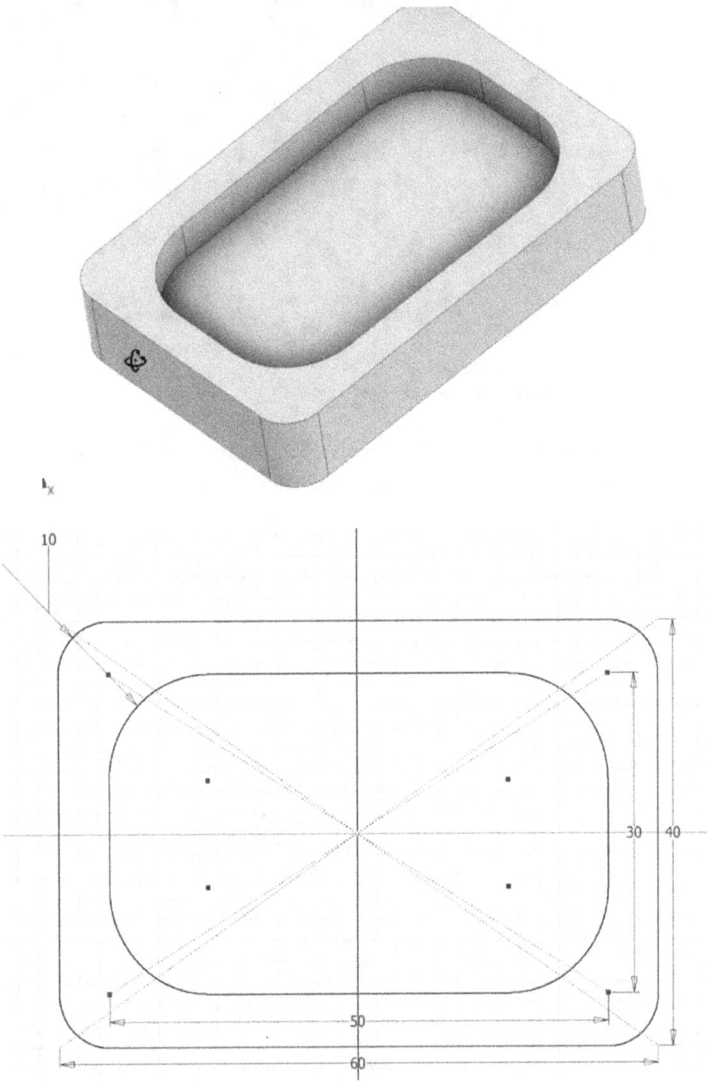

Figure 297: Design this part; extrusion: 10 mm; depth of cutout: 5 mm

Then we add four 5 mm holes to our simple model, which should go through the component and have a distance of 5 mm to the upper and lower edge and 15 mm to each of the side edges.

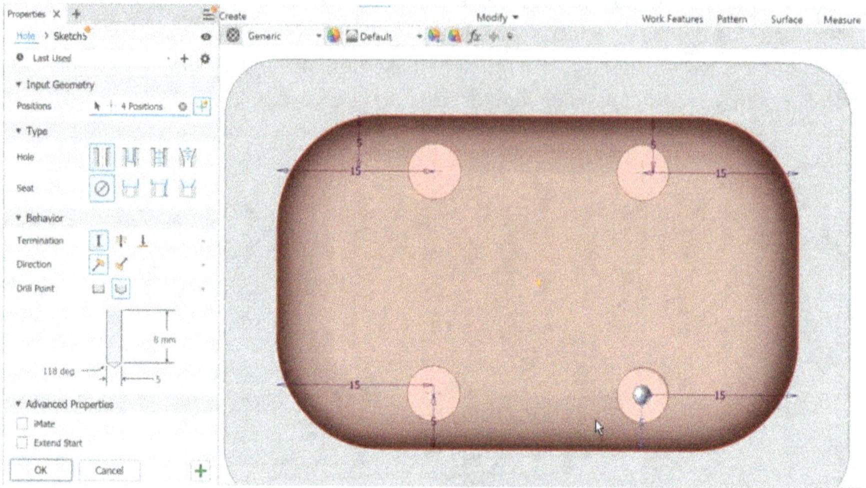

Figure 298: Then complete the part with four holes

To create a technical drawing from this CAD model, we create a drawing with "File" and "New". We first decide on a paper size or template.

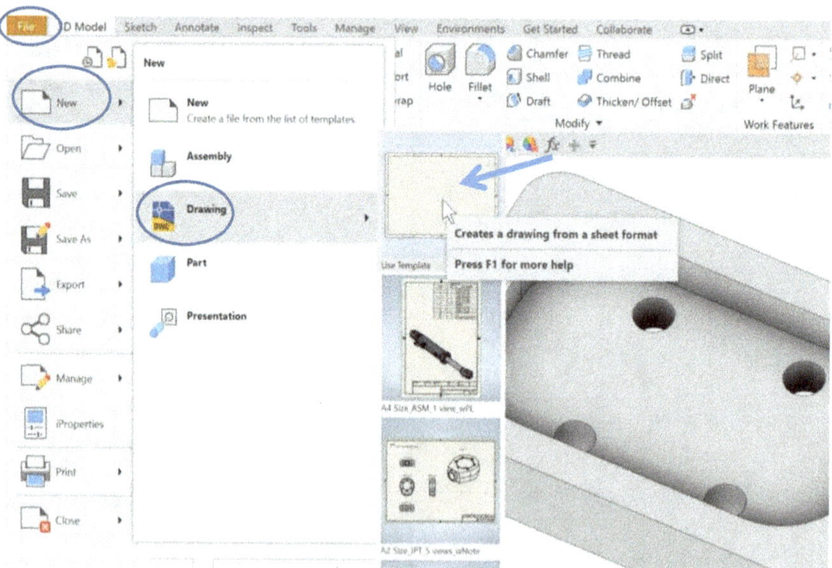

Figure 299: Selecting a template for the technical drawing

The program then takes us to the technical drawing environment. In the first step we have to place the base view of the component on the drawing. To do this, we select the "Base" command and then the component or its location. We can also make many other settings here, but we don't need them - except for scaling - for now. After we have scaled the drawing view a little larger, for example, we create the first view with "Ok".

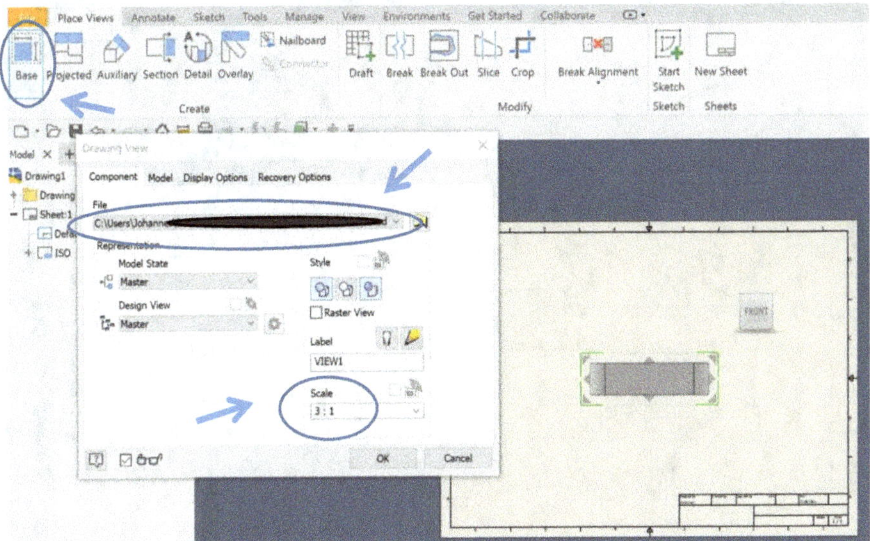

Figure 300: The first view of the component with "Base"

A technical drawing is created in the form of a three-panel view, depending on the so-called folding. In simple terms, this means that the component is shown from above, from the side and, if necessary, from the front in order to be able to place all the necessary dimensions and other designations. In addition, an isometric view is usually added to facilitate spatial imagination. To place a new view, in this case a derived view on the sheet, we use the "Projected" command and create a desired second view by clicking on the component from which we want to derive a view.

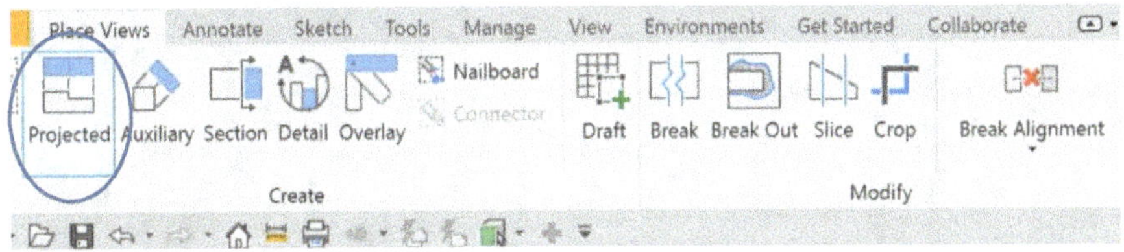

Figure 301: Creating derived views of a component with "Projected"

Depending on where we move our mouse cursor, the referenced view is derived. For example, if we move up or down, the view from the front or back of the component is displayed, and the same applies to the sides. If we move diagonally, we are shown an isometric view. To place one or more views we click on the drawing layer. When we have placed all the views we want, we create them by right-clicking and selecting "Create.

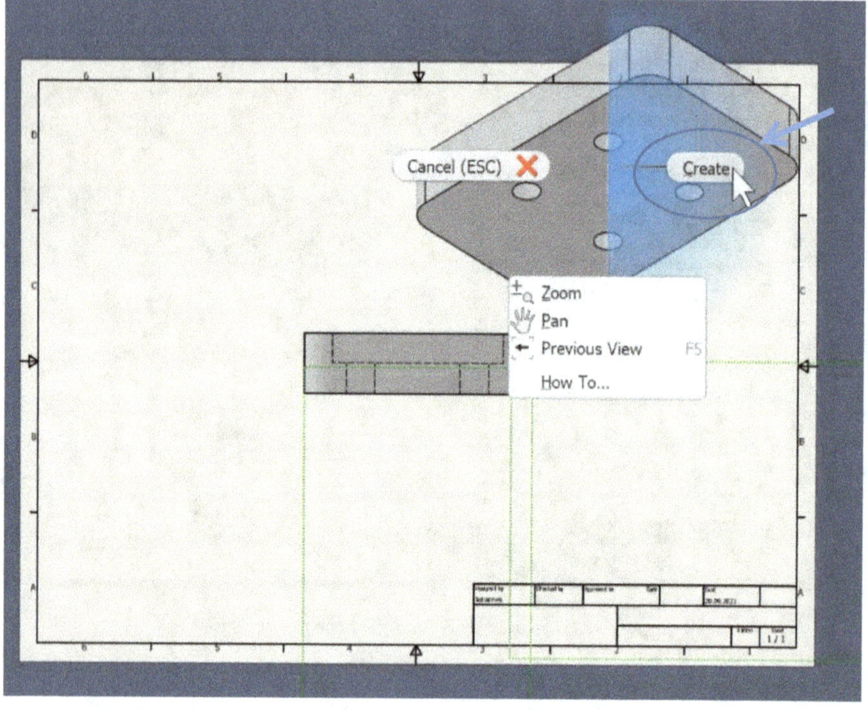

Figure 302: Place multiple views (green frames) and create them with right-click and "Create"

The isometric view seems a bit too big, so we edit it with a right click and "Edit View". We can then choose a different scale, e.g. 1:1.

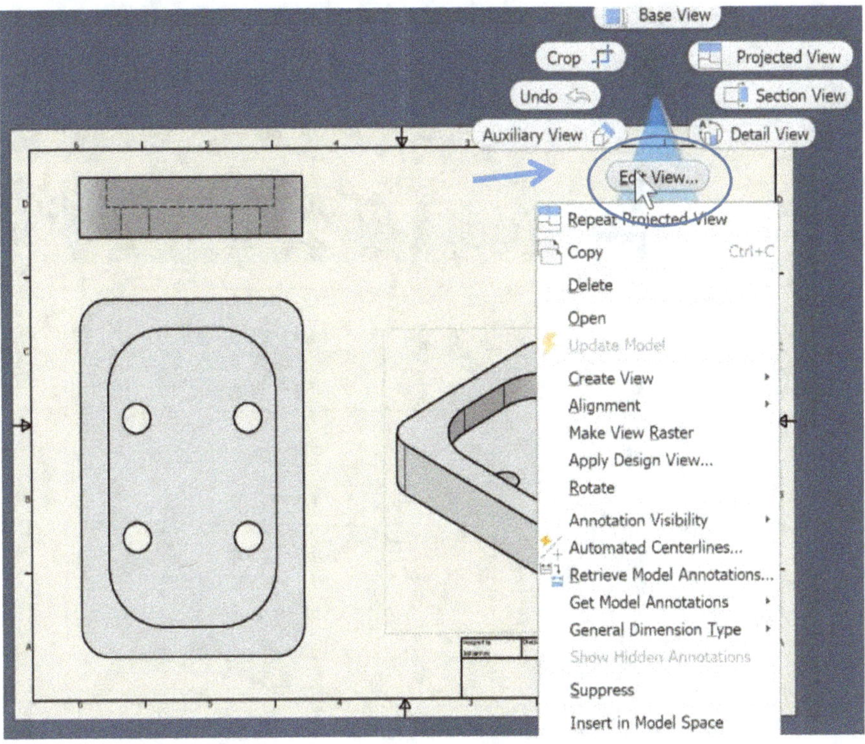

Figure 303: Editing the isometric view or any other view with "Edit View"

In the top left menu we could also create a section view: "section", a detail view: "detail", a break out: "break out" and more.

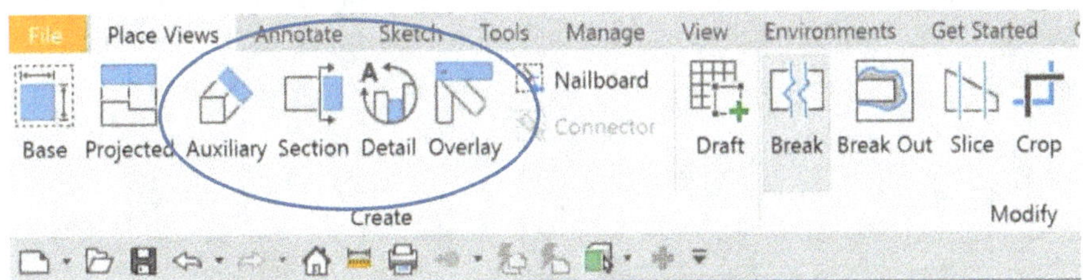

Figure 304: Add different view types

The main dimensioning function and various annotations are located in the "Annotate" menu section.

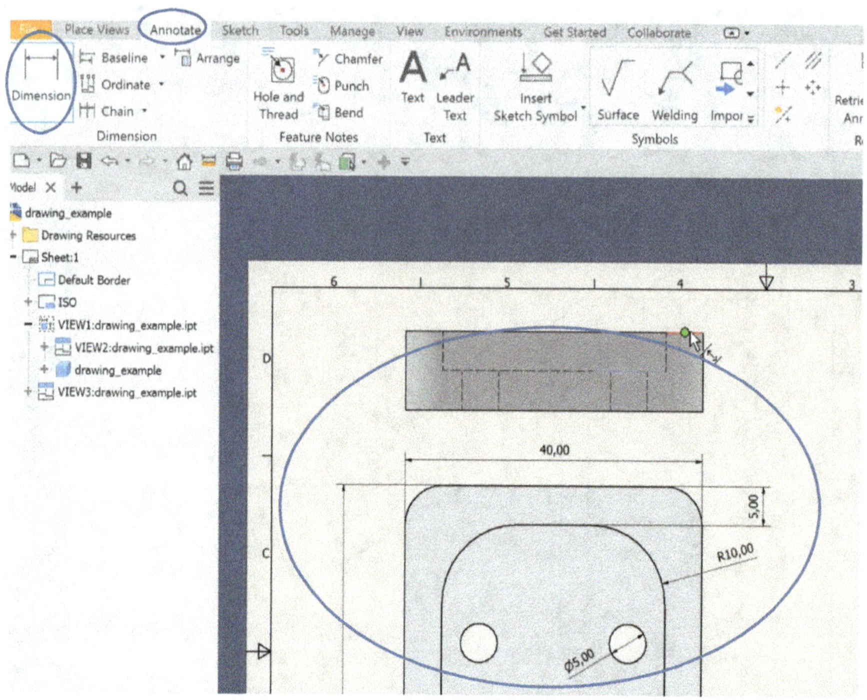

Figure 305: Adding the dimensions for the technical drawing with "Dimension"

With the help of "Dimension" we can create dimensions for our component. This is almost the same as creating a 2D sketch, except that in this case we provide our finished part with dimensions that are already defined and serve as information for manufacturing. With the elements in the "Symbols" area, we can also draw in geometric information, such as a center line or, in this case, symmetry lines and circle centers.

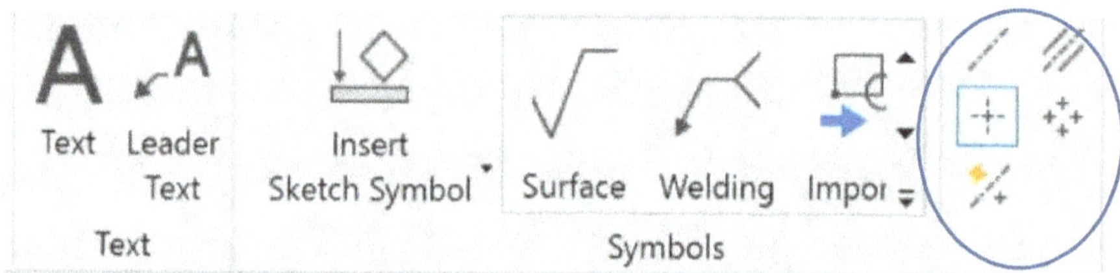

Figure 306: Add symbols like circle centers and symmetry lines

For the symmetry line we simply select two parallel lines of the component and for the circle centers we simply select the desired holes or circles. By the way, with a click on the dimension designations we can also edit them or add further data, such as a number. Perfect, now all the information that a company needs for manufacturing would already be on the drawing.

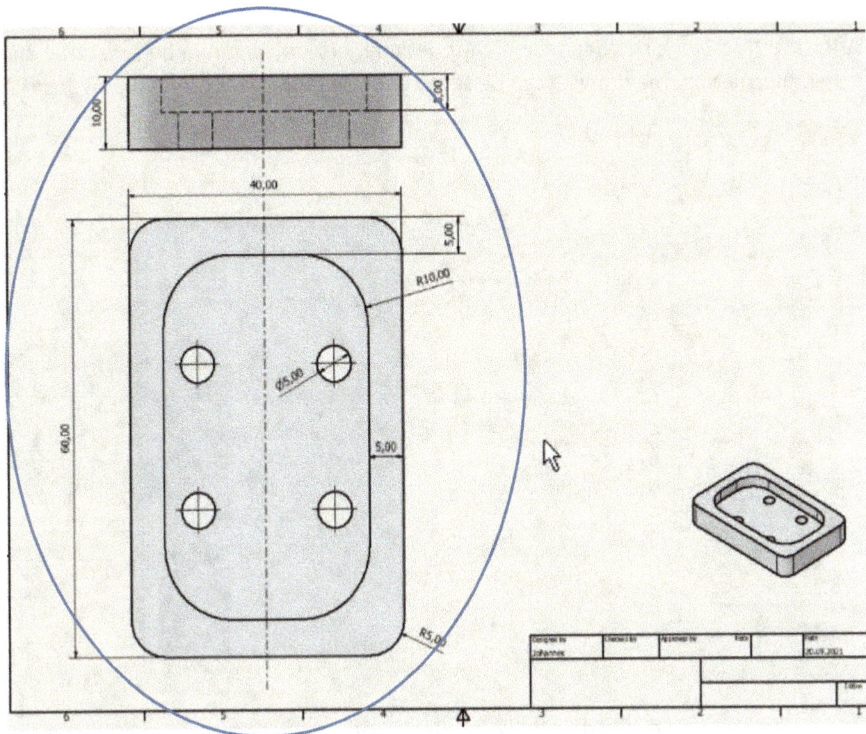

Figure 307: The fully dimensioned technical drawing

All lengths and widths, as well as the positions of the holes and recesses are dimensioned. If special characters are needed to indicate shape and position tolerances, surface finishes or even other texts, they can also be found in the "Symbols" area. The easiest way to create another sheet is to right-click and select "New Sheet" if we do not have enough space on one page.

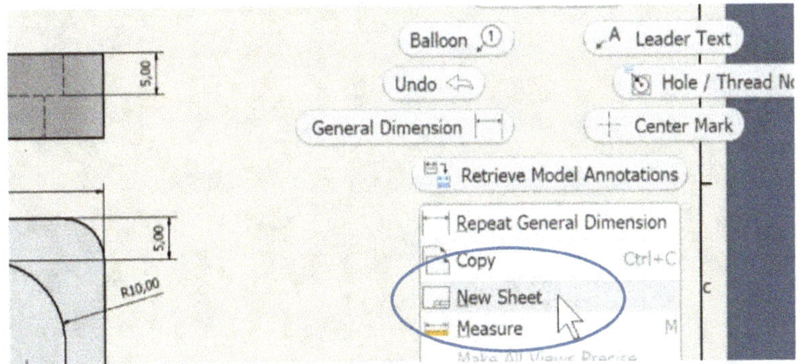

Figure 308: Adding a new sheet with a right click and "New Sheet"

After the title block has been filled with designation, drawing number, material and other information, the drawing can be saved and printed with "Export" e.g. as ". pdf"!

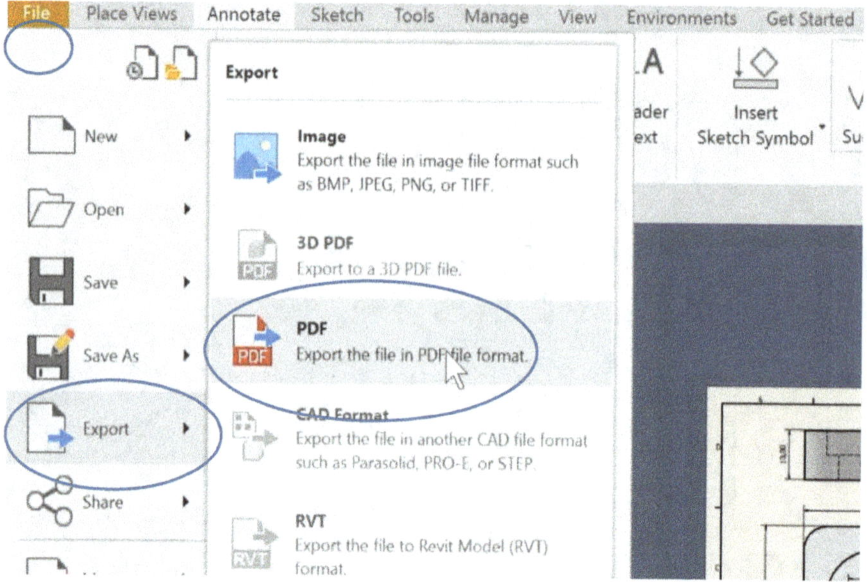

Figure 309: Exporting the technical drawing as a "PDF"

Closing words

Very good! You did it, with this chapter we finish the beginner course for the program "Inventor" from Autodesk!

Now it is your turn to deepen what you have learned and, above all, to apply it. You should now have a command of the most important functions of "Inventor" and you can tackle new projects, CAD designs, simulations and everything that goes with it on your own responsibility! Congratulations!

All relevant operations and features for beginners you have learned in this course. This allows you to design, simulate, render, animate and fabricate your own CAD files in a quick and easy way. Together we have accomplished quite a bit in this course! Be justifiably proud of yourself if you have made it to this lesson!

And as mentioned at the beginning of the course, take a look at 3D printing as well. It's tremendous fun and has great benefits when you can materialize your own designs.

This way, you can create parts out of thin air and have a solution at hand for all kinds of unavailable but urgently needed spare parts or anything else. The best way to do this is to use my book: "3D Printing | Step by Step" and get a copy for yourself at home today.

If you liked the "Inventor" course, I would be very happy if you leave me a rating and a short feedback, as well as recommend the book! Thank you very much for that!

Books you might also like

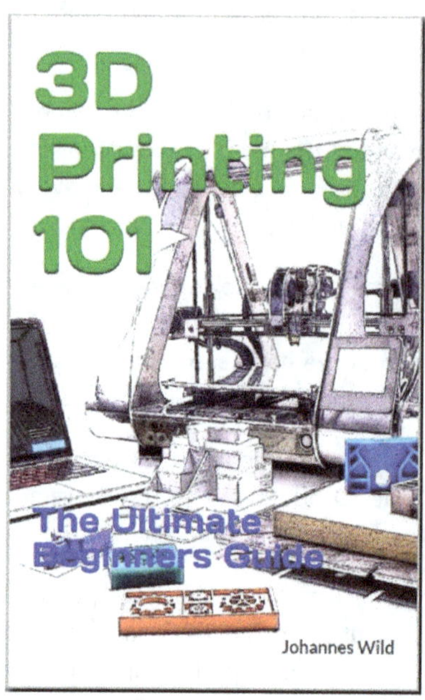

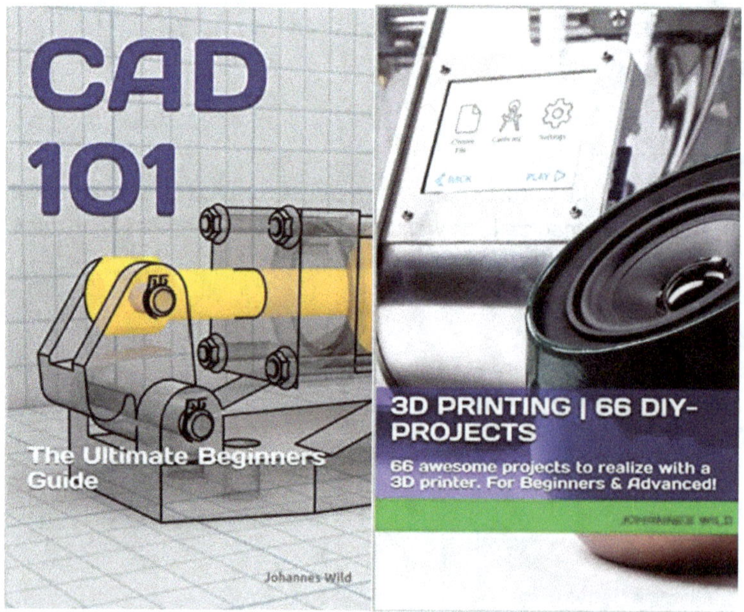